FOR
JOSEPH VERNER REED

Conversation with Max

MAX BEERBOHM
Self-caricature 1952

Conversation with Max

BY

S. N. BEHRMAN

HAMISH HAMILTON
LONDON

First published in Great Britain, 1960
by Hamish Hamilton Ltd
90 *Great Russell Street London WC*1

Copyright © 1960 *by S. N. Behrman*

The contents of this book originated
in *The New Yorker* as a series of articles

PRINTED IN GREAT BRITAIN
BY EBENEZER BAYLIS AND SON, LTD.,
THE TRINITY PRESS, WORCESTER, AND LONDON

CONTENTS

ILLUSTRATIONS

ACKNOWLEDGMENTS

My thanks are due to the executors of the Estate of the late Sir Max Beerbohm for permission to reproduce eighteen of his drawings in this book and to make numerous quotations from his writings. I should also like to thank Mr. Rupert Hart-Davis for much helpful advice, Sir John Rothenstein for permission to reproduce the drawing 'Some Members of the New English Art Club' which is in his possession, and also, for similar permissions, the Garrick Club, the executors of the Estate of the late Sir William Nicholson, the National Portrait Gallery, London, and the Ashmolean Museum, Oxford.

Further acknowledgments are due to the following publishers for permission to quote from books by Max Beerbohm: William Heinemann Ltd. (*A Christmas Garland, Seven Men, And Even Now, A Survey, Rossetti and his Circle, Observations, Mainly on the Air* and *A Variety of Things*); Rupert Hart-Davis Ltd. (*Around Theatres*) and The Bodley Head Ltd. (*The Works of Max Beerbohm* and *More*). Most of the Beerbohm drawings reproduced here are taken from the following books: *Caricatures of Twenty-five Gentlemen* (Leonard Smithers), *The Poets' Corner* (Penguin), *A Book of Caricatures* (Methuen), *Fifty Caricatures* (Heinemann), *Things New and Old* (Heinemann) and *Observations* (Heinemann). I have also to thank Mrs. George Bambridge and Messrs. Macmillan & Co. for permission to quote from *Rudyard Kipling* by C. E. Carrington. And finally Mr. Allan Dent for his astute and comprehensive Index.

S.N.B.

COMPARE ME

THE HERO of J. D. Salinger's novel *The Catcher in the Rye* judges authors by the simple test of whether he has an impulse, after reading something, to call the author up. It seems to me that all my life I have felt like calling up Max Beerbohm. I first made Max's acquaintance, one might say, in the Public Library on Elm Street, in Worcester, Massachusetts, when I was a boy, and I later deepened it in the Widener Library, at Harvard, so that long before the Maximilian Society was organized by his devotees on his seventieth birthday, in London, I was already a Maximilian. When, as a young man making my first visit to Italy, I looked out of the window of my compartment on the Paris–Rome Express and caught sight of the station sign 'RAPALLO' (the Paris–Rome Express does not stop in Rapallo unless you arrange it beforehand), I felt a quick attachment to the place, because I knew that Max Beerbohm lived there. I felt like getting off, but the train was going much too fast. On subsequent trips to Rome, I always looked for the flicker of that evocative station sign. That I would one day actually get off at Rapallo for a prearranged meeting with its renowned inhabitant never remotely occurred to me. But life is seething with improbabilities, and so, in the summer of 1952, it came about.

Sir Henry Maxwell Beerbohm, probably because from the beginning he signed his caricatures 'Max', was known everywhere by that brief, familiar name, but this does not mean that he was hail-fellow-well-met. Many years ago, I learned from old friends of his that with age he had become more and more reclusive. I didn't know his telephone number, but even if I had known it, and used it, there would have been no likelihood that he would run to answer the phone. He tolerated the instrument, but he didn't coddle it. Moreover, he habitually didn't answer letters. Sir William Rothenstein, one of Max's closest friends, told in his *Men and Memories* how he used to address his letters to Max, so little did he hope for an answer: 'Sir Max Beerbohm, The Caves of Silence, Rapallo.' Once, one of Max's friends, reproaching him for the intervals in his correspondence, said, 'No wonder people think you are dead, Max. No one ever hears from you.' 'I am *not* dead, am I?' inquired Max, always on the *qui vive* for interesting information. This bit of dialogue did nothing to change Max's ways. As long as he could be alive, he was rather pleased to be thought dead. I assumed that Max enjoyed his exaggerated reputation of mortality because it kept visitors away; I was reconciled to the austerity of 'respecting Max's privacy', as his friends put it, and to whizzing through Rapallo for the rest of my life. Then, one day, although I had not called Max up, or even written to him, *I* heard from *him*. He had liked something I had written, and wrote me a warm letter about it. This letter led to an exchange of letters between us, and to Max's inviting me to visit him. On my next trip to Italy, my railway ticket read, 'Paris–Rapallo'. It was the first of many visits, and the beginning of a friendship.

The first time I called on Max was on the eve of his eightieth birthday, four years before he died. It is uncommon, I believe, to make a new friend at eighty. In fact, even though I was twenty years younger than Max, I was not on the look-out for new friendships myself. Yet somehow the conditions, if not the chronology, were right for a new friendship. During these last years, Max was frail and tended to isolate himself. 'I am what the writers of obituary notices call "an interesting link with the past",' he had said on one of several B.B.C. broadcasts he made when he was in London during the Second World War. But he had an immense and lively interest in the present, and especially the present in America. And to Max I seemed to arrive bearing reports of the American present. He couldn't hear enough about the New York theatre and the personalities and styles of contemporary American writers and artists. He even wanted to hear about the fantasies of Senate investigations; he confessed to a 'macabre' interest in Senator McCarthy. Max was, of course, one of the most amusing talkers who ever lived; he was also, to use a word he himself often used, one of the most amusable listeners. To my delight, I found that I was able to amuse him. The atmosphere generated by mutual amusability was one that enabled Max to talk freely about everything and everybody; it made conversation easy. Because I would like to set his side of our conversation down, to record it as fully as possible, I shall on occasion quote myself, and for doing that I hope I'll be forgiven. I had the good fortune, late in my own life and later in Max's, to filch this clear friendship from the welter of improvisation and uncontrolled circumstance that engulfs us, and now I wish to recall some of the hours we spent together.

In London, in the summer of 1934, I bought from Sir William Rothenstein a charming pastel he had done of Max at the Villino Chiaro, Max's home in Rapallo. This pastel has hung in my various workrooms ever since. It shows Max, a diaphanous slight figure, leaning over the parapet of the flagged terrace of the Villino and contemplating the Mediterranean. Great vases of mimosa are set in the corners of the terrace; behind Max is the door to the blue-walled study in which he finished writing *Zuleika Dobson* and *Seven Men* and in which he drew innumerable caricatures. I remembered Rothenstein's saying, 'Max presumably goes to the terrace to work, but usually he does what I show him doing—just contemplates.' The drawing has been, through the years, a comfort, a delicious justification for doing nothing. Strenuous writers with a big output might find it enervating; for me it has been a palliative. It was clever of Rothenstein to make Max's figure diaphanous; that was a way of conveying the impression of incorporeality one always got from Max. In the years before I met the model for the relaxed figure leaning over the parapet, I often reflected that Max must occasionally have straightened up, crossed the terrace, and immured himself in that workroom. He must have sat at a desk and exhaled some writing. But the mere possibility of such exertion seems remote in Rothenstein's drawing. It is a study in contemplative—even sensuous— immobility. It conveys the spirit of a man who knows how precious the passing moment is, containing, as it does, an expanse of sea and sun, of mountains in a blue haze, of villas purring at the water's edge—who cherishes too intensely this evanescence, this miracle of sight and sound, to replace it with the vulgar self-assertion of work.

In June of 1952, sitting in my compartment on what I now thought of as the Paris–Rapallo Express, staring out at the calm, innocently blue sea that had drowned Shelley, speeding by the summer resorts that line the coast—the rainbow-coloured houses, the almond, lemon, and orange trees—some lines of verse that I had learned in German class at the Classical High School in Worcester came droning through my mind:

> *Kennst du das Land, wo die Zitronen blüh'n,*
> *Im dunkeln Laub die Goldorangen glüh'n,*
> *Ein sanfter Wind vom blauen Himmel weht,*
> *Die Myrte still und hoch der Lorbeer steht—*
> *Kennst du es wohl?*
> > *Dahin! Dahin!*
> *Möcht ich mit dir, o mein Geliebter, ziehn!*

We had been made to sing this in Schumann's setting. The teacher told us of the '*Drang*' towards Italy, with its sun and colours, that had been irresistible to northern Europeans in the eighteenth and nineteenth centuries. Had Max also obeyed that *Drang* when he quit London for this ineffable shore? Suddenly remembering that those lines were by Goethe, I opened my travelling bookcase, took out Max's book of essays *And Even Now*, and read again the slyest, perhaps, of all his pieces, and surely one of the most Maxian—'Quia Imperfectum', which he wrote in 1918. Reading it now, I wondered how my nice teacher in Worcester, who dilated so expansively and minutely on Goethe's greatness, would have responded to Max's insinuation that, however great Goethe was, he was also a bit of a bore. I shuddered.

Max starts by sighing for a museum of unfinished master-pieces:

> Mr. Pickwick and the Ancient Mariner are valued friends of ours, but they do not preoccupy us like Edwin Drood or Kubla Khan. Had that revolving chair at Gad's Hill become empty but a few weeks later than it actually did, or had Samuel Taylor Coleridge in the act of setting down his dream about the Eastern potentate *not* been interrupted by 'a person on business from Porlock' and so lost the thread of the thing for ever, from two what delightful glades for roaming in would our fancy be excluded! The very globe we live on is a far more fascinating sphere than it can have been when men supposed that men like themselves would be on it to the end of time. It is only since we heard what Darwin had to say, only since we have had to accept as improvisible what lies far ahead, that the Book of Life has taken so strong a hold on us and 'once taken up, cannot,' as the reviewers say, 'readily be laid down'. The work doesn't strike us as a masterpiece yet, certainly; but who knows that it isn't—that it won't be, judged as a whole?

Among the uncompleted masterpieces Max wants in his museum—where 'the public shall throng to steep itself in the splendour of possibilities'—are Penelope's web, the 'half-done marvel of the Night and Morning' of Michelangelo, the original designs for the Tower of Babel, the draft made by Mr. Asquith for a reformed House of Lords, and the notes jotted down by the sometime German Emperor for a proclamation from Versailles to the citizens of Paris. He thirsts for the score of an early unfinished Beethoven symphony and for the manuscript of Racine's fragmentary *Iphigénie*. The unfinished score is his favourite Beethoven symphony, in preference to the completed nine, and his longing for the partial canvas of Whistler's 'Miss Connie Gilchrist' would be unbearable were it not for the existence of an incomplete masterpiece that makes him forget all the others. This is an unfinished portrait of Goethe by a painter named Wilhelm Tischbein, who was Goethe's cicerone when the latter made his famous and highly documented tour of Italy. Max dotes on Tischbein. He dotes on him particularly in relation to Goethe. Where life throws the lion and the mouse together, Max's heart is invariably captured by the mouse, and

in this case Tischbein is the mouse. Max takes you into his
confidence about Tischbein:

> Wilhelm Tischbein is hardly a name to conjure with, though
> in his day, as a practitioner in the 'historical' style, and as a
> rapturous resident in Rome, Tischbein did great things; big
> things, at any rate. He did crowds of heroes in helmets looked
> down at by gods on clouds; he did centaurs leaping ravines;
> Sabine women; sieges of Troy. And he did this portrait of
> Goethe. At least he began it. Why didn't he finish it? That is a
> problem as to which one can but hazard guesses, reading
> between the lines of Goethe's letters. The great point is that
> it never was finished. . . . Goethe has more than once been
> described as 'the perfect man'. He was assuredly a personage
> on the great scale, in the grand manner, gloriously balanced,
> rounded. . . . Endearing though failure always is, we grudge
> no man a moderately successful career, and glory itself we will
> wink at if it befall some thoroughly good fellow. . . . Of Goethe
> we are shy for such reasons as that he was never injudicious,
> never lazy, always in his best form—and always in love with
> some lady or another just so much as was good for the develop-
> ment of his soul and his art, but never more than that by a
> tittle. . . . Yet, in the course of that pageant, his career, there
> did happen just one humiliation—one thing that needed to be
> hushed up. There Tischbein's defalcation was; a chip in the
> marble, a flaw in the crystal, just one thread loose in the great
> grand tapestry.

Max, reading between the lines of Goethe's letters, goes on
to develop the theory that what happened between Tischbein
and Goethe was a comedy, which began with Tischbein's
proposal that Goethe pose for a heroic portrait sitting on a
fallen obelisk while draped in a white mantle, and ended with
Tischbein's abandoning Goethe, the obelisk, and the portrait
in order to pursue the young and pretty Emma Hart. Miss Hart
then lived in Naples and managed the household of the British
Ambassador, Sir William Hamilton. She also managed to be
more attractive to Tischbein than Goethe was. Tischbein began
to play a tantalizing game with Goethe, which is exactly what
Miss Hart was doing with Tischbein. At one point, Tischbein
returned to Rome to go on with Goethe's portrait. Goethe,
happy, resumed his seat on the obelisk. He was very comfortable

on it when Tischbein skipped out on him again to go back to
Naples and to Miss Hart. The incident knocked Goethe out.
It knocks Max out also:

> Incredible! We stare aghast, as in the presence of some great
> dignitary from behind whom, by a ribald hand, a chair is
> withdrawn when he is in the act of sitting down. Tischbein
> had, as it were, withdrawn the obelisk.

I sat, with the book in my lap, watching the flying *Zitronen
blüh'n*. Thinking of Goethe, Tischbein, Beerbohm, and
posterity, I began to feel faintly apprehensive. Was I intruding
on Max's privacy? Was I an intruder from posterity? As the
phrase 'intruder from posterity' occurred in my mind, quotation marks formed around it. Where had I read it? It tantalized
me, but only for a moment. I picked up *And Even Now* again,
and turned to the essay 'No. 2, The Pines', where I quickly
found it. That's what Max felt himself to be when, in 1899,
he made his first visit to Swinburne, in Putney. Max's description of his own tribulation before ringing Swinburne's doorbell
rather bucked me up. He had sent a little book of his to a friend
of Swinburne's, and had got an invitation to come to lunch.
When Max received the invitation, he felt as if he had been
asked to meet Catullus.

> On the day appointed 'I came as one whose feet half linger'.
> It is but a few steps from the railway-station in Putney High
> Street to No. 2, The Pines. I had expected a greater distance
> to the sanctuary—a walk in which to compose my mind and
> prepare myself for initiation. I laid my hand irresolutely
> against the gate of the bleak trim front-garden, I withdrew
> my hand, I went away. Out here were all the aspects of com-
> mon modern life. In there was Swinburne. A butcher-boy
> went by, whistling. He was not going to see Swinburne. He
> could afford to whistle. I pursued my dilatory course up the
> slope of Putney, but at length it occurred to me that un-
> punctuality would after all be an imperfect expression of
> reverence, and I retraced my footsteps.
>
> No. 2—prosaic inscription! But as that front-door closed
> behind me I had the instant sense of having slipped away from
> the harsh light of the ordinary and contemporary into the
> dimness of an odd, august past. Here, in this dark hall, the past
> was the present. Here loomed vivid and vital on the walls those

women of Rossetti whom I had known but as shades. Familiar to me in small reproductions by photogravure, here they *themselves* were, life-sized, 'with curled-up lips and amorous hair' done in the original warm crayon, all of them intently looking down on me while I took off my overcoat—all wondering who was this intruder from posterity.

The train slowed down at Rapallo just as Max was taking off his overcoat in Swinburne's front hall. It was a considerable relief to realize that Max had been as edgy when about to meet Swinburne as I was when about to meet Max. Intruder or not, I got off the train and asked a taximan to drive me to the Excelsior Hotel.

At the Excelsior, I quickly tried to establish myself with Signor Turco, the concierge. I had travelled enough in Europe to know how important it is to get on the right side of the concierge. Signor Turco is an impressive figure. Tall and solid, yet agile, he has the easy authority of a man who knows he is master of all the intricacies of his trade. Turco, I found out later, is the president of the Italian Society of the Golden Keys. The Golden Key is the conciergish symbol. Turco lives on his presidential eminence comfortably and with humour; I eventually got to calling him *Il Presidente*. As a short cut to ingratiation, I let him know casually that I was in Rapallo to see Max Beerbohm. Turco has an expressive face, with lively dark eyes, but it expressed nothing when I made this portentous announcement. It developed that he had never heard of Max. This ignorance seemed to me astonishing, considering that Max had moved to Rapallo in 1910 and had, except when he returned to England during the wars, been living there ever since. The year before, I had travelled by car from Venice to the French Riviera to visit Somerset Maugham. When the French Customs man at the frontier asked my destination and the purpose of my visit, and I told him, he at once gestured to a colleague who was examining my luggage to close the bags. That was that! I reflected on the curious paradox that although Max had been well known in the Elm Street Public Library in Worcester in 1910, he was not known by the concierge of the leading hotel in his adopted town in 1952. If Max had transplanted himself to Rapallo to achieve privacy, he had certainly achieved it.

My room had a balcony, and I stepped out to look at the town, the bay, and the surrounding mountains. I saw the same view that Max was staring at in Rothenstein's pastel in my workroom in New York. I took out Max's letter of invitation and read it again. It was written in pencil, in the calligraphy with which I had long been familiar, from the legends that accompany his caricatures. This letter and the others I received from him take a curious and invariable form; the paragraphs balloon outwards on the left-hand side, the first line short, the second a little longer, and the widest line at dead centre; then the lines begin to draw in again, so that the left side of each paragraph makes a perfect crescent. The letter was written, on the stationery of the Villino Chiaro, from a Catholic hospice that took paying guests and that he was temporarily living in, on Montallegro, outside Rapallo, and it concluded as follows:

> I am in weak health, and the air down in Rapallo has been stifling, and I am therefore on this higher and more salubrious level—which is reachable by motor-car or (in six minutes or so) by a funicular railway. I am looked after with very great care and kindness by Miss Elisabeth Jungmann, of whom you will have heard. I am already better for having come from the above address to the far abover one where I am now.
>
> Will you please telephone to her saying when you could come to luncheon or to dinner?

I telephoned to Montallegro and asked for Miss Jungmann, who had been Max's secretary since Max's wife, Florence, died the year before. She was most gracious, and said that Max would be very happy if I could come to lunch the next day. She gave me instructions on how to get there, and we exchanged forward-looking courtesies. In Paris, on the day I left, I had had lunch with an old friend of mine from Hollywood, a cultivated film scenarist and humorist. When I told him where I was going, he asked me to convey his thanks to Max, because he, Max, had paid for my friend's education, in Philadelphia. I inquired how this long-range philanthropy had come about, and he told me. There was a rich Philadelphia bibliophile who was very eager to obtain the original manuscript of *Zuleika Dobson*. Knowing that my friend, then a college student, was more literate than he was, and wishing to give the young man a business opportunity, the collector asked him to become the intermediary between himself and Max. My friend wrote to Max to ask whether this manuscript was for sale and how much. Max wrote a polite letter—decorated with a few pencil drawings—telling him that he had no idea what to ask and suggesting that his London publisher might know. The patron bought this letter on the spot. My friend saw a new way of life looming; he kept writing to Max and getting short but decorated replies. He did not take up Max's suggestion about writing to his London publisher, because he feared that this might terminate the negotiations. The bibliophile never got the manuscript of *Zuleika*, but he did acquire all of Max's adorned letters, and my friend was able to complete his education. I wondered whether Max might enjoy hearing the story.

Turco arranged for a taxi-driver named Charlie to be assigned to me during my stay in Rapallo, knowing that I spoke scarcely a word of Italian and that Charlie did speak a kind of English. Charlie, a chunky little man with bright-red cheeks, had once worked in Pittsburgh and now had two married daughters living in the Bronx. The trip by car to the hospice is breathtakingly perilous. Montallegro seemed to me, as we were climbing it, to be the highest mountain in the world. We made it through a terrific thunderstorm that shut out everything but the very edges of the abysses we skirted; they seemed bottomless, and the mountain itself topless. We finally got there, however, and on time.

The hospice—a modest two-storey stucco house fronted by a yard—looked forlorn. I made my way across the yard, choosing the lesser puddles, and pushed the door open. In the lobby were some busy nuns and some cooped-up children of guests. I made my presence known. At the same moment, a tall woman came up and introduced herself as Miss Jungmann. She apologized for the weather. She was stricken that the view she had intended to show me of the valley below, which, she assured me,

was 'like a valley in the Bible', should have been made invisible
by the awful torrent. I told her that I could easily dispense with
it, that the view I had come for was of Max. At this, as if in
reward for my having said something that pleased her, she
offered me a Cinzano and led me to a sofa beneath one of the
streaming windows. 'Darling Max,' she said. 'He hasn't been at
all well. He'll be down in a few minutes. He is so looking forward to seeing you. We hardly ever see anyone these days, you
know.'

The Cinzanos arrived, and as we sipped them I got a chance
to observe Miss Jungmann. In her middle fifties, she was not
only tall but very strong-looking, with clearly defined features,
fine blue-grey eyes, and thick brown hair slightly touched with
grey. Miss Jungmann told me that, without Max's knowledge,
she was making certain changes in the interior of the Villino
for his convenience, and she wished these changes to be completed before she brought him back. 'Max hates changes,' she
said. '*Any* changes. But I know that he will be more comfortable
after he gets used to them, and then he will forget that they are
changes. Poor Max, he doesn't know anything about practical
matters at all; he's never so much as had a lira in his hand. Nor
does he speak Italian. I had a job in the Foreign Office in
London, but I gave it up in a minute—there was never any
question in my mind—when I felt that Max needed me. It is
wonderful to be able to do things for him.'

I said I could understand that.

'The trouble is, you see, that the heat in Rapallo in the
summer is unbearable, and in the winter it is so cold. The
heating in the Villino is inadequate. I have thought of putting
in a new heating system, but that would be so very expensive.
We can't afford it.'

I suggested electric heaters.

'I've thought of that,' said Miss Jungmann, 'but the current
is too weak. The town doesn't do much about supplying
current.'

We seemed to have reached an impasse on the heating problem in Rapallo in the winter.

Miss Jungmann said, 'Max told me how distressed he was

that you should be coming on such a day as this. And he is worried about the lunch, because'—her voice dropped, so that no passing nun would hear—'the food here isn't very good.'

I said that the lunch didn't matter at all, that I would be perfectly content just to listen to Max.

'Max,' Miss Jungmann responded quickly, 'says that he doesn't like listeners who never talk and talkers who never listen.'

This came out with such precision that I knew it was a direct quote. My heart sank. I had been prepared just to listen. Miss Jungmann's remark had the effect of a red flag, waved warningly on the very edge of the declivity of boredom down which, at any cost, I must not let Max slide.

I gradually discovered Miss Jungmann's story. She had been for many years the secretary of the German playwright Gerhart Hauptmann. Hauptmann lived *en prince*; he had three homes— one in Germany, one on an island in the Baltic, and one, rented, in Rapallo. 'Hauptmann loved Rapallo,' Miss Jungmann said. 'Rothenstein, on a visit here, introduced Max to Hauptmann. That is how I met Max. We used to have such good times. But then the war came and it all ended. I got a job with the British Foreign Office.'

I remarked on how lucky it was for Max that he had her to look after him, and inquired how it had come about.

Miss Jungmann laughed. 'Oh, Max! I always adored him when Hauptmann was alive. Hauptmann adored him, too. Max used to call me Diana . . .' Her voice trailed off for a moment, in memories of the happy past. 'Well, you know, Florence became very ill. She was ill for a long time. Everybody said, "What will become of Max when Florence dies?" I made up my mind. I dropped everything. I came to the Villino. There Max was, sitting before the little fireplace in the Villino —you'll see it when you visit us there. I said to Max, "Max, if anything happens, you have only to call me and, wherever I am, whatever I'm doing, I'll come the moment I hear from you—*the moment*." He said, "Oh, Elisabeth, that's awfully nice of you, it's most tremendously kind of you." Then I went back to London. When Florence was dying, and the time came for me to return to the Villino, I found Max sitting where I had left him sitting. There were tears in his eyes. Three hours later, Florence died. I have never left Max since that day.'

Miss Jungmann jumped up. 'But here he is. Darling Max!'

I stood up also. Walking down the stairs, slowly, was a frail, elegant little figure. One hand slid along the banisters; the other carried a cane. It was hot and close in the room—a bit steamy from the downpour—and one felt like taking one's jacket off, but Max was dressed *à quatre épingles*, in the style of 1910. He wore a double-breasted suit of grey flannel with a primrose sheen, and a low-cut waistcoat that had wide, soft lapels. On his head was a stiff straw hat set at a rakish angle. His costume suggested that he was going for a promenade on a fashionable boulevard in Nice; it defied the facts of his present environment—an isolated house on a mountain-top in a driving rain. Also, he was wearing neat, well-fitting patent-leather pumps and white socks, and these contradicted any ambulatory ambitions his suit may have had. Miss Jungmann and I walked to the foot of the stairs, waiting for him. Since Max, concentrated on his descent, did not look at us until he reached the floor, I was able to observe him. He looked as I had imagined he would look; his looks were just right for him. There was no frailty in his face. His skin was pinkish and clear; it did not have at all the parchmenty look that the skins of old men often have, as if held in place by a fixative. His moustache was white and trim, his forehead serene. But what struck me was his eyes. I knew those eyes. I had seen those eyes. Where? Whose? Then I remembered. Some years before, I had seen a coloured photograph of Max as a child of six or seven—Max Minimus. I had been struck, in the photograph, also, by the eyes—blue, candid, inquiring, slightly protuberant, innocent. They were the same eyes; it was the same look.

Max smiled at me when he reached the bottom step. We exchanged greetings. Max's voice also was what I had expected —beautifully modulated, soft yet edged, and with a vibration of exquisite courtesy. His diction was lapidary. He made one aware of how beautiful spoken English can sound. Max put his hat and cane on a chair, and we went into the dining-room, a bleak refectory. Miss Jungmann talked about the weather; Max suggested that perhaps there was nothing to be said about it that wasn't readily observable. A waitress came up and consulted Miss Jungmann about the order, in Italian, which Miss Jungmann spoke perfectly. Max, with an experienced look at me, said that this ceremony occurred twice daily—at lunch and at dinner—and that while there was an illusion of choice, actually there was very little choice. 'The food, I am afraid, is inevitable,' he said.

Remembering Miss Jungmann's briefing—that Max liked listeners who talked—I jumped in. Before I left New York, having found Max's books unobtainable except in libraries, I had discussed with a friend the possibility of getting all of Max's works together in a Modern Library Giant. I now told Max about this project. I explained to him that there were Giant Faulkners, Giant Hemingways, and so on.

'How would you like to be a Giant, Sir Max?' I asked.

'I should have to get an entirely new wardrobe,' he said regretfully, with the air of a man who already has all the clothes he wants. 'Many people have tried to make a success of me,' he added, by way of apology for having doused a well-meant effort. 'It cannot be done. Lord Northcliffe was one of those who tried. He failed.'

I inquired about the details of this, and learned that Lord Northcliffe had believed in Max, and had sent him to Italy, in 1906, to write pieces for the *Daily Mail*, and that Max had gone and done them, and Northcliffe had printed them, but they were no good. Max hadn't liked them and, of the ten he wrote, had printed only parts of two of them in a book. But at least he had discovered Italy, and on that visit had determined to come one day and live there.

The talk veered to writing and publishing and making a living by writing. I decided to tell him the story of my friend the scenarist. Max became very animated. 'Would you like to see a publisher's statement?' he asked, and turned to Miss Jungmann. 'Elisabeth! Do get that publisher's statement that came from Knopf.'

Miss Jungmann rose and left the table.

'Mr. Knopf has had the intrepidity to reissue a book of my essays called *Yet Again*,' Max said.

I said that I had just been reading his later book of essays, *And Even Now*, on the train. I ventured into a story about Goethe that had been told me by Franz Werfel. The greatest of the German annotators of Goethe had annotated a new edition of Goethe's autobiography. After Goethe's confession 'With her, for the first time in my life, I really fell in love!' the scholarly editor had put an asterisk that drew you to an authoritative footnote: 'Here Goethe was in error.' Max chuckled. Whenever he chuckled, his narrow shoulders shook with mirth. He took time off to laugh; he devoted himself to it. And his eyes held you while he laughed.

'Thackeray, you know, said that an audience he had with Goethe was like a visit to the dentist,' Max said. ' "If Goethe is a god," he said, "I'm sure I'd rather go to the other place." '

Miss Jungmann returned with the publisher's statement. Obviously, Max couldn't wait to show it to me. '*There's* a publisher's statement!' he carolled as he handed it to me. His soft but penetrating voice conveyed the jubilance of an author whose book has just been accepted by the Book-of-the-Month Club. Prepared for astronomical figures, I stared at the statement. On the right-hand side was an unbroken column of zeros. 'Not one copy!' crowed Max in triumph. 'NOT ONE!' It was an understandable paean from a man who cherishes privacy.

As Giantism didn't appeal to Max, I tried another tack. I spoke to him about an undertaking in which a friend of mine, Wolcott Gibbs, had been for some time passionately engaged— the preparation of a stage version of Max's novel about Oxford, *Zuleika Dobson*. As Max knew, I said, Gibbs was a devotee of his writing, and was also, as Max himself had been, a well-known drama critic. With all the kindness in the world, Max was bearish about this undertaking, too. He was aware of it, he said, but he was not optimistic about it. He felt, he said, a bond of sympathy with a fellow drama critic, and he asked me to advise Gibbs that the attempt to dramatize *Zuleika* was bound to be a failure. 'One of my books, *The Happy Hypocrite*, I dramatized,' he said. 'It was produced by Mrs. Patrick Campbell, as a curtain-raiser. My friend William Archer turned traitor'—Max smiled at me—'and condemned it in the *World*. He condemned it in two columns; the critique was longer than the poor piece itself, don't you know. To amuse him, and to avenge my ruffled feelings, I did a caricature of him, which I sent him.'

I was familar with this caricature. It is called 'Breaking a Butterfly', and shows Archer, a blindfolded entomologist, pushing a wheel and aimlessly waving a butterfly net to capture a butterfly that has flown far behind him. The legend reads, 'My dear W. A. Breaking a butterfly on a wheel is all very well, but —you must "first catch your" butterfly! Yours ever, Max.'

'Well, as a curtain-raiser *The Happy Hypocrite* did fairly well,' Max went on, 'but years later Ivor Novello, satiated with success, determined to play Lord George Hell, the hero-villain of *The Happy Hypocrite*. Clemence Dane made a full evening's version of it. Novello received great praise, but he had to be content with that. The financial report of Novello's earnings'— Max leaned forward, somewhat excited, as if financial statements were the medium in which he flourished—'read something like this: "1928, profit, thirty-five thousand pounds; 1930, fifty thousand pounds; 1934, sixty-five thousand pounds".' He paused to let this formidable figure sink in. 'And then—*The Happy Hypocrite*. The unfamiliar spectre—loss. Forty-three pounds, eleven shillings'—his voice dropped to an awed and reverential whisper—'and twopence.' Max leaned back, elated at having worked up to this superb climax.

After lunch, Max and Miss Jungmann and I sat in the rather bleak lobby of the hospice. I referred to a letter Max had written to Bohun Lynch, who subsequently included it in a biography he wrote called *Max Beerbohm in Perspective*. Probably no subject has ever written more discouragingly to a prospective biographer. The letter is dated Villino Chiaro, Rapallo, June 18, 1921, and begins:

DEAR BOHUN LYNCH,—
The sky is very blue here this morning, as indeed it usually

is, and your letter came like a bolt from it. After I had read the first 2 or 3 lines I instinctively sat down, somewhat blasted. I then read the whole letter manfully. And now I take up my pen. But I don't (it is a sign of the condition to which you've reduced me) know what to do with it. I don't quite know what to write. You are a much younger man than I am, and I think you might have waited for my demise—instead of merely hastening it. Had you said you thought of writing a little book about me, I should have said simply 'Don't!' But as you give me to understand that you *intend* to write a little book about me and have already been excogitating it, what shall I say? I know, at any rate, what I shan't say. I shan't say 'Do!'

I shan't offer you the slightest assistance—except of the purely negative and cautionary kind that now occurs to me. I won't supply you with any photograph of myself at *any* age, nor with any scrap of corrected MS., nor with any caricature of myself for a frontispiece (you yourself have done several brilliant caricatures of me, and I commend these to your notice), nor with *any* of the things you seem to think might be of interest. You must forage around for yourself. I won't even try to prevent you from using anything you may find. I eschew all responsibility whatsoever. I disclaim the horrid privilege of seeing proof-sheets. I won't read a single word till your book is published. Even if modesty didn't prevent me, worldly wisdom would. I remember several books about men who, not yet dead, had blandly aided and abetted the author; and I remember what awful asses those men seemed to me thereby to have made of themselves. Two of them were rather great men. They could afford to make awful asses of themselves. I, who am 100 miles away from being great, cannot afford such luxuries. My gifts are small, I've used them very well and discreetly, never straining them; and the result is that I've made a charming little reputation. But that reputation is a frail plant. Don't over-attend to it, gardener Lynch! Don't drench and deluge it! The contents of a quite *small* watering-can will be quite enough. This I take to be superfluous counsel. I find much reassurance and comfort in your phrase, 'a *little* book'. Oh, keep it little!— in due proportion to its theme. Avoid such phrases as 'It was at or about this time that the young Beerbohm' etc. My life (though to me it has been, and is, extremely interesting) is without a single point of general interest. Address yourself to my writings and drawings. And *surtout pas de zèle*, even here! Be judicial. Make those reservations without which praise carries no weight. Don't, by dithyrambs, hasten the reaction of critics against me. . . .

I suppose that it was because I wanted to get Max talking about Shaw that I adverted particularly to a later passage in this letter, in which he referred to the slogan that Shaw had attached to him and that tagged him all his life—'the incomparable Max'. When, in 1898, Shaw gave up his job as drama critic of the *Saturday Review*, in London, he was asked by the deputy editor John F. Runciman to endorse the appointment of Max as his successor. In his valedictory article, Shaw wrote, 'The younger generation is knocking at the door; and as I open it there steps spritely in the incomparable Max.' I told Max that recently an American humorist had written of him as 'the comparable Max'. He was delighted. 'Just what I told Lynch to do,' he said. 'To *compare* me.'

The passage reads:

> Years ago, G.B.S., in a light-hearted moment, called me 'the incomparable'. Note that I am *not* incomparable. Compare me. Compare me as essayist (for instance) with other essayists. Point out how much less human I am than Lamb, how much less intellectual than Hazlitt, and what an ignoramus beside Belloc; and how Chesterton's high spirits and abundance shame me; how unbalanced G. S. Street must think me, and how coarse too; and how much lighter E. V. Lucas' touch is than mine; and so on, and so forth. Apply the comparative method to me also as caricaturist. . . .

I was not inclined to do any of the things Max had asked Lynch to do, but I did venture to remind him that at least one of his standards of comparison was completely unknown except for the place he had among the writers Max parodies in his book *A Christmas Garland*. G. S. Street, I suggested, had the kind of immortality achieved by the imaginary Enoch Soames (one of the title characters in Max's *Seven Men*), who was to be discovered by readers in the British Museum at the end of the twentieth century under the card-catalogue entry 'Beerbohm, Max'. I then referred to another letter of Max's, which I had seen in a *Festschrift* volume on Shaw's ninetieth birthday. It was written to Stephen Winsten, the editor of the book, and reveals a distinct ambivalence in Max's feeling for his old friend and laudator:

DEAR MR. WINSTEN,

I like your idea very much. 'I suppose that the world itself could not contain all the books' that have been written about G.B.S., and I think it is high time that a book should be written to him. I wish I could be among the writers of it. But I think that no great man at the moment of his reaching the age of ninety should be offered anything but praise. And very fond though I am of G.B.S. and immensely kind though he has always been to me, my admiration for his genius has during fifty years and more been marred for me by dissent from almost any view that he holds about anything. I remember that in an interview published in Frank Harris's *Candid Friend* G.B.S., having commented on the adverse criticisms by his old friends Archer and Walkley, said, 'And Max's blessings are all of them thinly disguised curses.' I remember also a published confession of my own that I was always distracted between two emotions about him: (1) a wish that he had never been born, (2) a hope that he would never die. The first of those two wishes I retract. To the second one I warmly adhere. Certainly he will live for ever in the consciousness of future ages. If in one of those ages I happen to be reincarnate I shall write a reasoned estimate of some aspect of him and of his work. But now I merely send him my love.

Yours sincerely,
MAX BEERBOHM.

I asked Max whether it was true, as someone had remarked, that although Shaw hadn't an enemy in the world, none of his friends liked him.

'Well, he had a powerful brain, don't you know, but he was a cold man,' Max said. 'It's true I never had anything but kindness from him. Though I had written, in the *Saturday*, several sharply critical articles about him, it was Shaw who, in the absence of Frank Harris—Harris was on holiday, or whatever, in Athens—approved Runciman's slipping me in, rather, to the post of drama critic. Shaw was not vindictive. There was no element of vindictiveness in him. This is an admirable quality. In his case, it may have emanated, don't you know, from his absolute conviction—a conviction so manifest that it did not require assertion—that there was no one living who was worthy of his animosity. He was——'
Max paused on the brink of an epithet, then decided to take the

plunge. 'He was a coarse man. I remember his inviting me to
lunch in his flat at Adelphi Terrace to meet Mark Twain.
Barrie was there, three or four others. At the end of a very
agreeable lunch, Shaw jumped up, said he had an appointment
with his dentist, and rushed off, leaving us alone with his guest.
It was somewhat embarrassing, don't you know. Might he not
have told us in advance that he had an engagement, so that
we should be prepared? In his plays, I really enjoy only his
stage directions; the dialogue is vortical and, I find, fatiguing.
It is like being harangued; it is like being a member of one of
those crowds he used to exhort on street corners. He uses the
English language like a truncheon. It is an instrument of
attack, don't you know. No light and shade, no poetry. His
best work, I think, appears in his books of drama and music
criticism and his stage directions. When I was living with my
mother and sisters in London—I had just come down from
Oxford—Shaw made an immense journey by bicycle to see me,
because he had heard that I had done some caricatures. He
came to be caricatured. I had indeed done some caricatures,
I was beginning to achieve a little reputation as a caricaturist,
but I hadn't really, at that time, done anything very good, you
know. Still, Shaw would rather have had a presentment by
anybody, no matter how incompetent, no matter how malicious,
than no presentment at all. One day, I visited Mme Tussaud's,
in preparation for an essay I was writing on that gruesome
establishment. To my astonishment, I was confronted by the
waxen effigy of G.B.S. A few days later, I dined with him and
twitted him about it. He rather flushed with embarrassment,
don't you know, but he said that Mme Tussaud had wished to
add him to her chamber of horrors and that he felt that it
would be snobbish to refuse. Considering that it was the
proudest day of his life, I think his account of it was rather
touching, don't you? Shaw was not, in those early days, very
attractive—dead white, and his face was pitted by some
disease. The back of his neck was especially bleak—very long,
untenanted, dead white. His hair was like seaweed. In those
days, you were lucky not to see G.B.S. from the back. But in
later years, with that wonderful white beard, he became very

MAX BEERBOHM 1905
From the portrait by Sir William Nicholson

MR. BEERBOHM TREE

MR. WILLIAM
NICHOLSON

handsome and impressive-looking. In a day when *everybody* carried a walking-stick, I used to see him, in Hampstead, strolling *without* a walking stick, just to be conspicuous. Instead, he was eternally accompanied by female Fabians in jibbahs and amber beads. They were always cinctured with great ropes of amber beads. When he died, he stipulated that his ashes be sprinkled among the roses in the garden at Ayot.' Max leaned forward, in distress. 'Imagine! Among the *roses*!' It took Max a moment to get over this affront to the roses, and then he went on, as if in explanation, 'G.B.S. had no sense of beauty. That is why he couldn't appreciate Henry Irving. One night at dinner at Philip Sassoon's, I found myself sitting next to Mrs. Shaw. G.B.S. was a safe distance down the table, don't you know, and I ventured to say this to her. After spraying G.B.S. with every variety of praise, I murmured, "But you know, Charlotte, G.B.S. has no aesthetic sense. He is not an artist." She leapt at this! She said that she was always telling G.B.S. that. She said that what he *really* was was a reformer.'

Miss Jungmann was alert to Max's distress. 'Shall we show our visitor the Henderson?' she suggested, clearly feeling that this would be a restorative. She was right.

Max chuckled. He looked at me tentatively. 'If you think it might amuse him——?'

I expressed an instant desire to see the Henderson. Miss Jungmann left us to fetch it.

Max leaned forward again, reanimated, as gleeful as if he had another perfect publisher's statement to show me. 'I did it for William Archer. I thought it might amuse him. I believe that, off and on, I worked on it for a year, don't you know. And then, when Archer came to stay with me just before he left for America to produce his play *The Green Goddess*, I gave it to him as a going-away present. I never thought I should see it again, but Archer was such a considerate man; when he died, he stipulated in his will that it should be returned to me. Did you know that Archer, who always wished to demonstrate that, though a drama critic, he could write a play, had one night of triumph when he felt that he had achieved a beautiful play? He told me this himself. One night, between sleeping and

2

waking, it seemed to him that he had evolved a perfect plot, saw the whole thing from beginning to end. He saw that it only remained to write it—like that!' Max snapped his fingers. 'Then he fell into a blissful sleep. When he wakened, he went over the whole plot again in his mind. He had a disillusioning, a frightful revelation. What he had dreamt was *Hedda Gabler*. But some time later he had a luckier dream. He dreamt *The Green Goddess*, and that was a great success, you know. It made things easy for Archer for the rest of his life, and his friends were all delighted. He made a great deal of dreams; I believe he was writing a book about them when he died. He was a great follower of Freud. . . .' Max passed his hand over his forehead, as if in bewilderment at the eccentricity of a beloved friend who had indulged in a pastime in which he himself couldn't see the fun. 'But here is Elisabeth with the book. I *do* hope it won't bore you. It amused Archer, and it was so agreeable to amuse him—he was so responsive, don't you know.'

Max rose and we went to a long table in the back of the lobby to examine the book. It was an early edition of Professor Archibald Henderson's worshipful *George Bernard Shaw, His Life and Works*. On the first page, over the title, in Max's own tiny handwriting, is written, 'For W.A. with affectionate regards from Max, Rapallo, June 1920.' Below the title, in a forged and entirely different handwriting, large and splashy, is an additional dedication: 'And from *me* too—Archibald Henderson [a great extrovert curlicue in ink], North Carolina.' The book has more than twenty-five full-page illustrations. Following some random impulse, this later Henderson—the one Max creates in the dedication—has redrawn every illustration in the book, often adding colour, and has written elaborate notes on the reincarnations. The redrawings transmute the subjects violently—not only Shaw but Harley Granville-Barker, Sidney Webb, William Archer, William Morris, and even a London street crowd that Shaw is addressing—from the sobersides they were in the original edition into a motley of somewhat macabre grotesques, and they have had an extraordinary effect on the later Henderson's prose style also. Facing page 116, for example, is a full-page photograph of

Shaw as the Socialist, and the change in the Socialist's appearance is startling, even diabolical. He coruscates with lurid colour: his teeth are incandescent; his green billycock hat sports a feather; below his chin are a vast dotted ascot, a pear-shaped pearl; and his eyes gleam like Dracula's. No wonder the later Henderson abandoned sober academic prose for another style altogether, in a note surrounding the photograph:

NOTE BY PROF. HENDERSON:

When Shaw rummaged out this coloured photograph and handed it over to me, I suggested that it should *not* be reproduced in the book. Shaw was adamant. He insisted that nothing in his career should not be known. Let it be frankly said then that there came a time when again Shaw's Puritanism was latent. In the spring of '91 Eleanor Marx had given to him, as a token of esteem, a green billycock hat which had belonged to her father in his *bourgeois* days. 'It went,' says Shaw, 'to my head.' He feverishly applied himself to the task of dressing 'up to' it. Having succeeded in doing this, he offered himself as a candidate for admission to the Marlborough House Set, but, owing to the influence of Baron Hirsch (who could not, or would not, forget that the hat had belonged to Karl Marx), he was rejected. In deep bitterness of spirit he fell back on the Tivoli Bar, where he perceptibly coarsened. This was a very sad time for all Shaw's friends. In vain did the Sidney Webbs tempt him with the most exquisitely cooked statistics. Vainly did John Burns square up to him and threaten to break every bone in his body. To no purpose did that sterling fellow, J. M. Robertson, offer to take him along on an Atheistical Mission Tour among the Fiji Islanders. Shaw adhered to the T.B. (as he affectionately called it): at length, on the advice of Wm. Morris, recourse was had to that expert in salvage, Theodore Watts[-Dunton]. Where others had failed, this remarkable man succeeded. Shaw, without knowing just how it happened, awoke one morning to find himself an inmate of The Pines, Putney. He says that he was kept there for several months, but his friends assure me that he was there only for several days. Whatever the period of his detention, he went back into the world a wiser and a water-drinking man. But the strange contrariety of his nature had not been wholly in abeyance even at The Pines. It was there that he contracted that prejudice against the Elizabethan and Jacobean dramatists which gave such lasting pungency to his articles in *The Saturday Review*. A. H.

Max laughed when I told him that I found the later Henderson more readable than the earlier one, that, indeed, I had not
at all suspected Henderson of having in him a vein so tangential
and a literary visage so deadpan—an Americanism that I had
to explain to Max. Miss Jungmann, too, laughed as she turned
the pages, and Max and I bent over the book.

A caricature of Shaw by Max is reproduced in the Henderson
book. Max's caption reads, 'Magnetic, he has the power to
infect almost everyone with the delight that he takes in himself.' The caricature shows Shaw in slippers standing with his
legs crossed. In the margin, the later Henderson devotes
himself to an archaeological comment on Max's caricature:

> NOTE BY PROF. HENDERSON:
> A certain licence is allowed to comic draughtsmen. But they
> must be careful not to overstep it. Shaw readily yielded to my
> request that I should, to prevent Posterity from a grave error,
> take a plaster-cast of each of his feet. I did so. It was a labour
> of love. Models were made, at Shaw's own suggestion and
> expense, in bronze, and have a place of honour in the museum
> of the University of North Carolina, but are so small that
> visitors often overlook them. Shaw's feet are the envy of all
> Chinese ladies. One can hardly call them feet. They are
> tootsica.—A. H.

Considering that the photograph of Shaw at the age of
twenty-three, taken in Dublin in 1879, now makes him look
distinctly foppish—he has carefully frizzled hair, a monocle, a
stick-pin, and a boutonnière, and a cigarette dangles below his
curled moustache—the later Professor Henderson had, per-
force, to explain this unwonted dandyism. He writes:

> This photograph, like the one that faces page 18, was taken
> by the afterwards-notorious Richard Pigott. Shaw—let it be
> frankly confessed—had got into a bad, a 'fast' set, and was in
> the habit of drinking, smoking, and dressing, to excess. 'I
> wanted,' he writes to me, 'to be the best-dressed man in Dublin,
> and I was.' Pigott himself, though no longer a young man, was
> a member of Shaw's set—and indeed, by reason of his seniority,
> a leader of it. 'He played Falstaff,' says G.B.S., 'to my Hal.'
> For a time it seemed likely that the young Shaw would himself
> become a forger; but the latent strain of Puritanism in him
> suddenly asserted itself. He gave up tobacco, he signed the

pledge, he sold his wardrobe, he shook the dust of Pigott's studio from his shoes; at one bound he ceased to be the Alcibiades of the Liffey.

The printers of the Henderson biography put under each illustration, in heavy type, the number of the page the illustration faces. Around the photograph of Shaw's rather ungainly country house, at Ayot St. Lawrence, the Professor muses, in afterthought:

> Shaw never ceases to surprise you. He is what the French call *imprévoyable*. With him you must always 'expect the unexpected'. The ordinary successful man chooses a country house facing South. Shaw chose one [*Facing p.* 418].

But it was not only about Shaw that Professor Henderson had afterthoughts, doubtless inspired, in many cases, by the new aspect of the illustrations. Confronted by a photograph of Sidney Webb with a string hanging from each lens of his glasses, the later Henderson makes an appropriate comment:

> 'Webb,' writes Shaw, 'is the most generous of geniuses. "Shaw," he has often said to me, "when your *Quintessence of Ibsenism* shall have become the Bible of the whole internationalized human race, I shall be remembered only as the inventor of the double-stringed pince-nez." '

On one of the illustrations, the later Professor Henderson made no comment, although Shaw is here transformed into a kind of Horatio Bottomley demagogue. The illustration is captioned 'The Cart and Trumpet' and shows Shaw addressing a street crowd, which reaches as far as the eye can see. The printed sub-caption explains, 'Shaw addressing the dockyard men outside dockyard gate on behalf of Alderman Sanders. G.B.S. is annoyed with the interrupter, but is ready with an instant retort.' But if the later Professor Henderson was not moved to comment, Max, as the three of us leaned over it, was. He ran his hand over the glossy surface of the crowd—workmen in caps, looking content or sullen or merely vacuous. The questions he asked seemed to be addressed to himself, rather than to Miss Jungmann or me. 'What has become of all of them?' he said. 'What are they doing now? What are they thinking? Are they better off? Do they remember what G.B.S. said to them? Has it clarified their minds? Are they kinder, more thoughtful, more civilized, happier?' He peered at me. 'What do you think? Is it a happier time?' He paused a moment to weigh it. 'G.B.S. himself, you know, was disappointed with the final effect of Fabianism on the Fabians.'

Miss Jungmann spared me from having to answer a difficult question. 'Max,' she said, 'you have missed your nap. You have overdone. You must go up and rest.'

Max and I followed Miss Jungmann towards the front of the lobby. 'Do you know,' Miss Jungmann said to me as we were walking out, 'that a representative of one of your great illustrated magazines was good enough to come here to see Max just a little while ago? A most charming man. He wished to pay quite a handsome sum to have this book photographed and reproduced in his weekly.'

'Why not?' I asked.

'Oh, quite a staggering sum,' she said. 'But Max wouldn't have it!'

I said that it was a pity Max hadn't allowed it, since it was a unique volume. I said that the new Henderson was a kind of comic masterpiece, and that it was too bad more people couldn't see it.

'I did it to amuse Archer, don't you know . . .' said Max, with the implication that you couldn't amuse Archer and at the same time make money out of what had amused him. And then he added, 'I shall probably leave it to the Ashmolean.'

We had reached the front of the lobby. Max was inclined to linger, to talk, but Miss Jungmann admonished again. 'You mustn't overtire yourself, Max,' she said.

The afternoon was indeed advanced. It was after four. Miss Jungmann turned to me. 'I'll just go upstairs and make Max comfortable.'

Max gave me his hand and smiled; he said he had enjoyed my visit and hoped that it could be repeated. He picked up his straw hat and his cane, put on his hat at the Maxian angle, and started upstairs. Miss Jungmann accompanied him, carrying the Ashmolean legacy. I watched him—an air of elegance clung about his tilted narrow shoulders, about the slightly stooped back in its snug Edwardian jacket—make his way slowly up the stairs, following the banisters, as he had when he came down, with his free hand. When he reached the landing, he paused a moment and then began the promenade to his room.

THE MIRROR

THE SECOND time I saw Max, it was on his home grounds—in the Villino Chiaro, on the Via Aurelia, in Rapallo. Since my visit to him at the hospice, I had been corresponding with Miss Jungmann, who reported faithfully on how he was feeling and what he was reading and doing, and I had received occasional letters from Max himself. In one of them he wrote:

> Elisabeth is as wonderfully kind and good and delightful as ever. I have had a return or two of gout—or rather of what is diagnosed as 'symptomatic gout', which sounds less important. Elisabeth found the other day in the garage an unpublished MS. which I had entirely forgotten, and I read it aloud the other day into a microphone imported by Douglas Cleverdon of the B.B.C., and it will figure in a Christmas programme. I was glad to find that I didn't seem to have lost the knack of microphony. . . . I have become conscious that this letter consists of a single paragraph, without one break in the dullness of it all. Forgive this fault.

As Max did not own a car, there was plenty of room in his garage for forgotten manuscripts. The garaged piece was *Hethway Speaking*. I presently read it. Hethway is a character whom Max invented for the purpose of satirizing the quirks of real people represented to be Hethway's friends—William Morris, Algernon Swinburne, George Meredith, Dante Gabriel Rossetti, the Carlyles. William Morris, for instance, comes into the drawing-room of Hethway's house, where the poor man has fancied himself perfectly comfortable, and immediately starts redoing it *à la* Morris. I wrote to Max to tell him how

funny I thought this salvaged piece was, and how grateful we
should all be to Miss Jungmann for haunting garages. I insisted
that Hethway was more real than Hethway's real friends, and
that Max was boasting when he claimed to have invented him.
Max wrote back:

> We laughed inordinately over your doubts about the un-
> reality of Hethway. I am so glad my description of William
> Morris's visit to him gave you such pleasure. The thought of
> him [Morris] has always slightly irritated me. Of course he
> was a wonderful all-round man, but the act of walking round
> him has always tired me.

Confident that, not being an all-round man, I would present
no pedestrian problems to Max—in an essay, he had said that
taking any sort of walk was uncongenial to him, for walking
automatically stops all activity of the brain—I checked in at
the Excelsior for the second time, in the summer of 1953.
I was met at the station by Charlie, who told me that he missed
Pittsburgh acutely. The ravishing Ligurian coast did not con-
sole him in the least for whatever it was that he missed in
Pittsburgh. *Il Presidente* greeted me at the Excelsior, and after I
had had a telephone conversation with Miss Jungmann, Charlie
drove me to the Villino—down the hill to the promenade that
skirts the sea, past the cafés and bandstands, and then up the
steep hill of the Via Aurelia, to No. 47. The motor traffic on
the Via Aurelia is terrifying; tremendous trucks go up and
down it incessantly on their way to and from Genoa. The
traffic did not permit Charlie to stop in front of the house,
which is on the far side of the road; he had to go almost to the
top of the hill, where there is a place to turn, and then come
back to Max's iron gate. Charlie had to huddle his car very
close to the gate to allow the trucks to pass by. Charlie knew
the house; he used to drive occasionally for the late Lady
Beerbohm. He opened the gate for me, and told me to walk up
the stone steps and ring the bell. I asked him to return at six.
It was now four, and I had been invited to tea. I walked up the
flower-bordered steps and rang. Over the door hung a curiously
designed octagonal crystal lamp—a gift, I found out later,
from Gordon Craig.

2*

A girl of about seventeen opened the door, bobbed, and said that the Signora would be in in a minute. I followed her into a tiny hall. Just as in Swinburne's hall when Max called on him at No. 2, The Pines, the past was the present. The young girl walked into a little library off the hall, meaning me to follow her, but I was drawn—as Max had been drawn when he went to Putney to call—by a girl with amorous hair; only she wasn't by Rossetti, she was by Max. It was Elizabeth Siddal. In a small, curved lunette at the top of the back wall, she stood in an attitude of calm abeyance between Swinburne and Rossetti; Swinburne, whose hair was rather longer than Miss Siddal's, was reaching across Miss Siddal to flourish an admonitory forefinger against the Gibraltar of Rossetti's chest, exhorting the later, far from emaciated Dante to do something of which Rossetti manifestly took a poor view. Miss Siddal was staring at Swinburne as at an object theretofore unclassified; Rossetti's look at Swinburne was so concentrated and inimical that it would have put off anybody in the world but Swinburne. Was Swinburne exhorting him to do right by Elizabeth, or what? Only Max knew.

Miss Jungmann came in and greeted me warmly. I admired the picture in the lunette. 'Max is unhappy about Rossetti's hair,' said Miss Jungmann. 'It has faded, and he is always saying that he must touch it up.' We both looked at the embattled trio. 'Do you know,' she said, 'Florence told me this. When Max published his book of caricatures *Rossetti and His Circle*, the people around here somehow heard about it, and Max for a time achieved a kind of local celebrity. They thought —they were sure—it must be about Colonel Giovanni Raffaele Rossetti, who was an Italian naval hero of the First World War. And then they found out it wasn't about their naval hero at all, and they lost all interest in Max, to his great relief. Max,' she went on, 'is dressing up for you. He is putting on his shade-of-primrose suit.'

She then ushered me into the little library. The room was filled with the thunder of the passing trucks. I asked Miss Jungmann how Max stood it; I said that it reminded me of a remark made by Gustav Mahler when he was taken to

see Niagara Falls—'*Endlich fortissimo!*' 'Max doesn't hear it,'
Miss Jungmann said, 'and yet if as much as a teacup clinks
unexpectedly in a room he is in, he jumps as if a cannon had
gone off!' She showed me the treasures in the little library.
There were two watercolours, in oval frames, of Max's grandparents, in eighteenth-century clothes and with powdered hair.
They were both very handsome. Miss Jungmann told me a little
of Max's family history. Max's father, who had emigrated
from Germany to France when he was eighteen, had lived for
several years in Paris. He was so impressive in appearance that
he had earned the sobriquet of '*Superbe Homme*'. 'You know,
Max's father was born in 1810. Think of it!' Miss Jungmann
said. She showed me, on another wall, a black-and-white
drawing by Max of his sister Dora Margaretta, who became a
nun, in her habit. 'Max adored her,' said Miss Jungmann.
'She was very worldly.' Then there was a large wash drawing
of Carlyle striding along the Chelsea Embankment, his face
writhing with dyspepsia and introspection. On another wall
was a flamboyant wooden signboard showing the Elizabethan
comic actor Dick Tarlton as the Harlequin, wearing a suit of
red, green, and yellow lozenges. He was dancing and flourishing a belled stick; he dominated the room. 'This is the change
I told you last summer that I was making,' said Miss Jungmann, with modest triumph, waving a hand towards a little
living-room off the library. 'I broke it through! So you can see
everything, both rooms, in the mirror—there! It took some
time for Max to get used to it, but he approves of it now.'
The rooms composing this enlarged vista were both so tiny that
I couldn't help thinking that it was an ideal house for a
miniaturist. We walked into the living-room, and I looked at
the mirror on the far wall—a perfect circle in a wide-trellised
gilt-and-ebony frame. It was a convex Regency mirror, and it
did indeed gather up everything in both rooms in a curved
embrace. The curtains of the living-room windows curled
towards it, as if impelled by a kind of tropism, and so did the
walls. Miss Jungmann made me stand dead centre, and there I
beheld myself, diminished but with a somewhat disturbing
clarity of outline.

Max came in from his bedroom, which adjoined the room we were in. He was wearing the full complement of the shade-of-primrose suit that I had met first on Montallegro. While he was greeting me, I was conscious afresh of the quality of his voice and of his speech, which had a way of endowing the sound of the English language with lost overtones from a more leisurely past. I complimented him on looking well and, since he had put it on for me, on the elegance of his suit.

His hand flicked across the soft rolled lapels of his waistcoat, cut in a low V. 'I like plenty of room,' he said. 'They do not cut them like that any more. Gives the chest plenty of breathing space, don't you know.'

Since we were standing in front of the mirror, I made some comment on that—how it infoliated the images and focused them, as in a burning glass.

'Well, you see, it is convex,' Max said. 'There is no poetry in a straight mirror—just a reproduction of life. But what one sees in a convex mirror is a complete picture, a composition, an *intérieur*. By miniaturizing, it concentrates and essentializes. It hung in my nursery, this mirror. Then, when, as a young man, I occupied rooms on the top floor of my mother's house, I had it moved up there. It has been with me ever since. My father bought it at the Paris International Exhibition of 1867. It seems to me that during my childhood I was half asleep, but as I grew a bit older, this mirror began to fascinate me. I began to think of all that it had seen since my father bought it; he used to have it in his rooms. And then, when I reached the age of twenty-one —the age of reminiscence, of *seasoned* reminiscence—I began to see this mirror as a collaborator, with memories of its own, a *temps perdu* of its own. I began to write a novel about it, an autobiographical novel called *The Mirror of the Past*. I wanted to corporealize all the backs the mirror had seen leaving my room. I have it somewhere, the fragments of that novel.'

I proposed to Miss Jungmann that we go at once to the garage.

Max chuckled. 'No, the fragments are in London—aren't they, Elisabeth?' he said. 'But it became too involved, you know, too complicated. I couldn't understand it myself. But

some character sketches I made for it—oh, it was more than
forty years ago; I put them by, don't you know—I have read
over the B.B.C., and people seemed to like them.'

Miss Jungmann went out to make tea. Max settled himself
in his armchair in front of a tiny, cheerful fire. He asked me
whether I had read Virginia Woolf's diary. I said I had, and
he began talking about it. Her acute and incessant concern
with what reviewers felt about her work was distasteful to him.
Her perpetual concern with herself was distasteful to him.
'Rossetti allowed his life to be ruined by, among other things,
an adverse review of his work,' he said. 'A pity he—and
Virginia as well—couldn't have taken to heart Turgenev's
view of such matters.' I expressed a wish to take it to heart, too,
if he would only tell me what Turgenev's view was. Max
waved a hand. 'You'll find it in Henry James,' he said.
'Turgenev appreciated that criticism is a delightful pastime
for the critics—that, even, it may be delightful to their readers.
But, he says, it has nothing whatever to do with the artist, nor
with the process by which art is achieved. A pity poor Virginia
couldn't have remembered that! It would have spared her so
much.' He stopped for a moment, apparently saddened. He
went on, 'And then this stream-of-consciousness business! All
of us have a stream of consciousness; we are never without it—
the most ordinary and the most gifted. And through that
stream flows much that is banal, tedious, nasty, insufferable,
irrelevant. But some of us have the taste to let it flow by, *not*
to capture it, not to amber it on the written page, to spare
communicating it. But then I always felt in Virginia an absence
of vitality. And, indeed, her end was the abdication of vitality.
When you think of Benjamin Haydon! He was a painter, and
full of work and projects, and yet at the end of each day he had
the vitality to sit down, don't you know'—Max's hand began
to scribble fast in the air—'and write those immense diaries,
which are so fascinating to read.'

I might have suggested to Max that it was odd to pose
Haydon's vitality against Virginia Woolf's anaemia, since
Haydon had committed suicide also, but I didn't, because
when Max said this I didn't know of Haydon's suicide.

I asked Max, in my turn, whether he had read the Shaw-Campbell correspondence, lately published. Max said he had begun it but had found it too nauseating to go on with.

I told Max that by giving up he had missed a delicious line of Mrs. Pat's, when she says to G.B.S., 'Joey, you're brain-proud!'

Max admitted that that *was* good—a kind of jewel of under-statement. He then said that he had done a series of four caricatures, in watercolour, of Shaw's pursuit of Stella, as he called Mrs. Pat. (I saw them later. They are very funny. In one of them, Shaw is leaping over a piano in chase of his beloved. Stella, a balloon in lavender, ducks coyly under this leap.) In his placid, unhurried voice, Max went on to dissect one sentence out of Shaw's vast *œuvre* that, he said, 'unnerved' him. I have never seen a man unnerved with such unclouded serenity. The sentence was from *Maxims for Revolutionists*, and had been often and admiringly quoted: 'He who can, does. He who cannot, teaches.' 'The arrogance of it, don't you know,' said Max, without resentment. 'He himself so manifestly *can*! Of course, it is simply untrue. Many teachers have done moving and delightful things—Lewis Carroll and A. E. Housman, for example. But even those who haven't—if they teach well, if they inspirit the young, they are perhaps more valuable than those who have done the moving and delightful things. But then G.B.S. had been talking rot for more than fifty years. Will anyone ever write a book on the vast amount of nonsense uttered with such brilliance and panache by G.B.S.?'

I drew Max back to the character sketches that he had written for *The Mirror of the Past* and had delivered with such success over the B.B.C. I made some comment on the viability of these prose pieces, which could be delivered, unaltered, nearly half a century later, through a medium undreamed of when they were written. I asked what some of them were, and why he had not published them years before.

Max waved his hand, and said, 'Oh, they were all friends of mine, don't you know, and I thought they might give offence to their subjects—George Moore, Irving the younger, Yeats, Hall Caine, Nat Goodwin . . .' At the evocation of Goodwin,

Max's face showed pleasure. 'He was a most amusing companion, Nat Goodwin. I met him in America, you know, when I went with my brother on the first of his American tours. I went as Herbert's press representative. I wasn't very good, I'm afraid. I wrote all my formal communications to the press in longhand. I have never had the secret knack of typewriters. Typewriters can't spell, you know. I was too slow. Herbert replaced me, but he allowed me to stay on awhile. But Nat Goodwin! He owned a house at Shooter's Hill that my brother rented at one time, and I used often to spend weekends with Nat. He was married at that time—Nat never did such things for long—to Maxine Elliott. Her sister Gertrude married Johnston Forbes-Robertson. Nat was orotund in speech—like Coquelin.' Max leaned forward in his chair and became orotund. ' "My love for my wife Maxine," he would say, "amounts to I-DOLATRY!" And yet, with the idolatry, he managed to retain detachment also, don't you know, as far as his judgment of acting went. Maxine was beautiful. I have never seen eyes like hers; the whites of her eyes were not white but brilliant blue. But'—Max's voice dropped to the whisper of a confidence, as if he were wary of being overheard disparaging the talent of a lady whose hospitality he had accepted —'Maxine was not really a very good actress. Now, Gertrude was really a fine actress.'

Max's voice boomed into orotundity again; ordinarily soft-spoken, he didn't mind being loud as long as he was quoting. 'Nat used to say, "Gertrude, on the stage, is great; Maxine, my wife, is not great . . . but . . . she touches on greatness." He was a passionate theologian. His favourite book appeared to be Paley's *Evidences*. He would insist to me on the truth of Paley's *Evidences* with truculence, as if I had contradicted him— a David without a Goliath, don't you know. He was a great partisan, also, of the Sermon on the Mount. He defended it vehemently in the face of no opposition whatever.' Max's voice became very loud, declamatory. ' "THE SERMON ON THE MOUNT," he would insist, "is ab-so-LUTE-ly ALL RIGHT!" But he had a non-theological side, too. He was a great singer of Negro songs. One, which I would never tire of hearing, was

about a man, broke in Memphis, who remembers suddenly
that he has a sweetheart, solvent, in Nashville. Nat's eyes used
to gleam with sentiment and avarice while he sang this song.'
Max leaned forward in his chair and sang:

> 'I guess I'll go and telegraph my baby,
> I need the money badly, 'deed I do,
> For Lucy is a very genuine lady
> And I can always touch her for a few.
> I find the Western Union most convenient,
> No matter where I roam,
> So I'll just telegraph my baby,
> She'll send ten or twenty, maybe . . .'

In the middle of Max's aria, Miss Jungmann came in with
the tea. She also brought strawberries.

'From our garden,' she said proudly.

'I always say,' said Max, with a quick, sly look at me, 'that
things from gardens just haven't got that special something
which you find in things bought in a shop, have they?'

I asked Max what he remembered of his American tour with
Herbert. He remembered a great deal, and he began to tell me.

On the sixteenth of January, 1895, Sir Herbert Beerbohm Tree,
the resplendent English actor-manager, who was then forty-one,
set sail from England for the first of his numerous American
tours. He took along with him as his press representative his
half-brother Max Beerbohm, who had recently come down
from Oxford. The offer was a windfall for Max; it couldn't
have come at a better moment, because he had just been having
a madly Platonic, and hopelessly one-sided, love affair with
the child star of the Tivoli Music Hall, Cissie Loftus, and was
glad of an excuse to get away from London. He was to find
alleviation for his bruised emotions over Cissie in America,
because he fell in love again, this time with a member of
Herbert's company, Kilseen Conover. Miss Conover was a very
pretty and rising young ingénue; in London, Max had listened
to little jokes about her at the Garrick Club, where she was
referred to as 'Kill-Scene Conover'. Whether this meant that
she enervated the scenes in which she appeared, or wantonly

'stole' them for herself, Max did not know. He twitted her about it later, when he fell in love with her.

Julius Ewald Edward Beerbohm, the father of Herbert and Max, had married, at the age of about forty, Constantia Draper. They had four children: Ernest, Herbert, Julius, and Constance Marie. When Constantia died, Julius, then about fifty, married Eliza, Constantia's sister. They had five children: Matilda Helen, Gertrude and Marie Agnes (twins), Dora Margaretta, and Max, the youngest. Two of Max's half-brothers, Herbert and Julius, were flamboyant characters, and Max adored them both. They were much older than he was, and he followed their careers with the fascination of a child reading *The Arabian Nights*. Max instinctively shrank from bigness, but he made an exception of Herbert. Herbert liked big things, Max little things. Writing of his brother in a memorial volume he edited after Herbert's death, he said:

> I do believe he took as much pride in my little career as I took in his big one. 'Big' is a word that attaches itself in my mind to so much concerning Herbert. His body was big, and his nature big, and he did so love big things! Mountains, cathedrals, frescoes, Shakespeare, summer skies, Wagnerian opera—his spacious temperament welcomed everything of that sort. Things on a small scale, however exquisite, did not satisfy him.

Max didn't care for Her Majesty's Theatre, which Herbert built and which was the apple of his eye. Max thought it much too big; he liked small theatres, and much preferred the Haymarket. He told me a story of Herbert's taking a famous contemporary manager, Sir Squire Bancroft, to see his theatre. Sir Herbert was lavish with money; Sir Squire Bancroft was the opposite. In a glow of pride, Herbert stood Sir Squire across the street to let him look at Her Majesty's in all its magnificence. 'There'll be an awful lot of windows to clean,' said Bancroft.

Max's brother Julius gave Max even more to wonder at. 'Herbert was (then and always) a hero to me,' Max once wrote. 'But, let me add, Julius was a god.' Their father had founded a successful trade paper, *Beerbohm's Evening Corn Trade*

List; it recorded the movements of ships and cargoes in the corn trade. The elder Beerbohm took on young Julius as a clerk, but Julius couldn't stick it. At the age of twenty-three, he went off to Patagonia, where he resided for two years among the local ostrich-hunters. He wrote a book in two volumes about his adventures there—*Wanderings in Patagonia*. On his return to London, he went in for finance and wrote poetry. He was known to his friends as Poet. One of his poems is a threnody on the death of Cecil Rhodes, whom he idolized. Julius's career in the financial world was characterized by an unerring instinct for failure. For one thing, he was absentminded; Constance Collier, Sir Herbert's leading lady at Her Majesty's and for a time Max's fiancée, tells in her memoirs that once Julius put down a deposit to buy a hotel near Marienbad and then, diverted by another gleam of fool's gold, forgot all about it. At one time, Julius was involved in a scheme to drag the Nile, with the idea of finding Pharaoh's jewels. But Pharaoh, as it turned out, had concealed them too cunningly. Julius was a compulsive gambler; whenever he did make any money, he lost it gambling in Dieppe and on the Riviera. According to a contemporary description, he had 'a long yellow moustache, blue eyes, a languid manner, a nonchalant air, smart clothes, drawling speech, and imperturbable deportment.' His was what is called 'a crowded life' and he was loved by everybody. Max worshipped Julius because, he said, he was 'so cool and calm and elegant'. There is a curious contrast in the temperaments of the two batches of the elder Julius Beerbohm's children: those of his first marriage ran to the grandiose; those of his second marriage ran to the contemplative.

I asked Max where Herbert got the name Tree.

'Well,' said Max, 'when he first went on the stage, he had the fantasy, which became actual, that he would one day be a star. I don't suppose he could imagine the gallery, after a triumphant performance, shouting with enthusiasm for "Beerbohm, Beerbohm!" He had the prescience, don't you know, to supply a shoutable monosyllable.'

While Max was a schoolboy at Charterhouse, Herbert had

the lease of the Haymarket Theatre. Max has said, 'My body was at Charterhouse. My soul was in the Haymarket.' As an undergraduate at Oxford, Max was able to wield the pleasant patronage of inviting his friends up to London, getting free seats for Herbert's performances, and taking them back-stage afterwards to introduce them to his volatile and magnetic older brother. At Oxford, Max wrote an essay on Oscar Wilde, which had been accepted by a magazine called the *Anglo-American Times*. Wilde was delighted. 'No other undergraduate could have written it,' he said. 'You must take up literature. You have a style like a silver dagger.'

Max brought the silver dagger with him to America, but, unfortunately, he seldom pointed it at the theatrical columnists. In spite of Max's hero-worship and Herbert's affectionate indulgence, the business arrangement between them on this American tour did not work out very well. Max not only communicated with the press in longhand but also answered all of Herbert's letters, including the fan mail, the same way. His handwriting was exquisite and his sentence structure cunningly architectural. Those who received his letters must have been pleased with them, but, owing to the unconscionable time it took Max to polish his dagger, many correspondents and many newspapers remained uncommunicated with. Max loved his brother, and before he became a drama critic he loved the theatre, but he had two other loves as well—the writing of prose essays and the drawing of caricatures. His attitude towards the professional duties he owed his brother was easygoing. Herbert found it necessary to dismiss Max from his post and to engage someone less fastidious. Prodigality was one of Herbert's notorious characteristics, and he continued to keep Max with him and to pay him his salary. Max took his lucrative demotion in his stride.

Perhaps Herbert would have been well advised to choose as his press agent for this first American tour a writer less famous than his brother. It is conceivable that Herbert, who had risen with incredible speed to the top of a profession that thrives on sensationalism, was misled by the fact that Max was himself already an established sensationalist. As Horace Gregory wrote

in his biography of James McNeill Whistler, Max 'had come
down from Oxford to London, and had captured the town.'
He was already famous as an essayist and caricaturist, and also
as a dandy. He regarded dandyism as a form of courtesy;
dandyism was something, he felt, to gladden the eye of the
beholder. In 1894, Aubrey Beardsley introduced Max to Henry
Harland, who was then in the process of founding the *Yellow
Book*, and Harland thought it worth-while to ask Max for a
contribution to the first number. Max contributed a bombshell.
Sitting tranquilly in his room at Merton College, Oxford, the
year before, Max had written an essay that was to rock literary
circles in London to their foundations. The explosive essay,
when it appeared in the *Yellow Book*, was called 'A Defence of
Cosmetics'. A well-known humorist of the time, Barry Pain,
was so shaken by it that he momentarily mislaid his sense of
humour. As Max had begun to frequent the Café Royal
during his London sojourns, Pain, upon the publication of this
scandalous essay, lumped Max with the other decadent
denizens of that café and blasted it with the withering remark,
in his newspaper column, 'A whiff of grapeshot would do no
harm there.'

Punch's poet went to town:

> ARS COSMETICA
> How would the little busy bore
>   Improve on Nature's dower,
> And praise a painted Laïs more
>   Than maidens in their flower!
> How deftly he dabs on his grease,
>   How neatly spreads his wax;
> And finds in dirty aids like these
>   The charm that Nature lacks.
> In barber-born, cosmetic skill,
>   'Art' would be busy too;
> And folly finds some business still
>   For popinjays to do!

The popinjay was relaxed about this attack and other ful-
minations directed at his essay. He had expected the barrage;
he had courted it; he had known, sitting there in the armchair his father bought him when he went up to Merton, in

1890, exactly what he was doing. Max included this essay in his first published volume, *The Works of Max Beerbohm*, under the more veracious title 'The Pervasion of Rouge'. The fact is that Max, far from being a defender of cosmetics, had no use for them at all. If Barry Pain had kept his temper under better control and read Max's incendiary essay consideringly before he began whiffing grapeshot, he would have discerned that Max's defence of rouge was half-hearted; the essayist was merely recording, somewhat regretfully, its pervasion. It would never have remotely occurred to his sisters or his mother, Max told me, to apply it, and had they done so, he would have been saddened, even outraged. Up to that time, only women of the streets resorted to rouge. 'Fashion,' says Max in his essay, 'has made Jezebel surrender her monopoly of the rouge-pot.'

Max was devoted all his life to the unassisted complexions of unfashionable English girls; the natural English female complexion of those early days aroused in him, in long retro-spect, a memorial dithyramb. Over the tea and strawberries, Max enlarged on this sort of complexion. 'It was a delicate rose pink, don't you know, and rouge would only have blemished it,' he said. 'In those days, the houses were very irregularly heated; the downstairs library might be quite warm and the hall outside freezing cold. The ladies moved from room to room, and their complexions had to guess the next temperature they would encounter. It was this act of guessing that kept their complexions suspended, don't you know, between the lovely pink, the lovely rose.'

I accused Max of acquiring an initial reputation on false pretences.

Max replied mildly, 'It was just an exercise in euphuism. Still, as far as anyone in literature can be lynched, I was.'

Feelings ran high in those days. The *Westminster Gazette*, referring to the drawings by Aubrey Beardsley that were also published in the first issue of the *Yellow Book*, suggested 'an Act of Parliament to make this kind of thing illegal'. Beardsley was badly mauled by the critics, and, in a memorial essay on

Beardsley, Max tells, with approval, how Beardsley did them in:

> Most of the qualified art-critics, also, were very angry. They did not know what to make of these drawings, which were referable to no established school or known method in art. Beardsley was not at all discouraged by the contempt with which his technique was treated. On the contrary, he revelled in his unfavourable press-cuttings, knowing how little they signified. I think it was in the third number of the *Yellow Book* that two pictures by hitherto-unknown artists were reproduced. One was a large head of Mantegna, by Philip Broughton; the other, a pastel-study of a Frenchwoman, by Albert Foschter. Both the drawings had rather a success with the reviewers, one of whom advised Beardsley 'to study and profit by the sound and scholarly draughtsmanship of which Mr. Philip Broughton furnishes another example in his familiar manner'. Beardsley, who had made both the drawings and invented both the signatures, was greatly amused and delighted.

Max's undergraduate success was substantial. In 1893, Sir William Rothenstein was sent up to Oxford by the publisher John Lane to do a book of lithographs of university celebrities. Lane's idea was that he should do dons; Rothenstein insisted on including a few undergraduate celebrities. Naturally, he drew Max, who by that time was himself well known for his caricatures and writings. (In his memoirs, Rothenstein describes Max, at their first meeting, as 'rather tall', by which he must have meant that Max was tall in comparison with himself. In the innumerable caricatures that Max was to do of Rothenstein, the latter is always minuscule, a Lilliputian among Gullivers. There is only one caricature in which there is anyone smaller than Rothenstein, and that is one in which Rothenstein's brother Albert is included. Max puts Albert under a table and William on top of it, so that he can argue on terms of equality with the painter Wilson Steer, who is sitting.) After Rothenstein had finished his Oxford lithographs, he found that John Lane had commissioned Max to do a book of Oxford celebrities also; Max wrote to Rothenstein to apologize for Lane, but said he felt confident that 'there is room for both of us'. Once Max had launched his bombshell in the *Yellow*

Book, he relaxed. He wanted notoriety only in order to coast on it. He coasted till he got to America—or, specifically, Chicago—when he took a long look at his spangled past and a controlled one at his future.

Herbert's company opened in New York and moved on to Chicago. The journey to Chicago was a fateful one for Max. Passing through the sleeping-car reserved for the unmarried ladies of the company, he was hailed by Kilseen Conover and another young actress, Una Cockerell. They looked very pretty in their nightgowns and were eating fruit out of hampers. Miss Conover gave Max an apple and Miss Cockerell threw him a banana.

In London, once, I visited Miss Cockerell's uncle, Sir Sydney Cockerell. This entrancing gentleman was in bed. He was over ninety when I went to see him, and his vitality and the extraordinary vigour of his mind made me reflect that perhaps a lifelong preoccupation with the arts can be a powerful factor in longevity. Sir Sydney had been William Morris's and Ruskin's secretary when he was young, had made a pilgrimage to Tolstoy, and, as his books reveal, had made an art of friendship with the great spirits of his time. The chief devotion of his later years was to the Fitzwilliam Museum, at Cambridge, of which he was curator. He was perhaps the closest friend of Bernard Shaw; he was instrumental in getting Shaw to write *St. Joan*, and he spoke words from *Pilgrim's Progress* at Shaw's funeral. We talked about Max. Speaking of Max's drawings, Sir Sydney said, 'There is no one like Max. He is in a class apart. At his best, his perception is unique and beautiful.' The first time he had ever encountered Max, Sir Sydney said, was when he had gone to Paddington Station to see his niece off on the boat train for Herbert's first American tour. He noticed a young man, dressed to the nines, walking abstractedly up and down the platform. He had never seen a young man so exquisitely dressed. That was Max. Sir Sydney didn't meet him till many years later. And when he did, he bought three of Max's drawings for the Fitzwilliam. But Max didn't know anything about Sydney Cockerell on the night he got the banana and the apple, and it was then that he fell in

love with Miss Conover. As he wrote to his close friend
Reginald Turner at the time, they rode about Chicago in
hansom cabs holding hands, and Max asked Miss Conover to
marry him. She gave him no reason to believe that she
wouldn't.

In Chicago, Herbert, who was adventurous, put on Ibsen's
An Enemy of the People. The reaction of the first audience was
mixed, even tumultuous. Max did not capitalize professionally
on the controversial aspects of this reaction, however. He did
not stay for the end of the performance. Instead, he did something that theatrical press agents do not ordinarily do. Leaving
the impassioned audience to come to terms with Ibsen and
his brother in its own way, he went back to his hotel room,
made himself comfortable with pen and ink and paper, and
wrote an essay on Walter Pater, which he first called 'Be It
Cosiness' and later called 'Diminuendo'. Max polishes Pater
off quickly, and devotes the rest of the essay to himself. The
second title is meant to convey that after the awful, dizzying
summit scaled in the *Yellow Book* essay the rest of his life must
necessarily be a prolonged anticlimax. This anticlimax he
welcomes; he defines its contours, and begins at once to make
himself at home within them. On his arrival in Oxford as a
Freshman, he begins, he encountered Pater himself in Ryman's,
where he went to buy an engraving. 'I think,' he says, 'I
nearly went down when they told me that was Pater.' Max
records that he later tried to draw Pater and failed; he could
never really do funny caricatures of people unless he admired
or, at least in some grudging way, liked them. And he cared
no more for Pater's literary style than he did for his personal
appearance:

> Not that even in those more decadent days of my childhood
> [when Max was writing this, he was twenty-three] did I admire
> the man as a stylist. Even then I was angry that he should treat
> English as a dead language, bored by that sedulous ritual
> wherewith he laid out every sentence as in a shroud—hanging,
> like a widower, long over its marmoreal beauty or ever he
> could lay it at length in his book, its sepulchre. From that laden
> air, the so cadaverous murmur of that sanctuary, I would hook
> it at the beck of any jade. The writing of Pater had never,

indeed, appealed to me, ἀλλ' αἰεί, having regard to the couth
solemnity of his mind, to his philosophy, to his rare erudition,
τινα φῶτα μέγαν καὶ καλὸν ἐδέγμην. And I suppose it was when
at length I saw him that I first knew him to be fallible.

After gracefully interring Pater in the cerements of a few
of his own sentences, the young press agent goes on to inter
his own past and to peer down the vista of his future. Actually,
Max told me, he overcame his original repugnance to the
author of *Marius the Epicurean* enough to attend several of his
lectures. Evidently, for Pater, giving lectures was a form of self-
communion; he whispered them. At one of Herbert's supper
parties, Max met, for the first time, Oscar Wilde. By way of
break-in, he asked Wilde, 'Did you hear Pater at Oxford? I
couldn't.' 'I overheard him,' said Wilde. In 'Diminuendo',
Max writes that Oxford, like Pater, is a visual disappointment
('*On aurait dit* a bit of Manchester through which Apollo had
once passed'); the charms of the traditions he expected are
obsolescent ('The townspeople now looked just like undergraduates and the dons just like townspeople'); the improve-
ment in the train service between London and Oxford has
made the latter a kind of suburb of the former, and when he
looks at London, though he finds it 'fascinating to watch the
ways of its children', he is sure that 'modern life' cannot be
for him. He contemplates, in a few elegiac paragraphs, the
excessive and turbulent and incessantly amorous life of the
Prince of Wales, and is saddened by the reflection that a life
so busy must connote an interference with thought. 'I do not
suppose,' he writes, 'that, if we were invited to give authenti-
cated instances of intelligence on the part of our royal pets,
we could fill half a column of *The Spectator*. In fact, their lives
are so full they have no time for thought, the highest energy
of man.'

Chicago does not usually evoke searing introspection, but it
did in Max; ignoring completely the audience reaction to *An
Enemy of the People*—a serious lapse on the part of a drum-beater
for a theatrical enterprise—he casts a rueful glance at his own
spotted past:

Once, in the delusion that Art, loving the recluse, would

make his life happy, I wrote a little for a yellow quarterly and had that *succès de fiasco* which is always given to a young writer of talent. But the stress of creation soon overwhelmed me. Only Art with a capital H gives any consolations to her henchmen. And I, who crave no knighthood, shall write no more. I shall write no more. Already I feel myself to be a trifle outmoded. I belong to the Beardsley period. Younger men, with months of activity before them, with fresher schemes and notions, with newer enthusiasm, have pressed forward since then. *Cedo junioribus.* Indeed, I stand aside with no regret. For to be outmoded is to be a classic, if one has written well. I have acceded to the hierarchy of good scribes and rather like my niche.

Miss Jungmann disposed of the tea things; the three of us had already disposed of the strawberries. I looked around the tiny circumference of Max's present niche—a living-room no bigger than a few strides in each direction, and furnished with the convex mirror, a small beige-upholstered armchair that Max sat in, a small tea-table beside the chair, two straight chairs, a small dining-room table, a small fireplace, and, above it, a white-painted mantelshelf on which there stood two photographs and a delicate bronze figurine of a girl with averted head. I encouraged Max to talk more about his American visit. In Chicago, he said, he had enjoyed the fires. Max was devoted to fires—rampant ones in the outdoors and more controlled, indoor ones, such as the tiny, brisk one in the grate before us. In an essay on domesticated fires, he says that they are 'to your room what the sun is to the world', and continues, 'Doubtless, when I began to walk, one of my first excursions was to the fender, that I might gaze more nearly at the live thing roaring and raging behind it; and I daresay I dimly wondered by what blessed dispensation this creature was allowed in a domain so peaceful as my nursery.' Chicago, he recalled—he had earlier recalled it in *The Works*, published more than half a century before—provided him with a magnificent ungrated fire. Most of all, Max liked the American *attitude* towards fires, so different from the English one and so compatible with his own. In his essay, 'An Infamous Brigade', he reproaches the fire department of his home town for its destructive attitude towards fires. Chicago wins his enthusiastic approbation:

> Americans, as yet inferior to us in the appreciation of most fair things, are far more spirited than we are about fires. Many years ago, when all Chicago was afire, the Mayor, watching it from the Lake-Side, exclaimed in a loud voice, 'Who will say now that ours is not the finest city in all the world?' I remember, too, that some years ago, on the eve of my departure from Chicago, a certain citizen, who was entertaining me at supper, expressed his great regret that they had not been able to show me one of their fires. And indeed it must be splendid to see those twenty-three story buildings come crashing down in less time than was required to build them up. In Chicago, extinction is not attempted. Little value is set on bricks and mortar. A fire is enjoyed; then the building is reproduced and burnt down again at leisure. But we, who pull down, year by year, old inns and almshouses, because they are obsolete in usage, despite their prettiness and their tradition, we, in London, suffer to be saved any wharf or warehouse, however beautiful its encircling flames, however hideous it.

Max had an agreeable memory of a New York fire, too. After his press-agentry, he and Herbert, he told me, were staying at the old Waldorf. One of the actors in the company, who lived in a more modest establishment, was burned out. He burst into Herbert's apartment to report on the experience. Everybody had rushed out of the burning building carrying souvenirs, but this actor, in his excitement, had forgotten to take one. He joined the crowd of spectators on the pavement, and since he now saw that the firemen were demolishing everything, he thought he'd help them out by breaking in a bow window; while he was at it, he dragged out an armchair that, he told Herbert, would do admirably for a prop in one of his productions. Herbert inquired gravely whether it was singed. 'No,' said the actor. 'Just wet.' Max went on to tell me he had been interested in an American book that described how frequently our theatres burned down during this period. 'There was no parallel in England,' said Max, 'because we didn't choose to burn our theatres down.'

Max told me that he had had a good time in America, especially after he lost his job. Relieved of the necessity of writing professional letters, he wrote professionally. He sold two pieces to *Vanity Fair* and two to a short-lived magazine published in Chicago. He got twenty-five dollars apiece for them. He also sold several caricatures. Nobody bought 'Diminuendo'; it was, he said, much too 'stark'. He went with Herbert to Cambridge, Massachusetts, where Herbert read to the Harvard boys—Hamlet's fourth soliloquy in the voice of Falstaff, and Falstaff's 'honour' speech in the voice of Hamlet—but the main thing besides the reading that Max could remember of that occasion was that all the undergraduates parted their hair in the middle. One of them he used as a model for Mr. Oover, the American Rhodes Scholar in *Zuleika Dobson*, which he began to write in 1898 and did not finish until 1911. In Boston, also, Joseph Jefferson, the actor who perennially played Rip Van Winkle, came to call on Max and Herbert, and of this little visit Max remembered that Jefferson kept his hat on the whole time. His eyebrows went up in mild consternation when he told me of this solecism committed by Jefferson's hat, and I did my best to muster an answering expression of shock. In New York, Max met Clyde Fitch, the playwright, who took him to see Edward Harrigan, of Harrigan and Hart, the comedians. Max remembered Harrigan's walk, 'as if threading his way among broken bits of glass, don't you know—at once comic and extraordinarily graceful.' Max greatly liked Fitch, and they became friends. Max wrote in a letter to someone at the time, 'He loves my writing, which is a bond. I have never seen or read anything of his, which is awkward.'

One memory he put in the category of the grotesque. He was approached by an American impresario to give a lecture tour. The impresario was quite insistent. Max handled him. He made a strict counter-proposal. He undertook to give one lecture but stipulated that it must take place at Castle Garden. In addition, there must be no more than twelve people present. The impresario refused to meet this demand, and the whole deal fell through. But the American recollection that gave him the greatest pleasure was of 'a triumph of commercial misjudgment'. It concerned the Paul M. Potter adaptation of George du Maurier's *Trilby*. Herbert, of course, could not go to any shows, since he was playing. In pursuit of a vestigial duty remaining from his original job, Max was sent by Herbert to see *Trilby*, as his play scout, and to report on it. Max's report was unequivocal; the play was absolute nonsense and was bound to be a resounding failure were Herbert so ill-advised as to produce it in London. A lucky instinct kept Herbert ill-advised. On his last day in America, having nothing else to do, he went to see *Trilby* himself. He bought the play at once, and later, playing Svengali, made a huge success in it. It was from the vast profits of *Trilby* that Herbert was able to build himself a vast theatre—Her Majesty's. 'He was luckier,' said Max, 'than poor Chapman, the publisher who turned down *East Lynne* because his reader, George Meredith, had submitted an adverse report on it. But we were both right— Meredith about *East Lynne* and I about *Trilby*.' With the stubbornness of a drama critic, Max held to his view. *Trilby* only demonstrated, as far as he was concerned, that a play could be simultaneously rubbish and a tremendous hit.

In Baltimore, Herbert asked Max to go out front and bring a distinguished fellow-countryman of theirs backstage. This was Rudyard Kipling. Max obediently introduced himself to Kipling. Kipling said, with some surprise, 'You are Max Beerbohm! So young to have a style!' This was graceful, but not enough to forestall a lifelong aversion that was to have tragic reverberations for Max, that haunted him even in his little niche in Rapallo. Perhaps of all the big things in the world that Max could not abide, the one he could abide least was the idea of a big England, and a big England meant British imperialism; perhaps that was what was behind the only virulent relationship in his life—his relationship with Rudyard Kipling. Max was as passionately English as he was passionately anti-chauvinist, but the Boer War revolted him. (Oddly, Shaw supported the Boer War; he felt that the Boers were backward and the British somehow forward, and that this gave the British the right to annihilate the Boers.) Max thought that Kipling, who was the minnesinger of the national orgy, had put his powers to the service of unholy ends.

In 1901, Max drew and exhibited a number of cartoons that were published ten years later under the title *The Second Childhood of John Bull*. It is as bitter as Daumier—unique in that way among Max's productions as a caricaturist. The first two cartoons set the tone of the collection. The first is called 'The Ideal John Bull, 1901'. 'I'm going to see this thing through' is the caption. It shows the traditional indomitable, stocky little figure striding along with a no-nonsense walking stick, one hand in his pocket, the stiff upper lip in an inexorable upcurve. The second is called 'The Real John Bull, 1901', and shows John, his silk hat wrinkled, his cheeks rubicund with wine, his body flabby, cringing with bland ingratiation, invoking (by rote) bygone glories and getting them cockeyed. The caption reads:

> Ah, well, but I ain't doin' so badly neither. There's Boney under lock and key at St. Helena. An' Drake he have stopped that there Armada. An' Burgoyne's goin' to teach them Colonists a lesson. Just you wait. What I say is 'Old England's old England still,' etc., etc., etc.

There is a wicked drawing reflecting Max's pain at the debauches of misplaced patriotism that swept the British public after the newspaper announcements of victories that were not victories. John is lying on the ground with a whisky bottle, and is being given severe glances by figures representing the other European countries. John is, in short, blotto. The first part of the caption reads:

> J. B.: 'What I shay ish thish. A man'sh ash young ash 'e feelsh, an' ash dignified.'

Below this Max appends a sober quotation from an imaginary historian:

> 'We are often taunted with being a phlegmatic and unemotional race; but the nature and the extent of the recent rejoicings will convince even our neighbours, etc., etc.'

The insularity, the Philistinism, the indifference to art, the cruelty and callousness engendered by the hysteria of a war blundering along on a momentum of guilt are anatomized in other relentless cartoons. When John Bull is drunk, he is disgusting, and when he is sober, he is callous, but he has one moment when he is all smiles and approval; that is when he is congratulating Rudyard Kipling. John, well fed again and rosy again, is drawing on a long-stemmed pipe. An obsequious puppy is on its forelegs before him, yielding him true obeisance. Kipling, a short pipe jutting out below the hedge of his moustache, is flourishing a sudsy beer-mug. The caption, the longest in the book, reads:

DE ARTE POETICA. J. B. to R. K. 'Yes, I've took a fancy to you, young feller. 'Tain't often I cottons to a Pote, neither. 'Course there's Shakespeare. 'E was a wonder. 'E was (*sentimentally*). "Swan of Avon" *I* calls 'im. Take 'im for all in all we shall not look upon 'is like agin. And then there was Tennyson—'im as wrote the ode to Balaclavy. 'E was a master-mind too, in his way. So's Lewis Morris. Knows right from wrong like the palm of 'is 'and, and ain't afraid to say where one begins and t'other ends. But most potes ain't like that. What I say is, *they ain't wholesome*. Look at Byron! Saucy 'ound, with 'is stuck-up airs and 'is stuck down collars and 'is oglin' o' gals. But *I* soon sent 'im to the right about. '*Outside*' said I, and out 'e went. And then there was that there friend of his, went by the name o' Shelley, 'ad to go too. 'E was a fair caution, was Shelley. Drownded hisself in a' I-talian lake, and I warrant that was the fust bath 'e ever took. Most of 'em is like that—*not wholesome*, and can't keep a civil tongue i' their 'eads. You're different, you are: don't give yourself no 'aughty airs, and though you're rough (with your swear-words and your what-nots), I will say as 'ow you've always bin very civil an' respec'ful to myself. You're one o' the right sort, you are. And them little tit-bits o' information what you gives me about my Hempire—why Alf 'Armsworth 'imself couldn't do it neater, I do believe. Got your banjo with you to-night? Then empty that there mug, and give us a toon.'

When I was a child, on Providence Street, in Worcester, Massachusetts, Rudyard Kipling was a very great name indeed. My elders were avid for culture, and one of them gave me a copy of *The Light That Failed*, by Kipling. I read it with awe. Many other people in Worcester read it with awe. The demand for it at the public library on Elm Street was terrific. Several years ago, after reading Max's review of the play made from *The Light That Failed*, in his *Around Theatres*, I read *The Light That Failed* again—this time with in-

credulity. The hero, Dick Heldar, has made his reputation as
a painter of war scenes in the Sudan, when General Gordon
was embattled at Khartoum; his two buddies are war correspondents, terribly he-man. After a day with his sweetheart,
Maisie, Dick longs to join them for 'man-talk'. When they have
exhausted their man-talk, they have sofa-pillow fights. When
they hear that there may be trouble again 'down there', they
salivate with anticipation; the sights, the smells, the mere
thought of war put them in a state of ecstasy. In his essay on the
dramatization of *The Light That Failed* by a playwright who
used the pseudonym George Fleming, Max ambushes this
rampant virility of Kipling's. Because 'George Fleming' is the
pseudonym of a woman, he hazards the opinion that 'Rudyard
Kipling' is also; he starts his review, under the heading
'Kipling's Entire', as follows:

> 'George Fleming' is, as we know, a lady. Should the name
> Rudyard Kipling, too, be put between inverted commas? Is
> it, too, the veil of a feminine identity? If of Mr. Kipling we
> knew nothing except his work, we should assuredly make that
> conjecture. A lady who writes fiction reveals her sex clearlier
> through her portrayal of men than through any other of her
> lapses. And in Mr. Kipling's short stories, especially in *The
> Light That Failed* . . . men are portrayed . . . from an
> essentially feminine point of view. They are men seen from the
> outside, or rather, not seen at all, but feverishly imagined. . . .
> '*My* men—*my* men!' cries Dick Heldar when a regiment of
> soldiers passes his window. He is not their commanding officer.
> He was at one time a war-correspondent. . . . He had always
> doted on the military. And so has Mr. Kipling. To him, as
> to his hero, they typify, in its brightest colours, the notion of
> manhood, manliness, man. And by this notion Mr. Kipling
> is permanently and joyously obsessed. That is why I say that
> his standpoint is feminine. The ordinary male fictionist has a
> knowledge of men as they are, but is preoccupied by a senti-
> ment for women as he supposes them to be. . . . Mr. Kipling
> is so far masculine that he has never displayed a knowledge
> of women as they are; but the unreality of his male creatures,
> with his worship of them, makes his name ring quaintly like a
> pseudonym. . . . Writing of George Sand, Mr. Henry James
> once suggested that she, though she may have been to all
> intents and purposes a man, was not a gentleman. Conversely,

The small hours in the sixties at 16 Cheyne Walk—Algernon reading 'Anactoria' to Gabriel and William
(Swinburne with Dante Gabriel and William Rossetti)

Some Persons of 'the Nineties'

From left to right: Richard le Gallienne, W. R. Sickert, Arthur Symons, George Moore, John Davidson, Henry Harland, Charles Conder, Oscar Wilde, William Rothenstein, Max Beerbohm, W. B. Yeats, Aubrey Beardsley and 'Enoch Soames'

it might be said that Mr. Kipling, as revealed to us in his fiction, is no lady. But he is not the less essentially feminine for that.

On the whole, Max praises Miss Fleming; he thinks she has caught Miss Kipling entire. But he misses terribly two lines of the original. In one, Dick Heldar says of his sweetheart, 'Maisie's a bilious little thing', and the other is a heart-rending cry of the hero: 'When Dick, after blindness has overtaken him, ecstatically yells to the soldiers who have been ordered to fire the machine-gun on some skirmishing Arabs, "Give 'em Hell, men—oh, give 'em Hell." Sad not to have heard that noble heart-cry uttered on the stage—a heart-cry so inalienably characteristic of the Kipling hero.'

Max pursued Kipling inexorably. In *A Christmas Garland*, his book of parodies, caricaturing in prose the manner in which seventeen then famous authors would write a Christmas story, he starts 'P.C., X, 36', the Kipling one, with a parody of the *Barrack-Room Ballads*:

> . . .'Ustle 'im, shake 'im till 'e's sick!
> Wot, 'e *would*, would 'e? Well,
> Then yer've got ter give 'im 'Ell,
> An' it's trunch, trunch, truncheon does the trick!
> *Police Station Ditties*.

The culprit who gets the truncheon is Santa Claus, who is arrested, by Judlip, the police constable, as he is coming up out of a chimney, on the suspicion that he is a German. Kipling's obsession with technical minutiae is parodied in Max's description of Judlip's sigh:

> Now, when Judlip sighs the sound is like unto that which issues from the vent of a Crosby boiler when the cog-gauges are at 260° F.

It is a slow Christmas Eve for Judlip. He complains, ' 'Avent 'ad so much as a kick at a lorst dorg. Christmas Eve ain't wot it was.' But with the advent of Santa Claus, emerging from the chimney, things look up:

> Judlip's voice clove the silence. 'Wot are yer doin' hup there?'

3

The person addressed came to the edge of the parapet. I saw then that he had a hoary white beard, a red ulster with the hood up, and what looked like a sack over his shoulder. He said something or other in a voice like a concertina that has been left out in the rain.

'I dessay,' answered my friend. 'Just you come down, an' we'll see about that.'

Santa Claus was ill-advised to come down.

He didn't like the feel of Judlip's knuckles at his cervical vertebrae.

'Wot wos yer doin' hup there?' asked Judlip, tightening the grip.

'I'm S-Santa Claus, Sir. P-please, Sir, let me g-go . . .'

The captive snivelled something about peace on earth, good will toward men.

'Yuss,' said Judlip. 'That's in the Noo Testament, ain't it? The Noo Testament contains some uncommon nice readin' for old gents an' young ladies. But it ain't included in the librery o' the Force. . . . Hup with that sack, an' quick march!'

I have seen worse attempts at a neck-wrench, but it was just not slippery enough for Judlip. And the kick that Judlip then let fly was a thing of beauty and a joy for ever.

'Frog's-march him!' I shrieked, dancing. 'For the love of heaven, frog's-march him!'

C. E. Carrington, in his *Life of Kipling*, refers bitterly to the steady barrage Max levelled at Kipling:

Max Beerbohm published very little, and while he protested so prettily that his muse was no bigger than the servant-girl's baby, the literary world learned to wait expectant for each of his tiny little pronouncements, for Max had charm and talent. No one could deny, or did deny, that his work was polished, his wit penetrating—more penetrating with pencil than with pen. For fifty years anything spoken or written or depicted by Max called forth a shrill chorus of delight from the reviewers, and the present writer supposes himself almost the first to utter an unkind word about this incomparable master of the smirk and titter. Max was, as a rule, gentle, except when he touched upon one topic. He hated Rudyard Kipling. He set himself to destroy Kipling's reputation and, later, to assure the world that it had been destroyed, with no small degree of success among the literary coteries, but with no visible effect upon Kipling's ever-growing fame and influence in wider circles.

At least nine caricatures, two critical articles, and a ferociously malevolent parody of Kipling's style have been recorded as the work of Max Beerbohm, and while he discharged these arrows, Kipling, for thirty years, remained entirely unmoved by them.

There are two misstatements in Mr. Carrington's summary, of which he was probably unaware when he made them. One is that Kipling was unmoved by Max's attacks. When David Low wrote to Kipling asking to caricature him, Kipling refused, because, according to Low, he was still exacerbated by a caricature Max had done of him twenty years before, and on this ground he repelled all caricaturists. The other is that Max hated Kipling. As we sat by the fireplace, I told Max how extravagantly idolized Kipling was on Providence Street, and of my disillusioning experience in reading *The Light That Failed* after I had read his review in *Around Theatres*. I hoped that he would talk about his relationship with Kipling.

A truck thundered by; I thought perhaps he had not heard me, because he made no comment on my remark. Instead, he told me about the chair in which he was sitting—that it was the same chair his father had given him when he went up to Merton. 'Florence had it re-covered, and now Elisabeth has had it re-covered again—always with material similar to that which covered it in Oxford,' he said. 'It is really a very comfortable chair in which to sit and gaze at the fire. I deplore the passing of fireplaces. In flats, you can't usually have a fireplace; a house, no matter how tiny, with a fireplace in the living-room encourages conversation and companionship. In my mother's house, we always sat in front of the fireplace—my mother and sisters and I—and we had endless conversations about people and books and things. When I was a dramatic critic, I used to tell them about the plays I had seen and they used to tell me about the books they had read which I hadn't the time for because I was constantly seeing plays.'

I then got the feeling that he *had* heard my remark about Kipling, that the subject was painful to him, and that he didn't want to talk about it.

We sat in silence for a moment before the murmuring fire. Looking up at the mantelshelf, I studied the bronze figurine of the girl with averted head. I asked Max whether she had been with him in his rooms at Merton, too.

'Yes,' he said. 'My father bought her in Paris—at the same time that he bought the mirror.'

Miss Jungmann put a rug around Max's knees. She asked him if he was tired. He smiled at her and at me. 'Not yet,' he said. I offered to go. Max refused my offer. Miss Jungmann said she had a small errand to do, and excused herself. 'Show our visitor your two photographs,' she said as she turned to go out. 'They are Max's household gods—rather, goddesses. He can't bear to have them out of reach.' Miss Jungmann left us.

'Oh, yes,' said Max. 'Will you please take them down for me?'

I took from the mantelshelf the two photographs, a little larger than ordinary postcards. I gave them to Max, and he sat looking at them as if he had never seen them before. 'I always keep them by me,' he said. 'Look . . .' One showed two lovely girls in white, standing on a lawn beside a low wall on which there are huge urns. It is night. Above them are great beech trees, part of their slender trunks and their foliage white in the moonlight. 'Gordon Craig bought this in London in 1929 and gave it to me,' Max said. 'It had been in the library of Augustus Hare. It is a country house, Buttles, which Hare used to visit before the wars came, when the world was civilized. Now, I am told, in the drawing-room of that house they play billiards!' Max looked up at me from the photograph—a commiserating look, to ease the shock, to show me that he felt as bad about it as he imagined I did. 'But aren't they lovely? It is after dinner, probably, and the house is full of people, and perhaps they were bored and wanted to get off by themselves to gossip or to exchange romantic confidences. Aren't they lovely? Isn't it lovely? Vanished. That life and that era—vanished.'

He paused a moment longer over the two girls and then gave me the other photograph. This was a study in pure joy.

A little girl of three or four is standing beside a priest in full canonicals. The priest has just told her a funny story and the little girl's freckled, pug-nosed, homely face is crinkled with laughter; she is giving herself up to laughter without a let. You feel that she will go on laughing and laughing, and will laugh again whenever she remembers what the priest has said to her; the priest himself is smiling, revelling in the success of his joke. I asked where this photograph had come from. 'Oh,' said Max, 'it is a photograph from a book about Huysmans; it is the Abbé Mugnier with the little daughter of the Countess de Castries. I never look at it without its cheering me up. How happy she is! How happy they both are!''

Max took a farewell glance at the little girl and handed that photograph to me. His cheek muscles worked. 'You spoke to me of Kipling,' he said. He stopped for a moment. As rarely happened, his tranquillity was gone; he was tense. 'When first I met him, in Baltimore, he received me so nicely,' he said. 'He was charming. And later, in Herbert's dressing-room, so sympathetic, so kind. And then—you know—his books kept coming out, and occasionally I was asked to review them. I couldn't, you know, abide them. He was a genius, a very great genius, and I felt that he was debasing his genius by what he wrote. And I couldn't refrain from saying so. It went on and on. Friends of his and mine kept telling me that he was pained and shocked by what I wrote, but I couldn't stop. You know, I couldn't stop. As his publication increased, so did my derogation. He didn't stop; I *couldn't* stop. I meant to. I wanted to. But I couldn't.'

Max was suffering at this time from a severe inflammation of the lower lid of his left eye. He was very sensitive about it; he thought that it might be offensive to those who talked to him. As he leaned forward in his chair, he was still tense, and his eye seemed to water. He gripped the arms of the Merton chair as if to sustain himself against the pain of the memory induced by his feud with Kipling—as one instinctively grips the arms of the seat in an aeroplane during a sudden, violent dip. He went on, seeming determined, now that he had started, to tell the whole story. 'After that meeting in Baltimore, I saw him twice. Once in a hansom. I was in another hansom, and we passed each other in the Strand. He saw me and he knew that I had seen him. But as the hansoms passed, we each of us averted our eyes. Then, some years later, I saw him again, in White's Club. There was a table between us, and, looking across it, over the heads of the diners, I caught his eye. He was looking at me. I wished to get up. I very much wanted to go over to him and to say, "Mr. Kipling, I admire you. I admire your very great genius. If I have written harshly of you, it is because I do not believe you are living up to the possibilities of your genius." I so much wished to do this. But I didn't. Why didn't I do it? Why didn't I unbend? Why did I go on persecuting him? And now he is dead and it is too late.'

There was a silence. Max was still bent forward. His hands still clutched the arms of his chair. His eye was still watering. 'But it had to be so. I had to do it. He was a great genius who didn't live up to his genius, who misused his genius. . . .'

Miss Jungmann came back. She looked at Max. He sank back in his chair. 'Now, Max,' she said. 'You *are* tired. You must have a rest.'

I rose to go. I asked Max not to get up, but he did. I walked out of the room dead centre, conscious that the mirror, which had seen so many exits over so many decades, was miniaturizing and essentializing my back.

Miss Jungmann saw me out through the little hall, and we said good night under Gordon Craig's lamp. I apologized for staying so long.

'No,' she said. 'I think it's good for Max. Your visits are therapeutic.'

She peered out at Charlie, his car jammed against the rubble wall of the Villino. She called to him, in Italian, to back up to the gate. 'Charlie thinks that I am Max's daughter,' she said. 'All the tradespeople do, too. Don't disillusion him!' She waved to me as I got into the front seat beside Charlie.

'Very nice lady, the old gentleman's daughter,' said Charlie. 'Speaks very good Italian.'

I asked Charlie to drop me at the little *bistro* down the road
from the Villino, which is the hero of Max's essay 'The Golden
Drugget'. Charlie protested. 'This is no place for you,' he said.
I suppose he meant that it was much too lowly for a guest of the
Excelsior. But I overrode him. I asked him to wait, and went
inside, sat at a zinc-topped table, and ordered a Cinzano.

Max wrote his essay in England in 1918. He had gone back
to England to live for the duration of the war. From England
he remembered the kindly light shed from this humble little
bistro on a dark night:

> Primitive and essential things have great power to touch the
> heart of the beholder. I mean such things as a man ploughing
> a field, or sowing or reaping; a girl filling a pitcher from a
> spring; a young mother with her child; a fisherman mending
> his nets; a light from a lonely hut on a dark night. . . .
> These words are written in war time and in England.
> There are, I hear, 'lighting restrictions' even on the far
> Riviera di Levante. I take it that the Golden Drugget is not
> outspread nowanights across the high dark coast-road between
> Rapallo and Zoagli. But the lonely wayside inn is still there,
> doubtless; and its narrow door will again stand open, giving
> out for wayfarers its old span of brightness into darkness, when
> peace comes.

The light from the hostel on dark nights, Max says, offered
a promise that 'you will find here a radiant company of angels
and archangels.' Max never tested it; he never once went
inside. I did. I saw no angels, of any degree, but it was consoling,
just the same, to sit here. I thought of the two girls in white
whispering romantic confidences under spreading beech trees,
of the laughing little girl and the smiling priest, of Max
struggling, in unregretful remorse, to resolve in his own mind
his feud with Kipling. As any great humorist must be, Max was
incessantly and acutely aware of pain and sorrow, of the
evanescence of human life, of the savagery and the impulse to
destructiveness that are beneath everything and from which,
somehow, we must try to pull ourselves up. Though he himself,
as he wrote somewhere, was 'thickly veneered', he nevertheless
knew, since he belonged to the human race, that he had only
lately emerged from the cave. Some of the most casual and

lightly begun of his essays modulate into this tragic awareness, and none more poignantly than this one. I paused, as Max does at the end of 'The Golden Drugget', 'to bathe in the light that is as the span of our human life, granted between one great darkness and another.'

III

ON THE TERRACE

IN DECEMBER of 1926, I made my first journey to England, in the company of two older friends—Crosby Gaige, a prominent New York theatrical producer with bookish tastes, and his wife, Hilda, who fiercely admired the distinguished actor Sir Gerald du Maurier. Mrs. Gaige knew when we sailed, on the *Majestic*, that Sir Gerald was closing in Frederick Lonsdale's *The Last of Mrs. Cheyney* at the St. James's Theatre on the Saturday the ship was due to dock at Southampton. From the boat, she radioed to London, asking for seats for the final performance. The boat train reached London late in the afternoon; the Gaiges scarcely had time to register in their hotel and I in mine before we all met to gulp a hasty dinner and take a taxi to the theatre. After the performance, we went back to see Sir Gerald. It used to be said of Sir Gerald that he did not so much act as *behave* on the stage; he performed with an air of absent-mindedness, as if he were thinking all the time of other, and more agreeable, things than the ones he was professionally concerned with at the moment—of tooled-leather bindings, perhaps, or a lovely still-life, or maybe just of what would be waiting for him for supper when he got back, with relief, to Cannon Hall, where he lived. His dressing-room was a suite, and his dresser offered us a drink in the salon while we waited for Sir Gerald to appear.

Actually, I remembered the period of waiting more vividly than the meeting itself, because I became engrossed in a caricature by Max Beerbohm that was hanging on one wall. The caricature itself, entitled 'Long Choosing and Beginning

Late', was arresting, and the story it told in the legend—in Max's calligraphic handwriting—was even sensational. How sensational I did not know till many years later. It told a singular love story, projected into an era following a Bolshevik revolution in England in 1972. Max imagines Edward Windsor, then the Prince of Wales, as an old gentleman falling in love with and eventually marrying—against the stern opposition of the bride's parents—the daughter of a boarding-house keeper, named Flossie Pearson. While Mrs. Gaige was staring in trancelike suspension at the door through which Sir Gerald was to emerge, I started copying on a pad the legend Max had written to commemorate the ceremony at which the Prince and Flossie were united.

But before I could get going on Max's forecast of how *The Times* would comment on this improbable marriage, Sir Gerald came in. He had a quick eye, and he saw what I was doing; I was embarrassed, as if I had been caught reading one of his letters. Sir Gerald responded with murmured appreciation when he was told that we had rushed from the docks at Southampton to his final performance. In the lacquered conversation that ensued, I managed to insert a query about Max's caricature. 'Oh, amusing, isn't it?' said Sir Gerald absent-mindedly. 'I bought it at the Leicester Galleries, where it was first seen, in 1923. Kicked up quite a storm, you know.' I wanted to inquire about the nature of the storm, but Mrs. Gaige was imploring Sir Gerald to come to America and telling him what a reception he would find there. Sir Gerald managed to convey simultaneously the impression that there was nothing in the world he would rather do and the impression that there was nothing in the world he was less likely to do.

I kept looking at the caricature. 'Do you know Max Beerbohm?' I asked Sir Gerald.

'Oh, rather,' he said. 'For ever.'

By this time, other people had begun to stream in, and we got up to go.

In the summer of 1929, I was in London again, and again at the St. James's Theatre. The Lunts were playing in an adaptation of a Central European comedy called *Caprice*. Mrs. Lunt had Sir Gerald's dressing-room, and I had the hope, when I went back to see her after the performance, that I would be able to get another look at Max's caricature. There it was! Sir Gerald had left his dressing-room intact, against his next engagement. I was far more at ease with Miss Fontanne than I had been with him, and I sat down before 'Long Choosing and Beginning Late' to read and copy what *The Times* would one day have to say about the wedding of Edward Windsor and Flossie Pearson:

> An interesting wedding was quietly celebrated yesterday at the Ealing Registry Office, when Mr. Edward Windsor was united to Miss Flossie Pearson. The bridegroom, as many of our elder readers will recall, was one time well-known as 'heir-apparent' of the late 'King' George. He has for some years been residing at 'Balmoral', 85 Acacia Terrace, Lenin Avenue, Ealing; and his bride is the only daughter of his landlady. Immediately after the ceremony the happy pair travelled to Ramsgate, where the honeymoon will be spent. Interviewed later in the day by a *Times* man, the aged mother-in-law confessed that she had all along been opposed to the union, because of the disparity between the ages of the two parties— the bride being still on the sunny side of forty. 'I had always,' she said, 'hoped that my Flossie was destined to make a brilliant match.' Now that the knot was tied, however, the old lady was evidently resigned to the fait accompli. 'I believe,' she said, 'that Mr. Windsor will make a good husband for my girl, for I must say that a nicer, quieter gentleman, or a more pleasant-spoken, never lodged under my roof.'

Five years later, I was once more in London. Sir Gerald had just died, and I was eager to find out what had become of that caricature. I sought out Sir William Rothenstein, because I knew that he was one of Max's closest friends. In *Enoch Soames*, Max describes Rothenstein's irruption into Oxford when he himself was still an undergraduate at Merton. 'He was Paris in Oxford,' Max says, in rapturous recollection. Sir William proved to be a small, mercurial man—though not quite as small as Max liked to draw him. It was on this 1934 visit to London that I bought from Sir William the lovely pastel of Max standing on the terrace outside his workroom, not working. Before that, however, Sir William invited me to the Athenaeum for lunch. There I told my host about having seen in Sir Gerald's dressing-room Max's caricature of the Prince of Wales and Flossie Pearson, and asked him if he knew what had become of it. Sir William, with an I-could-an-if-I-would air that was very tantalizing, slid off into some private grievance.

'Is the caricature in private hands?' I inquired. 'Did Sir Gerald sell it?'

'I believe he did,' Sir William said. 'Yes, I believe it is in private hands. In any case, it is inaccessible.'

'What about the storm over it when it was first exhibited?' I asked.

At this, Sir William's eyes lit up; where there was a storm, he was in his element. 'Oh, terrific!' he said. 'Max had to withdraw it. Du Maurier was lucky to have bought it in time. Max was accused of all sorts of things in the press. We've laughed and laughed over it together since.'

By this time, my host was in such a jolly mood that I ventured to threaten him. 'If you won't tell me where that caricature is,' I said, 'I will write to Beerbohm myself to ask him.'

Rothenstein made, for him, a large gesture. 'Of course you may write to him,' he said. 'He won't answer. Max never answers letters.'

If I could not force Sir William to tell me where the caricature was, I could at least, I thought, repair to the British Museum to calibrate the storm, and this I did. It had indeed been considerable. The caricature whose legend I had copied in Sir Gerald's dressing-room in 1929 came in for a hurricane of fury when it was shown in the Leicester Galleries in 1923. Hannen Swaffer, a drama critic but not a humorist, headed a diatribe in the *Daily Graphic* 'The End of Max Beerbohm', a prophecy that Max deflated by not ending. There were, elsewhere, suggestions that Mr. Beerbohm was 'either a stealthy Bolshevist or a shameless bounder'. In the same exhibition, Max had included a caricature of Edward Windsor's late grandfather, revealing him in Heaven, an overfed, haloed angel strumming a lyre. 'Dastardly attack on Royalty', 'teutonically brutal', 'infamous bad taste', and, conversely, 'an offence to good taste', were some of the tempestuous words flung at Max. Max, I learned, withdrew the royal caricatures. 'It seemed,' he said in a letter he wrote to the Leicester Galleries, 'that they were likely to be misunderstood by the general public and to worry it.' The last thing Max wanted to do was to worry anybody.

I did not carry out my threat to write to Max himself to find out what had happened to the Windsor caricature. In fact, twenty years passed and Sir William was nearly ten years dead before I found out. I was again in Rapallo and again staying at the Excelsior. Since Max was not inclined to receive callers in the evening, I usually spent the hours between four and six in the afternoon with him. One hot July night, some American friends who were staying in nearby Portofino invited me to join them for dinner there, and I accepted. I summoned Charlie to take me to Portofino. On the way, Charlie told me that I was lucky I was going there, because the Duke and Duchess of Windsor were aboard a yacht in the bay; if my luck held, he said, I might catch a glimpse of them, for they came ashore every night to dine. My luck did hold. After dinner that night, my friends and I walked to the esplanade, curving like a horseshoe around the little bay, and sat on the terrace of a café having drinks. Before long, Charlie's wish for me was realized. The Duchess and her hostess were striding purposefully along the quay. The hostess, a round little woman, was very bouncy, and the Duchess, walking beside her, was equally brisk. Following them, at some distance, was the Duke, alone and walking wearily. He carried his jacket strung across his sagging shoulders; he looked like a tired commuter trudging to catch the train that would presently take him back to the same old bungalow. I remembered, of course, the caricature in du Maurier's dressing-room; the romance of this same Duke with Flossie Pearson; the great storm; my interview with Rothenstein, when he wouldn't tell me—though obviously he knew—where that caricature was. And now I wondered whether Max, whom I intended to ask about it the following day, would be less reticent than Sir William.

The next day, when I rang the doorbell of the Villino at
four, Miss Jungmann opened the door. She was in a state of
breathless excitement. 'Max is on the terrace!' she said. 'We
are going to have tea on the terrace!' Behind her excitement
lay the fact that it was her constant effort to get Max to leave
his tiny living-room and move about a bit. That day, the
weather was so fine that he had gone up after lunch and was
there even now. I followed Miss Jungmann through the house
and up the outdoor staircase that led to the terrace, and there
found Max, his straw hat on his head and his cane in one hand,
lounging against the parapet and looking out over the Gulf of
Genoa, as he had been doing in my workrooms at home for
two decades. I lounged beside him. I told Max that the scene
was familiar to me, that I had bought him and it from Sir
William Rothenstein in 1934. I added that since his figure in
the drawing was diaphanous, I had been seeing through him
for years.

Max laughed, and began to reminisce about Rothenstein.
'Will was a propulsive character, don't you know. He had
a propulsive mental activity. My caricatures [Max always
emphasized the last syllable in pronouncing this word, and the
't' sounded very precise and pure] of him were cruel, I am
afraid. He knew they were, and yet he took it manfully.' Max
reflected for a moment, in wonderment, on this cruelty. 'As
a writer, I was kindly, I think—Jekyll—but as a caricaturist I
was Hyde. I always preferred the society of painters to that of
writers: Walter Sickert, William Nicholson, Wilson Steer.
Writers, including myself, don't you know, like to make an
effect, put their best foot forward. But painters are another
story. Steer, for example, had no interest whatever in the
impression he made; he was just interested in painting. One
day, Sickert said to me, "Your caricatures of dear Will and of
Oscar Wilde were so deadly. I know how Oscar feels about
them—he can't bear them—but doesn't Will resent them?
Isn't he angry?" "More frightened," I said to Walter, "than
angry." But I loved Will; he was so kind. No one took such
trouble over young artists, to help them; there was nothing
he wouldn't do. But Oscar——'

Max leaned over the parapet, looking across the gulf. I encouraged him to say what he was thinking of Oscar.

'Well, in the beginning he was the most enchanting company, don't you know. His conversation was so simple and natural and flowing—not at all epigrammatic, which would have been unbearable. He saved that for his plays, thank heaven.'

As an illustration of Wilde's imperturbability at the beginning of his terrible debacle, Max repeated a story told him many years before by Lewis Waller, a matinée idol of the time. Waller was walking down Piccadilly with Allan Aynesworth, another accomplished actor. Waller was playing Sir Robert Chiltern in *An Ideal Husband* and Aynesworth Algernon in *The Importance of Being Earnest*. The Wilde scandal looked like closing both plays. The two actors were deep in talk about the source of their imminent unemployment when, to their horror, they were hailed cheerily by their disemployer, riding blithely down Piccadilly in a hansom cab. They returned his greeting pallidly, hoping Wilde would ride on, but he didn't. He got out and came up to them. 'Have you heard,' he inquired, 'what that swine Queensberry has had the effrontery to say?' Writhing with embarrassment, they both protested that no rumour of the Marquess's allegation had reached their chaste ears. 'Since you haven't heard it, I'll tell you,' said Wilde, with the eagerness of a tutor avid to fill in a gap in folklore. 'He actually had the effrontery to say'—and he fixed his eye on Waller—'that *The Importance of Being Earnest* was a better-acted play than *An Ideal Husband*!' He smiled radiantly, waved, got back into his hansom, and rode off down Piccadilly, leaving his victims gasping.

Max then spoke of his friends Ernest and Ada Leverson. He used to see a lot of them in their large, comfortable London house. Ada Leverson—the Sphinx, she was called—was a staunch friend to everyone who wrote or painted anything. She has survived best, perhaps, as having been the only person in London who would receive Wilde when he was out on bail between his two trials. Max said that she deserved credit for this, but that no one ever gave any credit to poor Mr. Leverson, who consented to let Wilde stay in his house. The Sphinx, Max said, cared only about the opinion of the artistic set, but 'Mr. Leverson had larger responsibilities. He was a prominent figure in the City and had much more to lose.' On the morning of Wilde's return from prison, Max continued, Mrs. Leverson got up very early in order to greet Wilde, who was coming straight from prison to the home of a clergyman named Stewart Headlam. She was in an agony of apprehension—how to greet this broken figure whom she had known, and received in her house, as the most sought-after lion in London. By the time she reached Headlam's house, she was in a panic. Then Wilde came in. He ran to her, smiling—a schoolboy greeting a pet aunt after a dreary semester—threw his arms around her, and crowed with appreciation, 'Sphinx, how marvellous of you to know exactly the right hat to wear at seven o'clock in the morning to meet a friend who has been away. You can't have got up; you must have sat up.' Ada had no worries after that.

'But, you know'—Max's eyes darkened with regret, and his brow furrowed—'as Oscar became more and more successful, he became . . .' Max paused, as if he couldn't bear to say it, but he did say it. 'He became arrogant. He felt himself omnipotent, and he became gross not in body only—he did become that—but in his relations with people. He brushed people aside; he felt he was beyond the ordinary human courtesies that you owe people even if they are, in your opinion, beneath you. He snubbed Charles Brookfield, the actor who played the lackey in *An Ideal Husband*—he was a wonderful, unfailing actor in small parts, and was said to be an illegitimate son of Thackeray, you know—and Brookfield never forgave him. Brookfield was vindictive; Brookfield hated Oscar, and it was Brookfield who did him in—supplied evidence against him. And I myself——It did give me a turn——'

I waited to hear what had given Max a turn. He told me.

'One day, I found myself in the office of the police inspector who had arrested Oscar. I don't know why; perhaps I went there to get news of Oscar or to find out whether there might be some amelioration—I don't know. This police inspector had offended Oscar when he arrested him.' Max's voice thickened in imitation. ' "Gruss misdemeanour!" the inspector kept shouting, and the gross mispronunciation grated on Oscar. There I was in his office. The walls were covered with a grisly collection of criminal souvenirs—oh, knives and pistols and bludgeons, all the implements of crime—and there among them, as though it were evidence against the inspector's latest malefactor, was one of my own caricatures of Oscar. I hadn't realized till that moment how wicked it was. I felt as if I had contributed to the dossier against Oscar; it gave me quite a turn. How did I come to do it? My hand did it, don't you know.'

Max looked ruefully at his hand, resting on the sunny parapet. His eyes had an expression of pain and bewilderment, as if he could neither understand nor explain the dichotomy in his art and in his nature. After a moment, he looked up; the furrows in his brow disappeared and he returned, as to a green pasture, to Will Rothenstein. 'I used to stay with Will. It was wonderful to stay with the Rothensteins at Far Oakridge, in Gloucestershire. I finished there one of the stories in *Seven Men*—"Maltby and Braxton". You are perhaps familiar with it?'

I was familiar with it: it is a study in the pathology of social climbing, as demonstrated by two newly arrived novelists Max invented. Maltby had had a great success with a novel called *Ariel in Mayfair*, Braxton simultaneously with *A Faun on the Cotswolds*. Braxton went in for fauns and Maltby for aristocrats. They are both—Braxton in his gruff, churlish way, and Maltby in his bland, ingratiating one—madly snobbish. The great prize is to be asked to the 'almost blatantly immemorial' country house of the Duke of Hertfordshire, Keeb Hall. At a party at which both are present, the Duchess invites Maltby; she wants to invite Braxton, but Maltby tells her that Braxton would be offended by the invitation and she forbears. The story is the account of the horrendous week-end, made disastrous for Maltby by his sense of guilt, as represented by Braxton's spiritualized presence, which Maltby can't get away from. Three of Max's favourite non-imaginary caricature subjects are there also: Henry Chaplin, the Marquis de Soveral, Arthur

Balfour. The last tries to help Maltby through his final horror but without much success. The experience is so eroding that, after it, Maltby has to leave England. He settles at Lucca, where Max meets him and gets the story. Maltby is quite happy. He has married his elderly landlady, and he expresses to Max his felicity in the last lines of the story:

> Maltby looked at his watch. He rose and took tenderly from the table his great bunch of roses. 'She is [he says of his wife, in an ecstasy of snobbery] a lineal descendant . . . of the Emperor Hadrian.'

I asked Max who had been the models for Maltby and Braxton. He would not tell me, though he said that Thomas Hardy had always insisted that they were H. G. Wells and Arnold Bennett. 'When I had finished the story, I told the Rothensteins that I had done so and that I had used their demesne for local colour,' Max said. 'Thereupon they both insisted—Will and Alice, Alice perhaps even more clamorous— that I read it aloud to them after dinner. Will was electrically attentive, but dear Alice fell asleep. I read and read, and Alice slept and slept. When I was approaching the end, I felt that something had to be done to spare Alice the embarrassment of having slept through a masterpiece.' Max gave me a quick look that was the equivalent of a wink. 'Therefore, when I got near the end, I began to read very loud. I bellowed, and Alice, startled, woke up. She came in for the kill, don't you know. She was most enthusiastic. She had, indeed, loved the story, so she insisted that I read it again. But my throat was hoarse from shouting and I forbore.'

I asked Max whether he hadn't been disturbed by Lady Rothenstein's critique.

'No,' he said quietly, 'because I knew the story was good.'

I spoke of Rothenstein's three-volume *Men and Memories*, the final volume of which is dedicated to Max, and he was pleased that I had enjoyed it. He recited to me a poem he had written about Rothenstein, first explaining to me how resilient Rothenstein was in mood—'always matching your own, don't you know.' Max recited the poem with spirit:

Poem on a Certain Friend's Remarkable Faculty for Generalization

'How do you do?' Will asked of me.
'Very well, thanks,' said I. Said he,
'Yes. I invariably find
Abundant health in all mankind.'

Next morning, 'How d'you do?' asked Will.
I told him I was rather ill.
'Alas,' his voice toll'd like a bell,
'Mankind was ever far from well.'

After we had laughed over the poem, Max felt a twinge of conscience. 'Perhaps I shouldn't have told you that,' he said. 'It will hurt poor Will.' I don't think that Max had forgotten, even momentarily, that poor Will had long since died; Max had read the eulogy at Will's memorial service. It was probably that he did not wish, even in fun, to ruffle the memory of his dead friend.

Miss Jungmann summoned us to tea, and gave instructions to the young Italian servant-girl who was setting the tea tray on a little table under an umbrella in front of Max's study. Max put his hat and cane on a chair. At tea, I described to Miss Jungmann and Max the scene I had witnessed in Portofino the night before. Max chuckled when I remarked on how energetic the Duchess looked and how weary the Duke.

'Sometimes he seems to have become a butt,' said Miss Jungmann.

'Not as bad,' said Max tolerantly, 'as being an if.'

I planted my next remark carefully. 'Isn't it odd,' I said, 'that at one time the Duchess's mother ran a boarding-house?'

'Did she? Did she really?' said Max. 'Did you know a countryman of yours—a radio artist, I believe he was—Alexander Woollcott?'

This diversion pulverized my plant so thoroughly that I did not even bother to enlarge on Woollcott's occupations. When Max found that I had indeed known him, he went on, 'I met him in England during the war. He was brought by Thornton

Wilder. I looked forward eagerly to meeting Mr. Wilder. I wished to hear him talk. But Mr. Woollcott talked *all* the time and Mr. Wilder never said anything, and I began to wonder— you know, I began to wonder whether Mr. Wilder *could* talk. But then Mr. Woollcott left, and Mr. Wilder *did*, and most enchantingly.'

I began to re-mine. 'That caricature you drew of the Prince of Wales,' I said. 'I saw it first in Sir Gerald du Maurier's dressing-room in St. James's Theatre.'

Max remembered that du Maurier had bought it, and was much interested to hear that I had seen it.

I then told him that in 1934 I had pumped Sir William Rothenstein about it, with no result.

Max was extremely interested.

I said that Max had, in that fantasy, been prophetic.

'It is amusing, isn't it?' he said. 'No matter how fantastic one is in art, life always surpasses one.'

Miss Jungmann was seized with a bright idea. 'Do you mind, Max, if I show Queen Victoria's book?'

Max didn't mind.

Miss Jungmann rose and went into the study to fetch it. 'Have you read Queen Victoria at all?' Max asked me.

I confessed I hadn't.

'Whatever may be said of Queen Victoria's style,' Max went on, 'it has to be admitted, I think, that no one ever, before or since, has written like her.' Miss Jungmann appeared with the book. It was *More Leaves from the Journal of a Life in the Highlands.* It is dedicated

To
MY LOYAL HIGHLANDERS
and especially
TO THE MEMORY OF
MY DEVOTED PERSONAL ATTENDANT
AND FAITHFUL FRIEND
JOHN BROWN

'But wait,' said Miss Jungmann. 'There is another dedication!' She turned the page, and there, scrawled in pen, in a slashing schoolgirl handwriting, with great flourishes, was:

For Mr. Beerbohm
the never-sufficiently-to-be-studied writer, whom Albert looks
down on affectionately, I am sure—

From his Sovereign
Victoria R.I.
Balmoral, 1899

'Do you know,' said Miss Jungmann, 'Max studied the
Queen's handwriting and copied it exactly. She wrote exactly
so. And, do you know, a lady came here once and I showed her
this and she believed—she really *believed*—that the Queen had
given this to Max and written the dedication. She was so awed
she could hardly speak.'

I stared, fascinated, at the Queen's handwriting. It was
touchingly ingenuous.

Miss Jungmann got up. 'It is time for your nap, Max,' she
said. 'I'll just make our guest comfortable in your study, and
he can see for himself what you have done to poor Queen
Victoria.'

Max rose, smiled at me, and said he looked forward to my
next visit. He put on his straw hat and took his cane, and
started to cross the flagged terrace. Halfway to the staircase
leading down to his bedroom, he turned and came back. He
removed his straw hat and gave me a quizzical look in which
there was an aspect of pity. I saw that he was enjoying himself.
'That caricature,' he began, 'that Flossie Pearson caricature
you were asking poor Will about'—he made it seem as if I had
been asking poor Will a few hours ago—'I don't know where it
is, but a series I did of Edward VII was bought by the Royal
Family, don't you know. It is not generally known, but
they are at Windsor. The tenants keep them behind a panel
in the drawing-room. I am told that when they have people
they are cosy with, they take them out from behind the panel
and show them. I hope that, unlike this lady on a historic
occasion'—he made a flicking gesture towards Queen Victoria
—'they *are* amused.' He replaced his straw hat at its customary
jaunty angle, and went back towards the staircase.

Miss Jungmann ushered me into Max's study. Before
tackling *More Leaves*, I had a look around. In this room, Max

had written most of his maturest essays and drawn a great many of the innumerable caricatures that are scattered all over the world, in private and public collections, concealed in palaces and exposed in libraries, art galleries, universities—in Blenheim, at Harvard, and at Merton College, Oxford, where there is a room devoted to Max. The study was a square room of modest size, with blue-painted walls. Max's nursery had had blue-painted walls, and his rooms in Merton, and he had brought his colour scheme here. On the walls hung a series of caricatures done by Max in imitation of the style of the great Italian caricaturist Carlo Pellegrini—'Ape', as he signed himself—whom Max revered as a master of the craft. The caricatures were imitations, but the legends were Max's own. Genuine Pellegrini drawings cut out of *Vanity Fair* had hung in Max's rooms in Merton, and later in those he occupied in his mother's house in London. When Max was tired, he said— especially after an exhibition of his drawings—and had no ideas for new caricatures, his hand still wanted to draw, and he pacified it by allowing it to produce these Pellegrini forgeries. One of those in the study was of the young Disraeli in his dandiacal period; Max's legend is 'A Well Known Dandy, Who Afterwards Followed a Less Arduous Calling'. (Max had a quartet of subjects whom he never let alone: King Edward VII, George Moore, Balfour, and Disraeli.) There was a square wooden table in the centre of the room, and on the left, near the door to the terrace, the drawing table on which Max had done his caricatures.

To be drawn by Max came to be the *insigne* of arrival, but it had its penalties, too. Christopher Hassall, in his biography of Sir Edward Marsh, tells with what excitement Marsh received the news that Max had expressed the wish to draw him. But some of Max's subjects—Arnold Bennett, H. G. Wells, Oscar Wilde, the Marquis de Soveral— were restive under the penalties. Mrs. Shaw, in a fury, tore in two a caricature Max had done of G.B.S. and threw the pieces into the fire. Max was aware of the restiveness, and he once said of his drawing table, 'This unassuming piece of furniture has given much offence.' Logan Pearsall Smith tells

how Edmund Gosse consoled him when Max had Smith on his
list:

> 'I feel it my duty to tell you [Gosse wrote Smith] that some-
> thing has happened to you that sooner or later happens to us
> almost all. Max has got you! We don't like it, and you won't
> like it, but you must pretend, as we all do, that you like it.
> You can console yourself, at any rate, with the thought that
> it will give enormous pleasure to your friends.'
> Gosse was doubly right. Though at Max's next show I found
> all the other drawings laughable beyond words, the caricature
> of myself I considered the only failure of the exhibition. Not
> that I minded in the least; I simply saw nothing funny in it;
> and was greatly surprised, though pleased, of course, as well,
> that it gave, as Gosse predicted it would give, so much pleasure
> to my friends.

Three of the walls were lined, halfway up, with plain white-
painted wooden bookshelves. I sampled some of the books.
They were mostly presentation copies of books by the great and
lesser and forgotten authors who were Max's contemporaries—
George Moore, Arnold Bennett, Oscar Wilde, G. S. Street,
George Meredith, Herbert Trench, Edmund Gosse, Siegfried
Sassoon, Thomas Hardy, Henry James, G. M. Trevelyan,
Henry Arthur Jones, Richard Le Gallienne, Stephen Phillips.
I looked through *Herod, a Tragedy* by Phillips, who was once
rampantly successful but is now a forgotten dramatist. Rothenstein tells, in his memoirs, of the time that Richard Le Gallienne
had, during the height of Phillips's success, suddenly gone to
America. Someone asked Max why Le Gallienne had made this
sudden departure. Said Max, 'He is waiting for Stephen
Phillips to blow over.' The poor man did indeed blow over;
he knew the sudden declension of popularity and took refuge in
drink. But here was one of his great successes, with an inscription to Max in the style of a man who is well aware that he can
afford to be modest.

For many of these books, Max had amused himself by drawing what he called Misleading Frontispieces. They are mostly
in colour, and they do mislead you. If you believed, for example,
Max's title-page for George Moore's *Memoirs of My Dead Life*,
you would think you were in for the reminiscences of a hero of

the cricket field. There were two odd volumes—*The Poetical Works of Thomas Henry Huxley* and *The Complete Works of Arnold Bennett*. I didn't know that Huxley had written poems, and I wondered how *all* the works of Arnold Bennett could be contained in this narrow volume. Were they on microfilm? I started to remove the *Complete Works* to find out by what miracle of compression they had been so compactly assembled. The book resisted me; I saw then that it and the *Poetical Works* were only part of the wooden partition. The spines had been so cunningly fabricated that I tried again to take the books out after I knew that they weren't there. It was a relief, though, to find out that I wouldn't have to read *The Poetical Works of Thomas Henry Huxley*. I found it hard to keep from browsing. It seemed that all the authors of my youth, whom I used to take out of the Elm Street Public Library, were here in person, near and tangible: they had been generous; they had given their works away; they had taken the trouble to write affectionate dedications; and Max had taken the trouble to mislead their readers into paths the authors had not chosen. He certainly misled readers of the Queen, with whom I now settled down on a sofa.

Before examining what Max had done to the Queen, I thought I'd better see what the Queen had done for herself. I was fascinated. I couldn't stop reading—not even for Max's forgeries, scattered all through the book in the Queen's handwriting. I saw quickly what Max had meant; certainly no one had ever written like this, before or since. On the surely acceptable theory that nothing she does can fail to be interesting, Victoria describes all the minutiae of her daily life during her travels in Scotland. She has a nice feeling for nature, for the colours of earth and sky, and she sets down her observations prettily. She reads, she writes, she sketches, she plays the piano with the Princess Beatrice. She rides her pony. She drives in her carriage. And always, everywhere and every minute, she misses Albert. When it is a nice day, she grouses about it. What business has a day to be nice when Albert isn't there to take in its niceness? When the weather is bad, she finds it 'provoking'; this is an affront not to Albert but to herself. The poignancy of her loss stabs her in unexpected places. She suffers a minor accident while out driving:

> Almost directly after the accident happened, I said to Alice it was terrible not to be able to tell it to my dearest Albert, to which she answered: 'But he knows it all, and I am sure he watched over us.' I am thankful that it was by no imprudence of mine, or the slightest deviation from what my beloved one and I had always been in the habit of doing, and what he sanctioned and approved.

Once, her irritation with the weather is assuaged by the memory of Albert's advice on such occasions:

> A thick, misty, very threatening morning! There was no help for it, but it was sadly provoking. It was the same once or twice in former happy days, and my dear Albert always said we could not alter it, but must leave it as it was and make the best of it.

She decides then to leave it as it is, and has breakfast with 'our three little ones'. She misses Albert acutely when she has a good breakfast:

> Excellent breakfasts, such splendid cream and butter! The Duchess has a very good cook, a Scotchwoman, and I thought how dear Albert would have liked it all. He always said things tasted better in smaller houses.

On a little safari over the Scotch hills, she sees some stags:

> We saw eight stags together at a distance. Oh! had dearest Albert been here with his rifle!

From all her journeys the Queen returns to Balmoral with manifest relief. She always tells the time of her return, to the minute, and she invariably says that she returned 'safely', as if she had reached Balmoral after running a gauntlet. In Mr. Brown, her gillie, the Queen has managed to create an extraordinarily diverting character. There are many references in *More Leaves* to General Ponsonby, her chief equerry. Max later lent me a book by the general's son, Sir Frederick Ponsonby— *Recollections of Three Reigns*. Sir Frederick had the same job with

King Edward VII that his father had had with Queen Victoria. It is a very entertaining and honest book. Sir Frederick devotes several pages to Mr. Brown. He doesn't believe for one moment what many blasphemers among the Queen's subjects believed—that she was secretly married to Mr. Brown. A privately printed pamphlet of the time entitled *Mrs. John Brown*, with the Queen as its heroine, he dismisses as 'scurrilous'. The possibility that the Queen was in love with Mr. Brown and that Mr. Brown reciprocated her emotion he does admit, but he insists that if it was so, the tidal passion was unconscious, certainly suppressed. But that Mr. Brown's tremendous influence with the Queen was a nuisance to everybody he does not deny. Mr. Brown was an absolute autocrat with the other servants, and equally temperamental with higher-ups. History, as set down by the Queen herself in *More Leaves*, records that whatever else Mr. Brown might have been, he was one thing unquestionably—accident-prone. The Queen never feels safe unless Mr. Brown is sitting on the box of any equipage that is conveying her, yet the number of upsets and wrong roads and serious mishaps that the vehicle encounters even with that ballast is astonishing. Perhaps it is no wonder, considering Mr. Brown's knack for misfortune, that the Queen emphasizes the safety element in her perennial returns to Balmoral. Mr. Brown is a Scot, and wears native costume when he is at home. This is too bad, because on one occasion Brown wounds his leg painfully by cutting it with his wet kilt. The Queen is 'much distressed' over the bad behaviour of Mr. Brown's kilt. On another occasion, more serious, the whole carriage—the Queen is travelling in a sociable this time—is overturned, and the Queen's thumb is injured in the fall. 'I thought at first,' she writes, 'it was broken, till we began to move it.' Another time, Mr. Brown falls through a turret:

> A dull morning, very mild. Had not a good night. Up at a quarter-past eight, breakfasting at a quarter to nine (I had packed my large boxes with papers, etc., with Brown, before breakfast on Monday, as all the heavier luggage had to be sent on in advance), and at a quarter past nine left *Balmoral* with Beatrice and the Duchess of Roxburghe. . . . Brown on the

rumble of the landau, his leg now really fairly well, but he looks pulled.*

At one point, the Queen, evidently a little tired of constantly saying 'Mr. Brown was on the box', advises her readers that henceforth, unless she specifies to the contrary, they may assume that Mr. Brown *was* on the box and so feel the security that she enjoyed herself. Along with his predilection for accidents, Mr. Brown appears to have only the most rudimentary sense of direction. He appears to have a dependable instinct for the wrong road. Sometimes he goes off on a road that isn't a carriage road at all but a cart road. Although he is on the box, the Queen cannot ignore the fact that progress is very bumpy; she is considerably shaken about. On trains, compartment doors stick and Brown has a terrible time opening them.

The book ends with a heartfelt tribute from the Queen to Mr. Brown, and a poem:

> A truer, nobler, trustier heart,
>   More loyal, and more loving, never beat
> Within a human breast.

Having, for once, been diverted from Max by another author, I now turned to his emendations. The Queen, in her Maxian phase, had taken the trouble to copy out on the flyleaf, in her own handwriting, 'Some Opinions of the Press' on her book:

> Cuts deep. . . . Had Marie Bashkirtseff sat on a throne for a good long time she might have done something like this—but we can think of no one else.—*Ladies' Pictorial.*

> Not a book to leave lying about on the drawing-room table nor one to place indiscriminately in the hands of young men and maidens. . . . Will be engrossing to those of mature years.—*Spectator.*

---

*When we went on board the *Thunderer*, August 12, at Osborne, Brown had fallen through an open place inside the turret, and got a severe hurt on the shin. He afterwards damaged it again, when it was nearly healed, by jumping off the box of the carriage, so that when he came to Balmoral about a fortnight afterwards, it was very bad, and he was obliged to take care of it for some days previous to the fresh journey.

Romantic . . . Strange . . . Enigmatic . . . Where's our Queen Mary the noo?—*Scotsman.*

Bin readin' Vic's latest. Perfickly scrumptious, doncher-think?—*'Eve' in the Tatler.*

A style as pure as her Court, and we cannot give higher praise than that.—*Windsor Mercury.*

The Queen has two collies, of whom she is almost as fond as she is of Mr. Brown. On one journey she writes, on her own:

Dear good Sharp* was with us and out each day, and so affectionate . . .

There is a full-page lithograph of Sharp. Beneath it the incorrigible forger has written:

Such a dear, faithful, noble *friend* and companion, and for whom Albert had the greatest respect also.

VICTORIA R.

And over Noble, the other friend's photograph:

Never shall I cease to mourn this dear, *good* servant. His early decease plunged us all in the *deepest* grief. It was *most* heartbreaking and annoying.

VICTORIA R.

To divert the Empress Eugénie after the loss of her son, the Queen takes her to a little cottage, Glen Gelder Shiel. There is a full-page photograph of the Shiel and the trees surrounding it. Beneath this is written, at least in Max's copy:

This picture is *now* inexpressibly saddening to me to see. The tree that I have marked with a cross [there is a firm, black-inked cross over that tree] died *last* year. Knowing *how much* I liked that tree, they sent me some chips of the poor *dear* trunk after it had been felled. These I have painted black and they are a great pleasure.

VICTORIA R.

At the very end, Max has had the effrontery to add to the lines of the poem the Queen wrote to Mr. Brown:

Uncouth he was,
But not the less a courtier withal.

*A favourite collie of mine.

And beneath that there is a drawing of Mr. Brown, wearing the lethal kilt, bearded, and with a great expanse of tartaned behind, just lifting himself up painfully from the ground after some unhappy miscalculation.

Perhaps the most famous caricature that Max ever drew was of Queen Victoria and her son Edward. It is captioned 'The Rare, the Rather Awful Visits of Albert Edward, Prince of Wales, to Windsor Castle', and shows the future Edward VII, then nearing sixty, frock-coated, obese, standing abject and chastened, with his hands behind his back, in a corner of a drawing-room of his mother's house. In the foreground sits the Queen, now a very old lady and also very fat, and frighteningly formidable. But there is a difference in the two fatnesses; that of the Prince is the efflorescence of over-indulgence, that of his mother an accretion of righteousness. Victoria's hands are crossed over a handkerchief in her lap. Her heavy-lidded eyes are closed, as if to shut out the awful spectacle of her son's profligacies. The blubbery back of Edward's neck, forced out of his collar, ends abruptly and somewhat trivially in the bald dome of his head. The head is an anticlimax to such a back-of-the-neck. From the tension with which his hands are clasped behind him you feel that the Prince is praying, 'O God, will I ever get out of this room!' But the Queen has had her say and is just sitting there, and you feel that she will be sitting there, locked in an outrage too deep for utterance, for ever. There is the ageing Prince, with so many pleasant things waiting for him outside this room—enormous meals, women, games, shooting, practical jokes, trips to Marienbad, to Paris (where he was adored), the whole palpitating world—if only he could get at them, if only that implacable little old lady who has been haranguing him would open her eyes. But her eyes won't open; they are clamped shut eternally against the horrors of her eldest son's excesses.

Max initiated the pastime of royalty-baiting long before the birth of the Angry Young Men. He indulged in it unremittingly, in caricature and in prose, all his life. The last caricature he ever made—with the exception of one of George Moore—was one he did of Edward VII, in 1955. Showing it to me in the

Villino one day, he was moved to comment on the sharpness of the nose, as on a phenomenon his caricature had made him notice for the first time. 'The noses of fat men do not follow suit with the rest of them as they age,' he said. 'The noses become, if anything, sharper, thinner.' But Max, even when he was a young man, was not an angry young man. He was a civilized young man. His needling of royalty was acute, uncompromising, and funny, but it was never savage.

I had earlier been told that a poem of Max's, written for private circulation among his friends during the reign of King George V and Queen Mary, had delayed his knighthood for twenty years. Max loved writing and drawing things for private publication or private circulation. Fond of privacy for himself, he sought it for his work as well. Perhaps Max *wanted* to undermine his knighthood; perhaps, in some unconscious way, he was trying to fulfil an ambition he had expressed in 'Diminuendo' when he was twenty-three—never to be knighted. The poem is called 'Ballade Tragique à Double Refrain', and it is actually a one-act play:

SCENE: *A room in Windsor Castle*
TIME: *The present*

(*Enter a Lady-in-Waiting and a Lord-in-Waiting*)

SHE:
Slow pass the hours, ah, passing slow;
My doom is worse than anything
Conceived by Edgar Allan Poe:
The Queen is duller than the King.

HE:
Lady, your mind is wandering,
You babble what you do not mean;
Remember, to your heartening,
The King is duller than the Queen.

SHE:
No, most emphatically, no,
To one firm-rooted fact I cling
In my now chronic vertigo:
The Queen is duller than the King,

HE:
Lady, you lie. Last evening
I found him with a rural dean
Talking of District Visiting. . . .
The King is duller than the Queen.

SHE:
At any rate he doesn't sew;
You don't see him embellishing
Yard after yard of calico. . . .
The Queen is duller than the King.
Oh, to have been an underling
To (say) the Empress Josephine.

HE:
Enough of your self-pitying;
The King is duller than the Queen.

SHE:
The Queen is duller than the King.

HE:
Death, then, for you shall have no sting.
    (*Stabs her, and as she falls dead produces
phial from breast-pocket of coat*)
Nevertheless, sweet friend strychnine,
The King—is—duller than—the Queen.

    (*Expires in horrible agony*)

In the summer of 1923, the future Duke of Windsor was
about to pay his annual visit to the Duchy of Cornwall. Someone at Court suggested to him that on his way he should visit
Thomas Hardy. The Prince agreed to do so, and, in due course,
lunched with Hardy and his wife. Max heard about this.
Again, he wrote a poem, this one a Hardy parody called 'A
Luncheon':

    Lift latch, step in, be welcome, Sir,
    Albeit to see you I'm unglad
    And your face is fraught with a deathly shyness
    Bleaching what pink it may have had.
    Come in, come in, Your Royal Highness.

Beautiful weather?—Sir, that's true,
Though the farmers are casting rueful looks
At tilth's and pasture's dearth of spryness—
Yes, Sir, I've written several books—
A little more chicken, Your Royal Highness?

Lift latch, step out, your car is there,
To bear you hence from this ancient vale.
We are both of us aged by our strange brief nighness.
But each of us lives to tell the tale.
Farewell, farewell, Your Royal Highness.

It was not until the next day that I was able to discuss with
Max his collaboration with the Queen and his verses on royalty.
I was returning to America, and Miss Jungmann had arranged
a farewell lunch for me at the Villino. Again the weather was
flawless. When I rang the bell, Miss Jungmann opened the
door. 'Max is in the Vining Room!' she said triumphantly. 'We
are going to have lunch there. He loves it there.' I followed Miss
Jungmann through the house, up the stairs, past the terrace,
and to a tiny auxiliary outdoor area, which she called the
Vining Room, just above the terrace. Beneath the canopy of
a vine from which white grapes were hanging, Max, straw-
hatted, was sitting at a table doing *The Times* crossword puzzle.
He got up to greet me, putting his hat aside.

It was an idyllic day, and we had a gay lunch. We began
talking about Victoria's prose style.

'It is rather nice, in the book, don't you think,' said Max,
'that when the Queen is asked to write her name in Sir Walter
Scott's diary, which is shown her, she refuses to do it—she
considers it a "presumption"? I thought that delicate.'

I asked Max whether King George and Queen Mary had
ever read the 'Ballade Tragique à Double Refrain'.

'Yes,' he said dryly. 'Kind friends sent it to them.'

'How did they like it?' I asked.

'They were vexed,' he said, with an innocent look at me.

I asked him whether it was true that this ballade had delayed
his knighthood for twenty years.

He said he did not know.

Considering how he had treated the successive generations

The rare, the rather awful visits of Albert Edward, Prince of Wales, to Windsor Castle

Are we as welcome as ever?

of the British Royal Family, I said, it was a wonder he had been
knighted at all; in fact, I wasn't sure that his residence in
Italy was entirely voluntary.

Max chuckled; his shoulders shook. 'You must remember,'
he said quietly, 'it was *British* royalty.'

'That is so,' Miss Jungmann said, looking at me seriously.
'There are no people in the world like the English. I am a
foreigner—I am a German and I can say it. I had a job in the
Foreign Office during the last war—I believe I told you. I shall
never forget the day Dresden was bombed. I can't tell you the
pain that was felt there in the Foreign Office. *Pain!* It was a
massive bombing, you remember. It had to be done, but no one
was happy about it. Just the contrary. I'll never forget the
atmosphere in the Foreign Office that day, overcast with gloom.
That could happen only in England. Only the English are
like that!'

Max began talking about King Edward VII. 'He spoke
English with a heavy German accent, very guttural.' Max
imitated the King's speech. 'When he was still Prince of Wales
and living at Marlborough House, Sir Sidney Lee, the Shakespearean scholar, came to the Prince with a proposal. It was
on the eve of the publication of the *Dictionary of National
Biography*. It was Sir Sidney's idea that the Prince ought to
give a dinner to those responsible for the completion of this
monumental work. The monumental work had escaped the
Prince's attention, don't you know, and Sir Sidney had painfully
to explain to him what it was. The Prince, you know, was not
an omnivorous reader. Sir Sidney managed to obtain his
grudging consent. "How many?" asked the Prince. "Forty,"
said Sir Sidney. The Prince was appalled. "For-r-ty!" he
gasped. "For-r-ty wr-ri-ter-rs! I can't have for-r-ty wr-ri-ter-rs
in Marlborough House! Giff me the list!" Sir Sidney gave it
to him, and the Prince, with a heavy black pencil, started slashing off names. Sir Sidney's heart sank when he saw that the
first name the Prince had slashed was that of Sir Leslie Stephen.
He conveyed, as tactfully as he could, that this was a bad cut,
since Stephen was the animating genius of the whole enterprise.
Reluctantly, the Prince allowed Sir Leslie to come. Eventually,

Sir Sidney put over his entire list. The dinner took place. Among the contributors present was Canon Ainger, a distinguished cleric whose passion was Charles Lamb, on whom he was considered a very great authority indeed. He had written the articles on Charles and Mary Lamb for the *Dictionary*. Sir Sidney sat at the Prince's right and found it heavy weather, don't you know. The Prince must have found it heavy going also; to be having dinner with forty writers was not his idea of a cultivated way to spend an evening. His eye roamed the table morosely, in self-objurgation for having let himself in for a thing like this. Finally, his eye settled on Canon Ainger. "Who's the little parson?" he asked Lee. "Vy is *he* here? He's not a wr-ri-ter!" "He is a very great authority," said Lee, apologetically, "on Lamb." This was too much for the Prince. He put down his knife and fork in stupefaction; a pained outcry of protest heaved from him: "On *lamb*!" '

Thinking of Edward put Max in a benign mood. 'My brother Herbert produced a play about Madame de Pompadour,' he said. 'The incidental music for it was written by a composer of the time named Edward German. You know, in those days the incidental music was quite a factor. The audience was affected by it; *I* was affected. When I listened to it, my heartstrings were twanged at. When it began to throb, I throbbed. People sobbed; I sobbed. King Edward expressed a wish to see my brother's production, and Herbert met him afterwards. The King said not a word about the production, or the play. All he wanted to know was who had written the incidental music, which had greatly moved him. Herbert was a bit miffed. "German," he replied to the King's question. "Oh, a German," said Edward. "Yes. Yes. I know many Ger-r-mans wr-rite music, but *which* German?" "Not," said Herbert, becoming a bit desperate, "*a* German but Sir Edward German, the composer. His name is German." Edward couldn't take it in; his gutturals thickened in vehement inquiry. Lady Tree intervened, but to no avail. It got worse and worse. It was never cleared up.'

Max remembered that someone had had the cruelty to insert in an Address from the Throne the phrase 'guerrilla warfare'.

The King's struggle to master this phrase was convulsive. Max imitated how it sounded—a consonantal chaos. The phrase was mercifully deleted.

I asked Max whether he cared at all for music that was not incidental.

'Anything above Puccini is above me, too,' he said, 'but I do love Puccini.'

I asked whether he had any Puccini records.

'Unfortunately,' said Miss Jungmann, 'we have no gramophone.'

Max took the deprivation more lightly than Miss Jungmann did; he was in a wonderful mood, and he began to tell, with tremendous gusto, and acting it out, about a shattering experience his friend Logan Pearsall Smith had once endured, when he found himself sitting next to Queen Victoria's son the Duke of Connaught at a lunch party. It was the day of the arrival of the surrendered German fleet at Scapa Flow, at the end of the First World War; the lunch was to commemorate the great occasion. 'When you are with royalty,' Max began, 'you are not supposed to start a subject; you are supposed to wait for them to start it and then you fall in. Logan knew this; he sat and sat through course after course, munching away in silence, waiting for the Duke to say something. The Duke didn't. Either he had no subject on which he wished to discourse or, if he did, he wasn't inclined to divulge it to Logan. The silence got on Logan's nerves; he decided, finally—he was American, you know; no Englishman would have done it—to take the plunge, and he was careful to make it what he considered a safe and conservative plunge. "Well, Sir," he heard himself saying, "this is an historic day." The effect on the Duke was devastating; whatever might have been drifting through his own mind had collided with something. A remark had been made; he had heard something, though not the remark. He turned on Logan; in a voice somewhat thunderous, he demanded, "What did you say?" Now that he was embarked on this line, there was no way for Logan to retreat. "I said, Sir," he repeated stoutly, "that this is an historic day." This time, the Duke did hear it—a remark so bizarre, so startling,

and, above all, so unasked for.' Max leaned forward and
whispered Logan's remark to himself as the Duke had done;
you could see that the vast implications of it were churning in
Max's mind as they had churned in the Duke's. It was barely
audible, Max's whisper: 'An historic day? An historic day.'
Emboldened, Logan repeated it out loud: 'Yes, Sir, this is an
historic day.' Max, who was inside the Duke's mind, kept
revolving it, turning it over, munching it; his lips kept forming
and re-forming the words inaudibly. Then a light began to glow
in his eyes and a smile to form on his lips. You could tell the
moment when the Duke made the molten connection between
the remark and the event; they fused suddenly, and this
illumination gave the Duke the thrill of creation. 'At last,' Max
went on, 'he had a subject; he had it firmly entrenched, and
was only too proud to introduce it, don't you know. He turned
to Logan and hosed him with it. He lavished upon the anonymous commoner the full power of his intuition. "THIS," he
said, "IS AN HISTORIC DAY!" '

Max went on talking about Smith. He said that Smith's
experience with the Duke might have been harrowing but that
Smith had submitted Max himself to an experience that was not
so much harrowing as humiliating. Smith was the son of
American Quaker parents from Germantown, Pennsylvania.
They were rich—the family owned a successful glass factory—
and were both internationally famous as applied salvationists.
Smith's father had applied salvation so intimately to his female
communicants in England that a hue and cry arose among the
pious and he retired into the shadows of contemplation, but
Logan's mother went on to the end, effulgent, preaching and
writing. Her inspirational books were best-sellers. Logan settled
down in London and devoted himself to literature. His greatest
success was with a little book called *Trivia*, which consists of
small, exquisitely polished paragraphs of worldly wisdom and
disillusion. Max had done a caricature of Smith. Its legend
reads, 'The Author of *Trivia* Submitting His Latest MS. to the
CONDUCTORS of *The London Mercury* (Mr. Logan Pearsall Smith,
Mr. J. C. Squire, Mr. Edward Shanks).' The caricature shows
Smith watching the two editors. He has just submitted the

manuscript to Mr. Squire, who is handing it ceremoniously to Mr. Shanks. The manuscript is the size of a postage stamp. One day, when Max was working for the *Saturday Review*, Smith gave him, for his edification, a small brochure written by his mother—*How Little Logan Was Brought to Jesus*. It appeared from it that little Logan had originally not been with Jesus. He was somewhat rebellious as a child; his mother had to bring him. Max received the book gratefully and promised to read it. He had a date at the Athenaeum for lunch, which he kept. In a cab, after lunch, he realized with horror that he had left the history of Logan's conversion at the club. He made a special trip to the club the next day to report his loss to the hall porter. The latter was lofty and elegant. Max flattered himself that he had a way with club hall porters—deferential, and with a hint of geniality restrained only by Max's own sense of decorum before the remote and august. He had always made a particular effort with the Athenaeum's hall porter, and felt that he had succeeded in winning his respect. Max reported his loss. 'And what was the book, Mr. Beerbohm?' the great man inquired. Max, since he had no alternative, answered, "*How Little Logan Was Brought to Jesus*". In that moment, Max recalled, something happened between the porter and himself. He lost status. The work of years of careful deference was undone. The porter merely said that he would inquire, but the intimacy was gone and the respect was gone. A few days later, Max returned. The porter handed him the book in a gingerly manner. It was carefully wrapped up and tied with string, so that the porter himself could handle it safely. Max knew that his day at the Athenaeum was over.

We started to leave the Vining Room. Max's eye caught the season's first gardenia in the flower border. We stopped to admire it. Miss Jungmann, with Max looking on approvingly, pointed out for me the acanthus, lemons, figs, bougainvillaea, geraniums. We stopped for a moment on the terrace, near the parapet. There was a great tree across the road before us. 'Do you notice,' said Max, 'that on the side facing us it spreads its branches way back, leans backwards—like Swinburne? There are the leaners-forward, you know, and there are the leaners-backward. H. G. Wells was a leaner-forward, but Swinburne was a leaner-backward, like that tree.'

Max stared at the tree, as if by looking at it he was again seeing Swinburne. From Swinburne his eyes wandered to the sea. He stared at it as if he were trying to extract from its tranquil, gleaming surface the answer to the riddle of those twin darknesses from which we emerge and towards which we move. I remembered a description by Max, at the end of one of his essays, of himself staring at another sea, on the coast of Sussex. The essay starts innocently enough: A nine-year-old architect is working rapturously and meticulously at constructing a sand cottage. Max is full of admiration at the completed work; other children come up and give their grudging admiration. Presently, the tide comes in and destroys the cunning fabrication:

> The unrestful, the well-organized and minatory sea had been advancing quickly. It was not very far now from the cottage. I thought of all the civilisations that had been, that were not, that were as though they had never been. Must it always be thus?—always the same old tale of growth and greatness and overthrow, nothingness?

To Max's surprise, the boys shout with joy as the cottage is demolished, and finally the architect himself joins in their jubilation:

> I myself was conscious of a certain wild enthusiasm within me. But this was less surprising for that *I* had not built the cottage, and *my* fancy had not enabled me to dwell in it. It was the boys' own enthusiasm that made me feel, as never before, how deep-rooted in the human breast the love of destruction, of mere destruction, is.

The spectacle arouses in Max a more intimate and fearsome speculation still: Is the English polity safe? Might it not share the fate of that cottage? He won't let himself think about it. 'I waived the question coming from that hypothesis,' he writes, 'and other questions that would have followed; for I wished to be happy while I might.'

IV

PARTITO MA NON ARRIVATO

I HAD a standing joke with Turco. When I asked him to summon Charlie for my daily drive to the Villino, I invariably appeared in the lobby on time, but Charlie was not as punctual. Turco would reassure me. '*Partito*,' he would say, '*ma non arrivato*,' Charlie had left the garage that employed him, but he had not yet arrived; he was, in other words, *en route*. I had told this to Max, and he had been amused by it; he said it applied to so many of his contemporaries—in fact, to almost everybody. Now, on a cold, rainy January day in 1954, I stood again in the lobby waiting for Charlie to drive me to the Villino, and I took the words of explanation out of Turco's mouth; we sang them in unison. They were, indeed, the only Italian words I knew, but I had full command over *them*. Charlie arrived and drove me to the Villino. We compared notes. He wanted to know whether I had received his Christmas card, and I wanted to know whether he had received mine. He was full of intimate information about our Ambassadress, Mrs. Luce, and he asked me for whatever news (it was marginal) I had of Pittsburgh.

I had sought domestic advice before I left New York, and bore presents for Max and Miss Jungmann. Shielding the packages under my overcoat from the rain, I rang the doorbell of the Villino. I looked at the tree that leaned backwards—like Swinburne. Denuded, and lashed by the rain, it seemed to have abdicated altogether. A young girl I hadn't seen before opened the door for me. She bobbed and nodded, and babbled in Italian. In the lunette at the far end of the entrance hall, Miss

Siddal, between Rossetti and Swinburne, had still not made up her mind. With an air of incredulity, she was still staring at Swinburne. I went into the little library. Max's grandparents were there, in their oval frames, and looked as handsome and well-adjusted as ever in their eighteenth-century clothes. Carlyle was still striding dyspeptically along the Chelsea Embankment.

Miss Jungmann came in and greeted me affectionately. I handed her my presents. 'Oh,' she said. 'I won't open mine till Max comes in. He'll be in in a minute. He didn't have a very good night. He had nightmares. He suffers terribly from nightmares. I think all creative people are subject to nightmares. Gerhart Hauptmann used to have nightmares. He remembered them in detail and used to tell me them, but Max never remembers the details—only a vague sense of terror. Perhaps he *does* remember them but wants to spare me. But it's cold in here! Come in and warm yourself by the fire.'

I walked through the little library and into the little living-room, where a fire was burning in the tiny grate. The Regency mirror noted my arrival; the bronze girl with the averted head was on the mantel; in the photographs flanking it the two girls in white were still confiding romantic secrets to one another, and the little pug-nosed girl was laughing at the Abbé's joke. Max came in. He was wearing a blue skullcap. Miss Jungmann displayed the two presents. Max was so ravished by the wrappings of the packages that I urged Miss Jungmann not to open them, to avoid an anticlimax. Max chuckled and encouraged Miss Jungmann to risk it. First, however, he took the packages and ran a hand over the glossy surfaces. 'How beautiful!' he exclaimed. 'Scarlet and silver!' But there was a residue of enthusiasm for the contents, too: a heavy sweater for Max, and a woollen stole for Miss Jungmann. Miss Jungmann made Max try the sweater on at once for size. 'I'll try it on for size,' said Max, 'but' —he smiled at me—'if you don't mind, I'll keep it on for warmth.'

Max, when it was agreed that the sweater fitted, settled himself in the Merton chair. Miss Jungmann hovered over him solicitously. 'Those dreadful nightmares of yours, Max! Was this one awful?'

'Have you noticed,' said Max, 'there is never any third act in a nightmare? They bring you to a climax of terror and then leave you there. They are the work of poor dramatists.'

I asked whether he could remember them after they were done with him.

'My nightmares are almost always abstract, don't you know —not personal. The only personal ones are those connected with my childhood.'

Miss Jungmann, aware that I knew of Max's aversion to psychiatry, chimed in, 'Maybe a psychiatrist could help cure you of those awful things?'

Max laughed. He turned to me. 'What would they do to me?' he inquired. 'I adored my father and mother and I adored my brothers and sisters. What kind of complex would they find me the victim of? Oedipus and what else?' He reflected a moment. 'They were a tense and peculiar family, the Oedipuses, weren't they?'

Miss Jungmann, explaining to me that the new servant was inexperienced, went out to manage tea.

Max had had a fan letter, from an American schoolboy, that had amused him greatly. He reached out to the little table beside his chair and picked up the letter and gave it to me. It was from Andover. The boy's English teacher, Dudley Fitts, had read aloud to the class Max's obituary essay on Ibsen from *Around Theatres*, as a stimulus to discussion at the next session. The boy, who was evidently thorough, had read up on both Max and Ibsen in the Andover library, and had found Max's first-person parody of Edmund Gosse, called 'A Recollection', in *A Christmas Garland*. In this piece, Max, pretending to be Gosse, a dedicated bringer-together of people who ought to meet each other, describes how, in Venice, he took Ibsen round to Robert Browning's for Christmas dinner, with disturbing results. The boy, taking Max's use of the first person literally, had written asking Max, as an old pal of Ibsen's, to give him some inside information. 'In 1878, when I imagined this dinner to take place,' said Max apologetically, 'I was only

4*

six years old. How can I tell this young man'—he tapped the letter—'that I was scarcely so precocious?'

In *A Christmas Garland* (which starts off with Max's parody of Henry James, 'The Mote in the Middle Distance'—perhaps the most famous of his parodies), Max, as the alleged Gosse, relates that he called on Robert Browning, who was spending the Christmas season in Venice. That same evening, he had an inconceivable stroke of luck. He ran into Ibsen in the Café Florian. As a young student of Scandinavian literature who had taken the trouble to master Norwegian, he had, of course, been in correspondence with Ibsen, and had been received by him some time earlier, in Rome. Max's Gosse picked up with Ibsen where he had left off, and there followed a halcyon period for the young scholar; he spent his afternoons with Browning, his evenings with Ibsen. He was in seventh heaven. There was one ever-to-be-cherished evening when Ibsen unbent so far as to read to the young student—in Norwegian, of course—one of his plays:

> He was staying at the Hôtel Danieli, an edifice famous for having been, rather more than forty years previously, the socket in which the flame of an historic *grande passion* had finally sunk and guttered out with no inconsiderable accompaniment of smoke and odour. It was there, in an upper room, that I now made acquaintance with a couple very different from George Sand and Alfred de Musset, though destined to become hardly less famous than they. I refer to Torvald and Nora Helmer. My host read to me with the utmost vivacity, standing in the middle of the apartment; and I remember that in the scene where Nora Helmer dances the tarantella her creator instinctively executed a few illustrative steps.

In an overflow of joy at the spectacle of Ibsen dancing the tarantella, and in constant transit between the two colossi, the young scholar became obsessed with a missionary zeal to bring his two idols together. This ambition he whispered to Browning. Browning had never heard of Ibsen, but so expansive was his nature that he fell in with the plan at once: 'Capital! Bring him round with you at one o'clock tomorrow for turkey and plum-pudding!'

The young middleman ran right back to Ibsen with this

invitation. Ibsen had never heard of Browning, either. 'It
was one of the strengths of his strange, crustacean genius,'
says the narrator, in a hushed aside, 'that he never had heard
of anybody.' But the middleman prevailed on Ibsen to accept
Browning's invitation, and on Christmas Day Browning sent
his gondola to fetch Ibsen and his palpitating guide. It was
understandable that the youth should be nervous, and he tried
to give Ibsen some hint of Browning's scope, translating
meticulously into Norwegian Browning's slogan 'God's in His
heaven, all's right with the world.'

When Ibsen and the young man arrived in Browning's
salone, their host was thumping out a toccata on the piano.
Browning swatted Ibsen heartily on each shoulder, wished
him 'the Merriest of Merry Christmases,' and led his two
guests in to dinner. There, things went less well. Ibsen sized
Browning up at once as a lightweight; he dropped him
even before he had taken him up. At dinner, the student of
Norwegian struggled manfully to translate Ibsen's tenebrous
remarks from Norwegian into English; he went on interpreting
like mad, slanting his translations to alleviate abrasion, panting
after the receding mirage of *rapport*. The debacle occurred over
a nice question of interpretation:

> The world of scholarship was at that time agitated by the
> recent discovery of what might or might not prove to be a
> fragment of Sappho. Browning proclaimed his unshakeable
> belief in the authenticity of these verses. To my surprise, Ibsen,
> whom I had been unprepared to regard as a classical scholar,
> said positively that they had not been written by Sappho.
> Browning challenged him to give a reason. A literal translation
> of the reply would have been 'Because no woman ever was
> capable of writing a fragment of good poetry.' Imagination
> reels at the effect this would have had on the recipient of
> 'Sonnets from the Portuguese'. The agonized interpreter, throw-
> ing honour to the winds, babbled some wholly fallacious version
> of the words. Again the situation had been saved. . . .
>
> I was fain to thank heaven when, immediately after the
> termination of the meal, Ibsen rose, bowed to his host, and bade
> me express his thanks for the entertainment. Out of the
> Grand Canal, in the gondola . . . he asked me whether Herr
> Browning had ever married. Receiving an emphatically

affirmative reply, he inquired whether Fru Browning had been happy. Loth though I was to cast a blight on his interest in the matter, I conveyed to him with all possible directness the impression that Elizabeth Barrett had assuredly been one of those wives who do not dance tarantellas nor slam front-doors. He did not, to the best of my recollection, make further mention of Browning, either then or afterwards. Browning himself, however, thanked me warmly, next day, for having introduced my friend to him. 'A capital fellow!' he exclaimed, and then, for a moment, seemed as though he were about to qualify this estimate, but ended by merely repeating 'A capital fellow!'

I told Max that Dudley Fitts had once written to me that one of his students at Andover had made the flat statement in a paper that Pontius Pilate was one of the twelve Apostles. Max was amused by this, but saddened, too. It led him into some reflections on the passing of Latin in the schools and the unfortunate effect this was having on the precise use of English. 'Gladstone used to quote whole strings of Latin hexameters, mostly from the *Aeneid*, in his parliamentary speeches, and the House understood him,' Max said. 'Already one discerns a debasement of English, and other debasements will follow that. With the blunting of precision in language, don't you know, comes muddiness in political policy, in morality, and in conduct.' Max went on to deplore the modernizations in translations of the Bible and the classics, which, according to him, were vulgarizations. He had been reading such a transla- tion of Cicero's letters. 'The translator,' Max told me, 'seems to be saying to the reader, "Look here, this fellow Cicero is just like you and me." ' Max gave me a consoling look to cushion the blow. 'He isn't!' he said firmly.

I then asked Max about Ibsen's obituary, which he had written for the *Saturday Review*. At the mention of this, his eyes darkened with an anxious look; his brow furrowed; he leaned forward tensely in the Merton chair. His strong, beautifully shaped, square forefinger tapped the Andover letter uneasily, in memory of an importunity that had been put upon him by the editor of the *Saturday* half a century before. 'Do you know, I remember that evening so well. It was May 1906. I had done my piece for that week, and was settled down cosily with a book in my rooms, on the top floor of my mother's house. I was luxuriating in the prospect of an evening in which I didn't have to go to the theatre. Then I was called to the telephone—an experience I have never much cared for. It was the editor. He announced that Ibsen had just died and that he wished me to write an obituary article. It quite spoiled my evening, you know! I am not a'—his hand waved into space— 'a dash-off writer. Writing is difficult for me, and over my weekly articles I agonized. They cost me anxiety and pain. The copy was always due on Thursday, and do you know that even on my holidays, away from England, when Thursday came around I was always conscious of this vague feeling of inanition, don't you know, of impatience—the sort of feeling a clock may have when it has not been wound up. And then, when I was revelling in the fact that my weekly piece was done, then came this telephone call——'

I could see that Max was hearing again, after half a century, the knell-like sound of the telephone. I did my best to reassure him.

'Well, Max,' I said, 'you really don't have to worry about it now. The piece is in, and a well-known teacher at Andover likes it well enough to recommend it to his pupils, so it must have been pretty good and you needn't worry!'

Max relaxed a bit. He smiled, giving me his quick, innocent look of gratitude for the relief of tension. Then he began to tell me about the obituary. He had sat down at home and written the piece in longhand. That was the first draft, and he gave it to the waiting copy-reader. (He spoke with affectionate remembrance of the copy-readers of the *Saturday*. They were charming and distinguished men, he said—scholars and writers *manqués*. They knew Latin and Greek, so when he used a tag from either language, he could be certain that it would come out all right.) Ibsen had been dying for a very long time; the stages of his disease had been minutely reported in the European press. In the obituary essay, Max wonders how the papers will keep coming out without the sustenance of Ibsen's interminable moribundity. But it had happened at last, and when it happened, Max took it robustly. 'Are we downhearted?' he asks in the obituary essay, and has the spunk to answer 'No'. The obituary is interesting, because it reveals something characteristic of Max; he felt about Ibsen the way he felt about Shaw, except that Shaw was funny and Ibsen wasn't. Even though he recognized that both were great writers, what they were as human beings mattered to Max—was, indeed, essential, in his view. In his obituary, he quotes a letter that Ibsen wrote to the Danish critic, Georg Brandes. 'Friends,' confides Ibsen chattily, 'are a costly luxury, and when one invests one's capital in a mission in life, one cannot afford to have friends. The expensiveness of friendship does not lie in what one does for one's friends, but in what one, out of regard for them, leaves undone. This means the crushing of many an intellectual germ.' Max comments on this avarice for intellectual germs:

> Ibsen had no lack of friends, so far as his genius attracted to him many men who were anxious to help him. And he used these men, unstintingly, when he had need of them. That volume of his correspondence, published not long ago, reveals him as an unabashed applicant for favours. Nor is this by any means to his discredit. The world was against him. He was poor, and a cast-away. He had to fight hard in order that he might fulfil the genius that was in him. It was well that he had no false delicacy in appealing to any one who could be of use to him. But, throughout that correspondence, one misses in him the sense of gratitude. One misses in him the capacity for friendship. Not one 'intellectual germ' would he sacrifice on that altar. He was, indeed, a perfect type of the artist. There is something impressive, something magnificent and noble, in the spectacle of his absorption in himself—the impregnability of that rock on which his art was founded. But, as we know, other men, not less great than Ibsen, have managed to be human. Some 'intellectual germs' may thereby have perished. If so, they are to be mourned, duly. And yet, could we wish them preserved at the price that Ibsen paid for them? Innate in us is the desire to love those whom we venerate. To this desire, Ibsen, the very venerable, does not pander.

Max doesn't think it is sentimental to accuse Ibsen of this limitation. He compares him to Swift. He says, 'Swift's strength lay in his intellect, and in his natural gift for literature; and a gigantic strength it was. But his harshness was not symptomatic of strength. It was symptomatic of a certain radical defect in himself. He was a Titan, not an Olympian. So was Ibsen . . . He was an ardent and tender lover of ideas; but mankind he simply could not abide. Indeed, I fancy he cared less for ideas as ideas than as a scourge for his fellow-creatures.' Max goes on to dissect the 'purpose' of Ibsen's plays. Max doesn't think that this much-written-about 'purpose' was to reform evil at all. 'Primarily, he was an artist, pure and simple, actuated by the artist's joy in reproduction of human character as it appeared to his keen, unwandering eyes. But he had a joy within a joy: joy in the havoc he wrought.' Ibsen hated peace, and he didn't care a snap of his fingers for liberty. Max quotes another of Ibsen's letters to Brandes, written after the proclamation of the Italian Republic:

> Rome was the one sanctuary in Europe, the one place that enjoyed true liberty—freedom from the political tyranny of liberty . . . The delicious longing for liberty—that is now a thing of the past. I for one am bound to confess that the only thing about liberty that I love is the fight for it; I care nothing about the possession of it.

'At any rate,' Max adds, in a sly postscript to Ibsen's letter, 'he cared nothing about other people's possession of it.'

I asked Max, who had piqued my curiosity by telling me something about how he had happened to get his job as drama critic for the *Saturday Review*, to tell me more.

'As you know, it was a kind of accident,' he said. 'I just slithered into it. Frank Harris was away in Athens when Shaw gave up the post; the suggestion came to me from Runciman, the deputy-editor.' Max wondered to Runciman how Shaw would feel about it, and Runciman said that Shaw approved; it didn't occur, evidently, either to Max or to Runciman to ask themselves whether Harris, who was, after all, the editor, might approve. But four years earlier, when Harris took over the *Saturday*, he had invited Max to write for the paper—anything he liked—and Max had done just that, so both he and Runciman assumed that it would be all right. Max undertook the job without getting even his own approval. He refused to

give himself a reference; his first contribution was a considered
essay, 'Why I Ought Not to Have Become a Dramatic Critic',
in which, without any conviction whatever, he hazards the
opinion that there are probably 'many callings more uncomfortable and dispiriting than that of dramatic critic,'
continuing, 'To be a porter on the Underground Railway must,
I have often thought, be very terrible. Whenever I feel myself
sinking under the stress of my labours, I shall say to myself,
"I am not a porter on the Underground Railway." ' Bucked up
by this negative solace, he prepared to go to the Savoy to
review *The Beauty Stone*, a musical comedy by Arthur Pinero,
Comyns Carr, and Arthur Sullivan. This was in May 1898. He
was twenty-five when he took the job, and thirty-seven when
he gave it up, in April 1910.

Frank Harris seems to have been the perennial type of the
genius-charlatan, who appears meteorically, soars to the top,
gets everybody excited, seizes the general imagination to such
a degree that for a time nobody else is talked about, and then
proceeds to disintegrate with a completeness that leaves, at best,
only the merest possibility of a shadow comeback. The reason,
Max told me, is egomania. 'When you believe yourself omnipotent, it is hard, don't you know, to reconcile yourself to mere
potency. Like all deeply arrogant men, Harris possessed little
or no sense of reality. His subsequent career proves it.' Harris
arrived in London, after wanderings in America and Europe,
in 1882, at the age of twenty-six. He was little and ugly. Within
five years of his arrival, he had, according to his latest and most
comprehensive biographer, Vincent Brome,* got to the absolute top in the London literary world, had married a rich
woman older than himself, had a house in Park Lane, and
entertained the best people. He had been editor of the *Evening
News*, he was now editor of the *Fortnightly Review*, and he was
soon to be the owner-editor of the forty-year-old *Saturday
Review*. He shook that paper up, got H. G. Wells and Shaw and
Max and Cunninghame Graham to write for it, and was—such
men always are—the talk of the town. He became known as the
Voice. According to Max, he had 'a marvellous speaking voice

*In *Frank Harris*, Cassell, London, 1959.

—like the organ at Westminster Abbey, with infallible foot-work.' He was also the Moustache. Brome tells how, in Berlin, Harris saw Bismarck riding by in a carriage. He envied Bismarck; that was the kind of power he would like, and intended, to have. He trained his moustache in imitation of Bismarck's ('It was a tremendous affair,' said Max, recalling Harris's moustache with admiration), and for a time he achieved the power, too.

Max always took Harris with what he called 'a stalactite of salt'. But women didn't. 'Women like men to be confident, and Frank did not lack confidence,' Max said. This was certainly a Maxian understatement about a man who thought nothing of letting his voice boom out formal lectures on the subject 'Shakespeare, Shaw, and Frank Harris'. Shaw, Max remembered, liked Harris and, when Harris was on his uppers, sent him an account of his love life, to help him finish his biography of Shaw.

Max was interested in my account of Gabriel Pascal, the film producer, whom Shaw also liked—who was, indeed, the confidant and friend and entertainer of his old age. Max was amused to hear that Pascal had once admitted to me, 'When I was nineteen, I was already a genius!' Max's narrow shoulders shook; such examples of precocity delighted him.

I asked Max whether he had ever known Harris to tell the truth.

'Sometimes, don't you know—when his invention flagged,' Max said.

After Harris got to the top, says Vincent Brome in his biography, 'there was no holding him.' There never is any holding them. These shattering careerists seem to follow a single pattern. Once they've reached, by spasms of will, the place where they want to be, some driving instinct inexorably impels them to destroy the pedestals their effrontery and egotism have erected, and to plummet to the gutter. It is as if they were driven by some *nostalgie de la boue*. During the First World War, when, having found it expedient to leave London, Harris was in New York, editing *Pearson's Magazine*, his magnetism was still strong enough to attract crowds to his lectures. Harris took it out on London for having put him in jail for contempt of court in 1914 by becoming a German propagandist in the First World War. At this, his friends, Arnold Bennett and Max among them, wrote him off. But always and everywhere, whatever he did and whatever his age, women abounded, caught up in the wake of his confidence. After the war, Harris went back to Europe, settling down in Nice, and there he wrote the bulk of the four volumes of his pornographic autobiography, *My Life and Loves*. Actually, it is a funny book, of that peculiar variety that can be achieved only by people who write about themselves with what Max called 'a sublimity of earnestness'—his euphemism for a total lack of humour. In it Harris tells, indiscriminately but with a nice feeling for juxtaposition, about his many love affairs and his adventures in the worlds of diplomacy and letters. At the end of one chapter, Harris describes a sexual episode the way an expert gymnast might describe an intricate manœuvre in callisthenics. And then, suddenly, you are confronted with the heading of the next chapter: 'How I Met Gladstone'.

During the years that Max worked for Harris on the *Saturday*, he found him admirable as an editor; everybody agrees that Harris really was a great editor. It was after Harris sold the *Saturday*, in 1899, that a little problem arose between Max and Harris. Harris was then editing *Modern Society*, one of the series of fly-by-night tattle sheets that he tried to galvanize into profit by the sheer power of his voice and moustache. Blackmail was a source of revenue that could not be recorded in the books, if there were any books. Brome tells substantially the same story Max told me. The novelist and playwright Enid Bagnold worked for Harris on this paper. Miss Bagnold has written about what he was like:

> We had a great *schwärmerei* from Frank which would come like measles and go as completely. . . . He was an extraordinary man. He had an appetite for great things and could transmit the sense of them. He was more like an actor than a man of heart. He could simulate everything. While he felt admiration he acted it and while he acted it he felt it, and 'greatness' being his big part he hunted the centuries for it, spotting it in literature, poetry, passion and acting.

While Harris was editing *Modern Society*, he was sued for libel, insulted the judge and was imprisoned for contempt of court. Miss Bagnold, desperate to get material for the next issue during the enforced absence of her chief, appealed to Shaw and Max for contributions. Shaw sent a nice letter refusing, but Max responded magnificently with a cartoon he gave Miss Bagnold 'on the solemn promise' that it should never be used either as a cover or as a poster. The cartoon, captioned 'The Best Talker in London—with one of his best listeners', is still in Miss Bagnold's possession; it shows Harris seated at one side of a table, expounding great ideas with large gestures. On the table is a bottle of wine. In another chair, Max is sitting bolt upright, listening. He is listening hard but, you feel, with a certain reserve. Under the drawing Max wrote, 'For my old friend Frank Harris this scribble in record of a scene which, happily for me, has been so frequent in the past twenty years.' Miss Bagnold took the drawing to Harris, in Brixton Jail. Harris was not pleased either with Max for having made his stipulation or with Miss Bagnold for having submitted to it, but he promised that the restriction would be faithfully observed. Needless to say, it was not. According to Brome, 'Within twenty-four hours the young girl who represented the advertising department of *Modern Society* visited the prison and received instructions to "go it strong on publicity" with Beerbohm's drawing, "and damnation take these fancy promises." ' After fifty years, Max's gratitude to Miss Bagnold for her share in circumventing the betrayal by the advertising department was still acute. 'It was Miss Bagnold,' he said, 'who spared me from seeing the cartoon on every hoarding in London.' This is Brome's account of how she did it:

> Presently she drove furiously in a cab to his [Max's] house, rang the doorbell and sent up an urgent message via the maid. Still not dressed, the gracious figure with the porcelain forehead came down 'in a wonderful dressing gown', and listened, his 'two very blue eyes . . . serious with anger'. Seeing how genuinely distressed she was, he dressed quickly and hurried out beside her, carrying a beautiful cane with a loop at the handle. They drove back to the office, examined the poster, dragged the roll into a cab and hurried round to the printers.

There, with some difficulty, they managed to commandeer the block. Twenty minutes later, they walked down the Savoy steps to the river, threw plate and posters wholesale into the black water, watched the block disappear and saw the posters unroll and begin to submerge.

Max was grateful to Miss Bagnold, but Miss Bagnold has every reason to be grateful to Max, because Max, just by his way of listening to the Best Talker, cured her of her measles. She recently wrote:

> I lunched at the Savoy with Frank Harris and Max Beerbohm and his first wife very shortly after they were married. And I have never forgotten Max's peculiar method of listening. His blue eyes wide with wonder, his forehead pink with admiration, but somehow, simultaneously, playing a ray of mockery—so light that it fell unnoticed on the Talker. I, who was all eyes and mouth open, learnt a lesson from that. It was the onset of my cure.

Some time ago, in the *Sunday Times*, I read the announcement of a book, by Sandy Wilson, to be called *Who's Who for Beginners*, which was to consist of a series of spoofs of young contemporary writers possessed of millennial and cosmic vision, those writers whose vaticinations embrace the future of the universe—dark, of course—and who offer prescriptions for lighting it. One of the young men, Mr. Reg Glupton, is nineteen years old and refers to himself as 'a mixture of the three "Ks"—Kierkegaard, Kafka, and Krafft-Ebing'. It sounded promising, and I thought I should like to buy the book when it came out, but an item in Mr. Glupton's entry really warmed my heart. This was that Glupton, while finishing his new book, *The Whip and the Butterfly*, was also contributing a series of articles to the *Onlooker* called 'World Disintegration—And After'. This warmed my heart because I knew immediately that Mr. Wilson was a reader of Max. When readers of Max meet—even when they don't meet—they experience a thrill of recognition. Mr. Wilson, I knew at once, had read and admired one of the juiciest of Max's pieces, his biographical study of T. Fenning Dodworth. Prophecy on the cosmic scale was T. Fenning Dodworth's stock-in-trade.

As we sat before the fire, I asked Max who had been the model for T. Fenning Dodworth, and he waved a hand and said vaguely, 'Oh, a Parliamentary figure of the time. I took quite a bit of trouble, don't you know, in the composing of his name, and I was pleased with the result: the bold "T.", like the statement of a portentous theme; the ominous and brooding vestibule of the Fenning; and then the broad, capacious good earth of the Dodworth.' Max tells you that T. Fenning Dodworth was a great wit and gives you examples of that wit, although he admits that, personally, he is not convulsed by them. He tells you that Dodworth, 'quite apart from his wit, seems to me one of the most remarkable, the strongest and, in a way, most successful men of our time.' And yet when he comes to analyse his hero's career, it emerges unblemished by the vulgar stigmata of success. He tried the bar, but he had to give it up, because, says Max simply, 'he got so few briefs.' He stood seven times for Parliament. Max writes, 'He escaped, every time, the evils of election. (And his good angel stood not less close to him on the three occasions when he offered himself as candidate for the London County Council.) Voters, like jurors, would not rise to him. At length it was borne in even on the leaders of his party that they must after all be content to rely on his pen rather than on his tongue.'

Max remembers having been moulded, when he was a schoolboy, by Dodworth's reasoned and weighty pronouncements in the political weeklies: 'The Franchise Bill—And After'; 'The Home Rule Peril—And After.' 'Both seemed to me splendid,' Max says warmly, 'partly perhaps because of their titles. Dodworth was, I believe, the first publicist to use that magical affix, that somehow statesmanlike, mysterious, intriguing formula, "—And After".' But later he grew more critical: 'Dodworth as a political thinker seemed to me lacking in generosity, lacking even (despite his invariable "—And After") in foresight.'

Dodworth took over the editorship of a newspaper, contributing to it his article—'substantially the same,' Max explains, 'as every article he had ever written; but, like some masterpiece of music, it never palled.' The newspaper folded. In the war, the

Minister of Information naturally summoned Dodworth, who
came through at once with a pamphlet that was translated into
thirty-seven languages and fifty-eight foreign dialects, and not
read in any of them. Max follows the rest of T. Fenning's career
breathlessly, through the peace that followed the war, and the
resumption of his top hat—for during the war he had 'worn
a thing of soft black felt, which I took to be a symbol of
pessimism'—and is with him on his visits to the House of
Commons. Max took such delight in his witticisms that Dodworth promised him a copy of his next book, *A Short Shrift for
Sinn Fein—And After*.

Dodworth wrote a play, produced by Sir George Alexander,
which Max attended, he says, in his professional capacity. He
reports on that momentous opening:

> All the leaders of both parties in both Houses were present
> on the first night, and many of them (rashly, so weak were they
> with laughter) were present also on the second, third and fourth
> nights, and would probably have been present on other nights,
> too; but (such was the absenteeism of the vulgar) there were
> no other nights.

Dodworth was undaunted. At a dinner given him by the
Playgoers' Club, he taunted Max and the other critics with their
failure 'to arrest the decay of dramatic art by elevating the taste
of the public.' Dodworth returned to his true field, article-
writing: 'The Assault on the Constitution—And After'; 'The
Betrayal—And After'; 'The End of All Things—And After'.
Max read all of them, generously recognizing, in spite of a
dislike of the author that he could not control, that Dodworth
was at his best in all of them. Max takes Dodworth to his
apogee—a public dinner at which the Prime Minister, Mr.
Lloyd George, proposed his health. The Prime Minister, when
he was 'a bare-legged, wild-eyed, dreamy little lad on the Welsh
mountains', had, like Max, been nurtured on the prophetic
writings of the guest of honour.

Max writes on the assumption that T. Fenning Dodworth is
the most successful man he has ever known. Why? Because of
his indurated conceit, the enviable congenital astigmatism that
enabled him to see the world as an arena in which the puny

contestants failed pitifully to measure up to an ideal visible
only to him, Dodworth, and by him, uniquely, so easily attainable. He had fought all the battles and won them in the trophied
caverns of his own self-esteem, and, says Max, taking on the
role of prophet himself for once, 'he will die game, and his
last words will be "—And After?" and will be spoken
pungently.'

I told Max that I had been looking at Fenning the night
before, in my hotel room, and that I had noticed, as I had not
when I first read it, that the last 'And After', which Max
predicted would be uttered by Dodworth when he was dying,
had a question mark after it.

'Ah, yes,' said Max. 'It's the first time Dodworth wasn't
sure!'

'He died a failure, then,' I said.

Max smiled. As an artist, he liked to get his effects simply.
And I could see that he was pleased that his cataclysmic
question mark had got over—a punctuation mark that conveyed the swift transition from certitude to agnosticism (a true
death-bed conversion), and from success to failure.

It was warm before the fire, but it was cold everywhere else
in the room. Miss Jungmann came in with the smallest hot-
water bottle I have ever seen and with a normal-sized one.
She put the normal-sized one on Max's lap—tucking it in
under the rug over his knees—and the small one behind his
neck.

'Our sunny Italian Riviera,' she said, 'is not so sunny
today. Max's room is *so* cold. I don't know *what* to do about it.'

'Have you ever noticed,' asked Max, 'that all hot-water
bottles look like Henry the Eighth?' He made the point clearer
by taking out the larger hot-water bottle, picking up a pencil,
and sketching on it the lineaments of the King—eyes, nose,
moustache, and chin—and the resemblance became indeed
remarkable. 'Holbein in rubber!' Max said, smiling.

'Tea will be ready in a minute,' Miss Jungmann said, and
excused herself.

I asked Max to tell me about the station hotels in which he

used to stay on his visits to London. I had read Logan Pearsall
Smith on the subject. Smith once wrote that Max would often,
on his visits to London, after he had made the rounds of all the
friends who were eager to see him, say formal farewells to them
as if he were going back to Italy and make straightaway for
the Great Western Railway Hotel at Paddington. Max would,
Smith wrote, 'remain there unknown to all for weeks and sometimes months. He found the monstrous horror of its 1860 decora-
tion (a horror that must be seen to be believed) and the awful
insipidity of its corn starch and custard cooking very congenial to his mid-Victorian tastes. He could hardly tear himself
away from it.'

'Yes, people used to wonder that I stayed in station hotels,'
Max said. 'They thought it quaint, I imagine. I stayed in
them because they were so comfortable. I adored them. The
early Victorians were great craftsmen, and they made the
furniture you find in the station hotels. Those great chests of
drawers! The drawers don't stick, as they are likely to do in
modern work; they come running out, like puppies when you
whistle for them, and run back at a touch, as if you had thrown
them a ball.' He smiled at me. 'I have been faithful to the
Charing Cross Hotel in my fashion, but I confess to a long
infidelity with the Paddington station hotel—the Great
Western, you know. I believe I have stayed there longer than
any man since it was built, and it was built at about the time the
first railways were laid down. And then the rooms! I am not a
tall man, but in the modern hotels, with their tawdry simplicity,
the doors and ceilings are so low. The public rooms are as big
as the Albert Hall, but they want to cram as many bipeds as
possible into as many storeys as possible, while the station hotels
—ah!—they give a man headroom, even a tall man. And you
look out of the window and see the columns of smoke pressed
down under the station roof and escaping as well as they can,
and you see the travellers emerging from the trains and
walking towards the hotel, as to an inn, for a night's lodging
after their journeys. There is a faint thunder always, a rever-
beration from the trains, catching all that movement, all that
going about. I like these Vulcan sounds. And in the lobbies—

the people who are sitting there are only there for the night, don't you know, and in all that transitoriness, by virtue of the fact that you are *not* travelling, you are *not* running about, well, you get a sense of immobility, of staying put, of tranquillity. Oh, yes, I loved dearly to stay at the station hotels.'

Max remembered with affection and exactitude the *maître d'hôtel* at the Charing Cross Hotel. 'He was tall and somewhat gangling, and he wore a frock coat with no silk facings on the lapels. He used to glide in and out among the tables, noiselessly and with great adroitness.' Max's hand glided in and out among the tables. 'My wife, Florence, wherever she was, used to come back to the hotel to have lunch with me. One day she couldn't come, but I neglected to cancel our usual reservation; it was a small table for two, in any case, and I lunched there alone. The *maître d'hôtel* saw me and glided through to me. I said that I would be alone this day. He made an incomparable gesture'—Max imitated the gesture with both hands, palms upturned—'a gesture of consoling me, don't you know, a gesture of tolerant understanding between one man of the world and another, a gesture of connoting heaven knows what, but counselling patience and tolerance in the face of such lapses among womankind.'

Even in Paris, Max ferreted out a station hotel and stayed in it. He tells about the delights of these sojourns in an essay he calls 'Fenestralia'. The view from the windows of the hotel in the Gare du Nord, he says, affords him a rapture he can't get anywhere else in Paris—not from sightseeing, not from walking, not from dining out:

> I looked forth early on my first morning, and saw a torrent of innumerable young backs, flooding across the square beneath and along the straight wide Rue Lafayette beyond. The fulness and swiftness of it made me gasp—and kept me gasping, while in the station behind me, incessantly, for more than an hour and a half, trainload after trainload of young men and women from the banlieue was disgorged into the capital. The maidens outnumbered the youths by about three or four to one, it seemed to me; and yet they were one maiden, so identically alike were they in their cloche hats and knee-deep skirts and flesh-coloured stockings, and in virtue of that erectly

tripping gait which Paris teaches while London inculcates an unsteady slouch. One maiden, yet hundreds and thousands of maidens, each with a soul of her own, and a home of her own, and earning her own wages. Bewildering! Having seen that sight, I needed no other.

Max is, in any case, partial to windows. He enlarges on the allurement of scenes and people seen through windows:

> I have set eyes on many great men, in my time, and have had the privilege of being acquainted with some of them (not of knowing them well, understanding them well, for to do that there must be some sort of greatness in oneself). And of all the great men whom I have merely seen the one who impressed me most was Degas. Some forty years ago I was passing, with a friend, through the Place Pigalle; and he, pointing up his stick to a very tall building, pointing up to an open window *au cinquième*—or was it *sixième*?—said, 'There's Degas.' And there, in the distance, were the head and shoulders of a grey-bearded man in a red béret, leaning across the sill. There Degas was, and behind him, in there, was his studio; and behind him, there in his old age, was his life-work; and with unageing eyes he was, I felt sure, taking notes of 'values' and what not of the populous scene down below, regretting perhaps (for he had never cast his net wide) the absence of any ballet-dancers, or jockeys, or laundry-girls, or women sponging themselves in hip-baths; but deeply, but passionately observing. There he was, is, and will always be for me, framed.

Max's favourite girls have what he calls 'the charm of windowhood'—the cottage girl at a small lattice window drawn by Rossetti, Mrs. Patrick Campbell windowed in *Mélisande*. Gladstone and Disraeli, he says, were at their most effective when they spoke through windows. The best sketch he has ever seen of Goethe was drawn by Tischbein while the great man was leaning out of a window of a Roman inn and looking down into the street below. 'It is a graceful, a forceful, and a noble back that we see there in that bedroom,' writes Max.

Miss Jungmann brought in tea and left again, and while we were sipping it, I returned to T. Fenning Dodworth and to Max's fondness for writing about failures—Enoch Soames, Savonarola Brown, Romeo Coates, and many others.

'I find failure endearing, don't you?' he said. 'Touching. And obsessive failure, from the point of view of the non-obsessed, can be so funny that you forget that it is touching.' He reached out and took up his own copy of *Zuleika Dobson*, which was published in 1911. The volume was much decorated by him. Among the publisher's notices printed on the inside of the jacket was a list of books and their authors. Max had drawn a little figure of himself standing below this list. He is reaching up to the list with a teacher's pointer and saying, 'Perhaps you prefer one of these?' Max stared at the list. 'Do you know one of them?' he asked.

I had to admit that none of the names, none of the titles, meant a thing in the world to me.

'And yet,' he said, 'these authors agonized over their works. There came a bright day when it was announced to them that their books would be published. There came a day when they *were* published. And now here we sit—it's not so *very* long ago, is it?—and you don't know any of them, and I myself, their contemporary, can scarcely remember them.'

I asked Max about a literary device to which he was addicted, that of having his fictional characters constantly involved with actual, historical ones: T. Fenning Dodworth with Lloyd George and other statesmen and personalities of the time; Enoch Soames with Will Rothenstein; Maltby (of Maltby and Braxton) in a Sunday-morning encounter with Arthur Balfour; the playwright Savonarola Brown appointing him, Max, as his literary executor. In *The Happy Hypocrite*, his early nineteenth-century allegory of good and evil, Max uses footnotes, as if he were writing an historical work, that refer to comments on his scapegrace hero, Lord George Hell, by known contemporaries: Banastre Tarleton, in an apocryphal work of his, *Contemporary Bucks*, and Lord Coleraine, in his *Correspondence*—both prominent Regency figures. Max said, 'The fantasist takes his imaginings seriously, you know.' When you wrote a fantasy, Max believed, between the improbable premise and the still more improbable conclusion you must be inexorably logical and realistic. He pursued this method with *Enoch Soames* and *The Happy Hypocrite*, pegging them to actuality with his contemporary references. On the inside back cover of his own copy of *Zuleika Dobson* he pasted a page out of Bradshaw, giving the hours of departure from Liverpool Street Station of trains to Cambridge. Around the departing hours he drew little circles, presumably designed to make things easier for other Zuleikas who have completed their dread work in Oxford to get on with more of the same in Cambridge.

I went on to refer to the fact that in *Poor Romeo!* the pathetic account of an early nineteenth-century gentleman of means, Robert Coates, who is known as Romeo Coates because of his misguided ambition to play Romeo, Max has embedded references to actual memoirists of the time. Here Max had me; here the references turned out to be genuine. There really was a Romeo Coates, and he did play Romeo, but the character is such a natural for Max that he might as well have invented him. Romeo was right up Max's street—a man obsessed with the wish to do something that he was simply unable to do. 'The lust for the footlights' glare,' Max says, 'grew lurid in his mothish eye,' and then he settles down to describe Romeo's début:

> The night came. Fashion, Virtue, and Intellect thronged the house. Nothing could have been more cordial than the temper of the gallery. All were eager to applaud the new Romeo. Presently, when the varlets of Verona had brawled, there stepped into the square—what!—a mountebank, a monstrosity. Hurrah died upon every lip. The house was thunderstruck. . . . Those lines that were not drowned in laughter Mr. Coates spoke in the most foolish and extravagant manner. He cut little capers at odd moments. He laid his hand on his heart and bowed, now to this, now to that part of the house, always with a grin. . . . The performance, so obviously grotesque, was just the kind of thing to please the gods. The limp of Hephaestus could not have called laughter so unquenchable from their lips. It is no trifle to set Englishmen laughing, but once you have done it, you can hardly stop them. Act after act of the beautiful love-play was performed without one sign of satiety from the seers of it. The laughter rather swelled in volume. Romeo died in so ludicrous a way that a cry of 'encore' arose and the death was actually twice repeated. At the fall of the curtain there was prolonged applause. Mr. Coates came forward, and the good-humoured public pelted him with fragments of the benches.

Informed by Max of Romeo's actuality, I later looked him up. Max says, at the end of his essay, that he wishes he had known Romeo, and I share his wish. He was very rich and lived, says the *Dictionary of National Biography*, in extraordinary style: 'His carriage, drawn by white horses, was in shape like a kettledrum, and across the bar of his curricle was a large brazen cock, with his motto, "Whilst I live I'll crow".' He eventually played in London, and his appearance there created such a sensation that a farce written about him, in which a popular comedian of the time, Charles Mathews, played Coates, had quite a success. Romeo found himself, therefore, not only acting but being acted. He returned to Bath, the scene of his first triumph, and played again. But the fickle audience got tired of laughing at him and began to hiss him. He died in a street accident after going to the theatre, crushed between a hansom and a private carriage. Max says of him, in summary, 'As his speeches before the curtain and his letters to the papers show, he took himself quite seriously. Only the insane take themselves quite seriously.'

Max professed to be flattered at my thinking that he had invented Romeo. I said it was natural, considering that he had invented Enoch Soames and Savonarola Brown. Probably those who haven't read anything else of Max's—except, perhaps, *Zuleika Dobson*—know these two sad histories. They are both masterpieces. Max's special method is beautifully exemplified in *Enoch Soames*. He begins:

> When a book about the literature of the eighteen-nineties was given by Mr. Holbrook Jackson to the world, I looked eagerly in the index for SOAMES, ENOCH. I had feared he would not be there. He was not there.

Holbrook Jackson's book *The Eighteen Nineties* has a chapter on Max—with the inevitable title 'The Incomparable Max'—and is dedicated to him. The book is a roster of everyone who figured in the literary and art worlds of the nineties. Max, saddened by the omission of Enoch from Jackson's book, goes on to describe the 'bolt from the blue' that flashed down on Oxford in the summer of 1893: the arrival of Will Rothenstein. It is a straight history of the beginning of his friendship with

Rothenstein. He tells how Rothenstein introduced him to
Aubrey Beardsley, to Chelsea, to the Bodley Head, to Walter
Sickert, and to that den of iniquity the Café Royal. Max goes
on to describe the famous domino room, 'haunt of intellect and
daring' :

> There, on that October evening—there, in that exuberant
> vista of gilding and crimson velvet set amidst all those opposing
> mirrors and upholding caryatids, with fumes of tobacco ever
> rising to the painted and pagan ceiling, and with the hum of
> presumably cynical conversation broken into so sharply now
> and again by the clatter of dominoes shuffled on marble tables,
> I drew a deep breath, and 'This indeed,' said I to myself, 'is
> life !'

Max is having dinner there with Rothenstein when a
shambling fellow walks by and lingers, obviously wanting to
meet Rothenstein. 'He had a thin vague beard—or rather, he
had a chin on which a large number of hairs weakly curled
and clustered to cover its retreat.' This is Enoch Soames, a
poet, who has just published a little volume called *Negations*.
Enoch wants to be painted by Rothenstein, but Rothenstein
snubs him. However, the fact that he *has* published a book and
has been to Paris impresses Max. 'If Rothenstein had not been
there,' Max says, 'I should have revered Soames.' Soames is at
work on another book. Max asks what the title will be, and
Soames says it will have no title, for he trusts to the content
to enchant the public.

> Rothenstein objected that absence of title might be bad for
> the sale of a book. 'If,' he urged, 'I went into a bookseller's
> and said simply "Have you got?" or "Have you a copy of?"
> how would they know what I wanted?'

When Rothenstein refuses to draw him—it was Enoch's idea
that the drawing of himself by Rothenstein should serve as a
frontispiece for his book—Max is pained.

> 'Why were you so determined not to draw him?' I asked.
> 'Draw him? Him? How can one draw a man who doesn't
> exist?'
> 'He is dim,' I admitted. But my *mot juste* fell flat. Rothenstein
> repeated that Soames was non-existent.

But Max, in spite of Rothenstein's scepticism, makes you believe in Soames's reality. He makes you believe so strongly in Soames's aspiration to be a famous poet that you are cheering for him to come through. Max keeps seeing Soames. He finds out that he is a Catholic Diabolist. Max reads his second book when it comes out—unadorned by a frontispiece by Rothenstein. It has a title after all—*Fungoids*. He quotes several of the poems. One of them rather puzzles him:

To a Young Woman

Thou art, who hast not been!
  Pale tunes irresolute
  And traceries of old sounds
  Blown from a rotted flute
Mingle with noise of cymbals rouged with rust,

Nor not strange forms and epicene
  Lie bleeding in the dust,
   Being wounded with wounds.

  For this it is
That in thy counterpart
Of age-long mockeries
Thou hast not been nor art!

The poem worries Max. He writes:

There seemed to me a certain inconsistency as between the first and last lines of this. I tried, with bent brows, to resolve the discord. But I did not take my failure as wholly incompatible with a meaning in Soames' mind. Might it not rather indicate the depth of his meaning? As for the craftsmanship, 'rouged with rust' seemed to me a fine stroke, and 'nor not' instead of 'and' had a curious felicity.

How can you not believe in the reality of a writer who is subjected to so fine an analysis by another writer? The story of a man thirsting for immortality is carried out to the end in ruthless fantasy. No other Catholic Diabolist had ever to take such punishment. And Max punishes not only Enoch but another contemporary, Bernard Shaw. After Soames has made his deal with the Devil and been allowed to look himself up in the reading room of the British Museum in 1997—only to find himself referred to as the subject of a satirical essay by Max Beerbohm, and no mention whatever of *Negations* or *Fungoids*—Enoch reports to Max on his astonishing experience. Everybody in the Museum, he says, was dressed as Shaw was—in Jaeger. Names had disappeared; everyone was numbered. And the report in which Enoch read about himself, by the Holbrook Jackson of 1997, T. K. Nupton, was written in phonetic spelling, for which Shaw was even then agitating and to which eventually he was to leave part of the fortune that he didn't, at that moment, have. This is what poor Soames had to struggle through:

> Fr egzarmpl, a riter ov th time, naimd Max Beerbohm, hoo woz stil alive in th twentieth senchri, rote a stauri in wich e pautraid an immajnari karrakter kauld 'Enoch Soames'—a thurd-rait poit hoo beleevz imself a grate jeneus. . . .

By this time, Max has made you feel so sorry for Enoch that it is really impossible to read further what T. K. Nupton will say about him, even aside from the pain of having to read the sterilized English.

Writing did not, Max told me, come easily to him. He suffered over it. 'Writing was always painful,' he told me. 'Whereas drawing I love—it comes easily to me, or did. My hand wanted to draw. Many years ago, I found that my caricatures were becoming likenesses. I seemed to have mislaid my gift for dispraise. Pity crept in. So I gave up caricaturing, except privately.' He constantly rewrote, because he could not bear to go on when he felt that what he had already written fell short of his own standard of perfection. 'The only things I ever wrote with joy—easily—were *"Savonarola" Brown* and the meeting between Ibsen and Browning in *A Christmas Garland*,' he told me. 'You see, Brown was such a bad writer that I was under no strain. It was easy to write better than Brown.'

As passionately as Enoch Soames wanted to be a poet, Savonarola Brown wanted to be a playwright. Unlike Romeo Coates, who could indulge his obsession to act, because he was rich, Savonarola was poor and had to rely, like most playwrights, on the market place. Max writes that he knew him

Some Members of the New English Art Club

MR. FRANK HARRIS

MR. REGINALD
TURNER

first when he was at school; his real name was Ladbroke, his unimaginative parents having christened him after the crescent in which they lived. Ladbroke dropped out of school, and Max didn't see him for a great many years, though he was occasionally tortured by the memory of the ragging to which he and his schoolmates had subjected poor Ladbroke on account of his unfortunate Christian name. Max became drama critic for the *Saturday Review*, and asked for second-night seats instead of first-night ones. He found the audiences at second nights less showy and more earnest. It was in this way that he ran into Brown again, because Brown was a confirmed second-nighter.

In an entr'acte meeting, Brown confided to Max that he was thinking of writing a play about Savonarola. 'He had thought of writing a tragedy about Sardanapalus; but the volume of the *Encyclopaedia Britannica* in which he was going to look up the main facts about Sardanapalus happened to open at Savonarola.' Brown was rather like that woman in Kaufman and Hart's *You Can't Take It With You* who became a writer because a typewriter had been delivered to her house by mistake. For nine years, Brown kept working on the play, and during those nine years Max kept seeking him out on second nights to get progress reports. In this way, Max saw him through four acts. But there was one to come, the final act, and this Max couldn't seem to get out of him. Max was impatient because Brown had refused to let him see the play until it was finished. One night, Max met him and found him rather glum. He had decided he must kill Savonarola in the last act, and he had by that time conceived such an affection for his protagonist that he hated to do it. As they were walking away from the theatre, Max remonstrated with him:

'But in a tragedy,' I insisted, 'the catastrophe *must* be led up to, step by step. My dear Brown, the end of the hero *must* be logical and rational.'

'I don't see that,' he said, as we crossed Piccadilly Circus. 'In actual life it isn't so. What is there to prevent a motor-omnibus from knocking me over and killing me at this moment?'

At that moment, by what has always seemed to me the

strangest of coincidences, and just the sort of thing that play-wrights ought to avoid, a motor-omnibus knocked Brown over and killed him.

He had, as I afterwards learned, made a will in which he appointed me his literary executor. Thus passed into my hands the unfinished play by whose name he had become known to so many people.

And this is how Max is able to present the four completed acts of *Savonarola* to the reader. The four acts are written in Shakespearean blank verse, some of which just misses being good. The hero, Savonarola, is supported by a distinguished cast: Dante, St. Francis of Assisi, Lucrezia Borgia, Lorenzo de' Medici, Leonardo da Vinci, Michelangelo. Even Pippa, in a stage direction, passes. The drama critic, Wolcott Gibbs, once told me that after he read this uncompleted tragedy all Shakespearean productions seemed faintly funny to him.

Max knows that the one thing in the world poor Brown wanted was a production. He offers the play to one manager after another:

> All have seen great merits in the work; and if I added together all the various merits thus seen I should have no doubt that *Savonarola* was the best play never produced.

Since the managers all say they can't produce an unfinished play, Max feels it his duty, as Brown's literary executor, to supply a fifth act. He writes the scenario of one, which seems to fit magically into Brown's own vein. But it doesn't satisfy Max. Brown had endlessly reiterated to him what he had heard —and what one still hears—from other playwrights; namely, that *they* don't write the play, it is the characters who write the play. The characters have such reality, so much vitality, that they take over, they dictate, they tell the author what to do. Max decides to wait for dictation from Brown's characters:

> I saw that Brown was, in comparison with me, a master. Thinking I might possibly fare better in his method of work than in my own, I threw the skeleton into a cupboard, sat down, and waited to see what Savonarola and those others would do.
>
> They did absolutely nothing. I sat watching them, pen in

hand, ready to record their slightest movement. Not a little
finger did they raise. Yet I knew they must be alive. Brown had
always told me they were quite independent of him. Absurd
to suppose that by the accident of his own death they had
ceased to breathe. . . . Now and then, overcome with weariness,
I dozed at my desk, and whenever I woke I felt that these rigid
creatures had been doing all sorts of wonderful things while
my eyes were shut. I felt that they disliked me.

In the end, Max throws in the sponge. He announces a competition, open to everyone who wants to try his hand at finishing
the play. As a reward, he offers the winner a seat for the second
night.

Another failure Max took a deep interest in was an actual,
though anonymous, clergyman. From the immense realm of
Boswelliana, Max picked out a single sentence, a single puny
question put one day by a poor clergyman to Dr. Johnson, and
fixed it, in his essay called 'A Clergyman', as an eternal symbol
of quenched human aspiration. The essay starts:

> Fragmentary, pale, momentary; almost nothing; glimpsed
> and gone; as it were, a faint human hand thrust up, never to
> reappear, from beneath the rolling waters of Time, he forever
> haunts my memory and solicits my weak imagination. Nothing
> is told of him but that once, abruptly, he asked a question,
> and received an answer.

The two-line drama was played on the afternoon of April 7,
1778, in Mrs. Thrale's house. Johnson was feeling fine; he'd
had a ride in a coach, which for him was 'the sum of human
felicity', and there was a good dinner in prospect, another sum.
How the poor little curate got there Max doesn't know; Max
thinks that perhaps he was attached to the neighbouring
church. He should have been content just to *be* there, but one
can forgive him for wanting more, for wanting fame, for wishing
to make a début, however modest, on the great stage of Johnson's attention. Johnson was being asked by Boswell for his
opinion of the styles of the various famous preachers of the time,
whose deliveries were analysed in the eighteenth century much
as we nowadays compare Olivier with Gielgud, or Lunt with
Guinness. Max describes the electrifying fantasy of success that

went through the little curate's mind as he sat there listening to
Johnson:

> He sits on the edge of a chair in the background. He has
> colourless eyes, fixed earnestly, and a face almost as pale as the
> clerical bands beneath his somewhat receding chin. His fore-
> head is high and narrow, his hair mouse-coloured. His hands
> are clasped tight before him, the knuckles standing out sharply.
> This constriction does not mean that he is steeling himself to
> speak. He has no positive intention of speaking. Very much,
> nevertheless, is he wishing in the back of his mind that he *could*
> say something—something whereat the great Doctor would
> turn on him and say, after a pause for thought, 'Why yes,
> Sir. That is most justly observed' or 'Sir, this has never occurred
> to me. I thank you'—thereby fixing the observer for ever high
> in the esteem of all.

What did happen is almost too cruel:

> 'We have no sermons addressed to the passions, that are
> good for anything; if you mean that kind of eloquence [Johnson
> says, according to Boswell].
> 'A Clergyman, whose name I do not recollect: Were not
> Dodd's sermons addressed to the passions?
> 'Johnson: They were nothing, Sir, be they addressed to what
> they may.'

Max continues:

> The suddenness of it! Bang!—and the rabbit that had
> popped from its burrow was no more. . . . In Johnson's massive
> and magnetic presence only some very remarkable man, such
> as Mr. Burke, was sharply distinguishable from the rest. Others
> might, if they had something in them, stand out slightly. This
> unfortunate clergyman may have had something in him, but
> I judge that he lacked the gift of seeming as if he had.

That was it. The clergyman was annihilated. He had had
no gift of selling himself, and Max's sympathy always went to
the great unsold.

Max never pretended to be as interested in success as he was
in failure. In fact, it was impossible for him to pretend to feel
anything he didn't feel. He could not pretend to admire what
he didn't admire, or understand what he didn't understand.

He has an essay, 'On Speaking French', that describes an awful experience which, perhaps, cured him for ever of pretending:

> To listen and from time to time murmur 'C'est vrai' may seem safe enough; yet there is danger even here. I wish I could forget a certain luncheon in the course of which Mme Chose (that brilliant woman) leaned suddenly across the table to me, and, with great animation, amidst a general hush, launched at me a particularly swift flight of winged words. With pensively narrowed eyes, I uttered my formula when she ceased. This formula she repeated, in a tone even more pensive than mine. 'Mais je ne le connais pas,' she then loudly exclaimed. 'Je ne connais pas même le nom. Dites-moi de ce jeune homme.' She had, as it presently turned out, been asking me which of the younger French novelists was most highly thought of by English critics; so that her surprise at never having heard of the gifted young Sévré was natural enough.

At a time when Yeats was fairly generally revered, Max admitted that he was bothered by the poet's preoccupation with the occult. In a sketch on Yeats, written in 1914, he says that he felt always 'rather uncomfortable [with Yeats], as though I had submitted myself to a mesmerist who somehow didn't mesmerize me.' Often, he says, Yeats engendered 'a mood in a vacuum'. When Max first met Yeats, the latter was full of the cult of Diabolism, to the Catholic branch of which Soames was committed. Later, it was spiritualism. In this same essay, Max uttered the blasphemy that the poetry of Tom Moore conveyed more of Ireland to him than Yeats's did. Max was not ashamed to tell me that Freud, too, was beyond his range. There were already some distinguished visitors in the realm of his admitted incomprehension. In the essay called 'Laughter', he had written:

> M. Bergson, in his well-known essay on this theme, says . . . well, he says many things; but none of these, though I have just read them, do I clearly remember, nor am I sure that in the act of reading I understood any of them. That is the worst of these fashionable philosophers—or rather, the worst of me. Somehow I never manage to read them till they are just going out of fashion, and even then I don't seem able to cope with them. About twelve years ago, when everyone suddenly talked to me about Pragmatism and William James, I found myself

moved by a dull but irresistible impulse to try Schopenhauer, of whom, years before that, I had heard that he was the easiest reading in the world, and the most exciting and amusing. I wrestled with Schopenhauer for a day or so, in vain. Time passed; M. Bergson appeared 'and for his hour was lord of the ascendant'; I tardily tackled William James. I bore in mind, as I approached him, the testimonials that had been lavished on him by all my friends. Alas, I was insensible to his thrillingness. His gaiety did not make me gay. His crystal clarity confused me dreadfully. I could make nothing of William James. And now, in the fullness of time, I have been floored by M. Bergson.

Max was floored also by some of T. S. Eliot and the 'obscure' school of poetry in general. He referred to it as 'the wooziepoozie school'. He was enchanted by Eliot personally. 'He is very modest and most impressive in appearance,' he told me, 'with the look of a great man, don't you know, but as for some of his poetry I can neither read nor understand it.' Max liked various of the Georgian poets—Siegfried Sassoon especially. Of Robert Graves he said to me, as if confiding a personal and probably—considering the trend—an unbelievable idiosyncrasy, 'My joy in him is not diminished because he is intelligible.' Max preferred Wordsworth's sonnets to those of Shakespeare. He said that often he had no idea what Shakespeare's sonnets meant, and he felt that many of their passionate admirers had very little idea what they meant, either. Max didn't take any more kindly to some contemporary art. Certain of its manifestations seemed to him departures from sanity. Sir Edward Marsh once wrote to Max on behalf of the Contemporary Art Society 'to find out whether there is any chance that you would fall in with a strong desire they have formed (prepare yourself for a shock) to commission Graham Sutherland to paint your portrait—I expect you have heard of his portraits of Willie Maugham and Max Beaverbrook, both of which seem to me masterpieces. . . . I understand that in Continental opinion he now ranks with Henry Moore, who for the first time has put English sculpture on the map of Europe.— Besides which he is a most charming fellow.' Max was later to express himself to me about Sutherland's portrait of Maugham.

Max said, 'Maugham looks in it as if he had died of torture.'
Having no wish to die that way, Max wrote to Marsh refusing
the honour. 'My dear Eddie, I, with my pencil, have been in
my time a ruthless monstrifier of men,' he wrote. 'And the
bully is, proverbially, always a coward. . . . "Henry Moore,"
you say, "has put English sculpture on the map of Europe!"
This being so, the younger Pitt would not now say "Roll up
that map!" It has been squashed down flat for ever.'

But what floored Max more than anything else was the
Freudian vocabulary that he kept increasingly hearing and
reading. The psychoanalytic argot his younger visitors so glibly
dispensed seemed to imply a mastery over the secrets of the
mind and the riddles of motive; these people, he thought, were
persuaded that vocabulary was an adequate substitute for
understanding. 'They are so spendthrift, don't you know, with
complexes,' Max said. 'They fling them about.' As Max and
I were finishing our tea, the conversation got back to psychiatry,
and from there we went on to Freudian jargon. 'Just the other
day,' he said, 'I was reading a biography of Kipling. Kipling
liked to have high hedges around his country house, at Rotting-
dean. The biographer made a great thing of that. He traced it
back to Kipling's fight with Balestier in Vermont; he inter-
preted the hedge in the light of that, and came to a bursting
conclusion that Kipling had a privacy complex. Well, what
fastidious man doesn't? I had to put the book down. I could
read no more of it. And then, in a biography of Tennyson, I
read an extraordinary interpretation of his elegiac poem on his
friend Hallam—I forbear to tell you of *that*! And what do you
think of this psychoanalytic interpretation of Henry James's
The Turn of the Screw—that the whole thing was a fantasy in
the mind of the governess to alleviate some psychic disturbance
in *her*, that it was the projection of some morbid complex within
herself? Nonsense! Henry James was simply trying to write a
powerful mystery story, that's all.'

Miss Jungmann came in. She suggested that Max had been
up long enough. 'And besides,' she said, 'I have been invited to
dinner! Unless'—she turned to me—'you have changed your
mind.'

I said I hadn't.

'Do you mind,' I asked Max, 'if I take Miss Jungmann out to dinner?'

Max reached out his hand to me. He smiled. 'Not at all,' he said. 'I have a giving-away complex!'

V

THE MENU

O N AN exceedingly cold afternoon, during my visit to
Rapallo in the winter of 1954, I saw an encouraging
announcement in the lobby of the Excelsior. *La Bohème*,
I read, was to be given that evening in a theatre, ordinarily
devoted to motion pictures, in the town of Santa Margherita
Ligure, a mile away. Since my room in the Excelsior was
extremely cold—about as cold as the Villino was, once you got
outside the immediate orbit of Max's fireplace—I assumed that
it would be warmer in the theatre, and asked Turco to get me a
ticket. The movie theatre turned out to be packed, and it *was*
warm, even stifling. The singers, according to the announcement, had illustrious histories; they had managed to escape,
momentarily, from the confines of La Scala, and Santa
Margherita was to be congratulated on having caught them
while they were on a busman's holiday. I had never before
sympathized so acutely with the efforts of Rodolfo and the other
starving artists in their garret to keep warm. When they fell
with such avidity on the food that one of them brought in, the
effect was not quite convincing, because the starvelings were
enormously fat and looked as if what they needed was strict
dieting, but the acrobatics in which they indulged to stave off
the cold were something I had learned to understand. They gave
each other huge slaps on the back; they hugged themselves
exuberantly; they danced about and jumped up and down to
get their circulation stirring. I left at the end of the first act;
it was much too warm. After driving back to the Excelsior, I got
into bed with a hot-water bottle and read Max's wonderful

description of George Moore's receding chin—it kept advancing and receding—in a reprint of a B.B.C. broadcast he had delivered in 1950 but had written in 1913, as a sketch for *The Mirror of the Past*.

The next afternoon, I arrived at the Villino at four o'clock, and I found Max sitting in front of the fire. He was wearing the heavy sweater I had brought him from America, plus the wool stole I had brought Miss Jungmann. I told him about my excursion of the night before, and his shoulders shook with laughter.

'Although you have never been given a release from La Scala,' I said, 'I hear that you are something of a singer yourself, even a radio singer—though not a crooner,' and I explained to Max about American crooners and what a vogue they had once had. I was referring to the fact that in another B.B.C. broadcast he made, on the music halls of his youth, he had ventured into song.

My remark set Max off. He began to sing from the repertory of one of the favourite music-hall comedians of his youth, George Robey. When Max sang, he leaned far forward in his chair, his expression immensely solemn. Assuming an air of honest indignation and injured innocence, he sang, in full Cockney but with unimpaired diction. Max's eyebrows became very active; they twitched in Pecksniffian outrage. The burden of the song was that Robey had been accused by malevolent spirits of playing Peeping Tom at the bathing machines at Brighton. When Max came to the end of the song, his voice and eyebrows cried out in gruesomely lascivious protest:

'Did I go near the bathing machine?
NAOW!'

Max had adored Robey. He smiled as he spoke of Robey's impersonation, in a sketch, of Queen Berengaria; evidently she was putting on the royal raiment *in* a bathing machine, and her sudden startled expression, half reluctant, half experimental, indicated that the Queen was herself suspicious that George Robey was lurking somewhere in the vicinity. When Robey died, Max said, he had been given a memorial service at St.

Paul's. This had afforded Max intense amusement, and, he said, it would have afforded the same to Robey. 'Pity he couldn't have been informed!'

Max then imitated Marie Lloyd singing 'Oh, Mr. Porter, Whatever shall I do? I want to go to Birmingham and they're taking me on to Crewe'. To Marie, Max, a few years before, had paid an obituary tribute over the B.B.C. 'It is strange,' Max had said, 'that of all the women of the Victorian Era the three most generally remembered are Queen Victoria herself, and Miss Florence Nightingale, and—Marie.'

When Max was sixteen, his half-brother Julius, who was then twice his age, had taken him to dinner at the Café Royal and then to his first music hall, the Pavilion, to hear The Great Macdermott—'a huge old burly fellow, with a yellow wig and a vast expanse of crumpled shirt-front that had in the middle of it a very large, not *very* real diamond stud.' It was at a moment of anti-Russian tension, because of repressive measures taken by the Tsar against the Nihilists, and The Great Macdermott, it appeared, had had an interview with the Prime Minister about it. This was odd—as if Eisenhower were to consult Jimmy Durante about certain Russian tensions now—but it was so. Macdermott, Max says, did not regard the interview as confidential. He sang about it the night Max first heard him:

> ' "What would you like to do, my Lord?"
>   I asked Lord Salisburee.'

Fond of tracing words to their sources, Max remembered that the word 'jingo', as a symbol of effervescent patriotism, had been introduced in a music-hall song by this same Macdermott. It was at a moment when Russia appeared to be threatening Turkey, then (as now) England's ally. Max, imitating Macdermott, became quite bellicose, unusual for him:

> 'We don't want to fight, but, by jingo, if we do,
> We've got the ships, we've got the men, we've got the
>   money, too!
> We fought the Bear before, and while Britons shall
>   be true,
> The Russians shall not have Constantinople!'

I chided Max for being so possessive about Constantinople. He relaxed from his belligerence and said that he didn't want it for himself, he just didn't want the Russians to have it.

I remembered that Miss Jungmann had told me he had once written a song for the music-hall entertainer Albert Chevalier, and I asked him about that.

'Oh,' he said, 'I wrote it, but I never offered it to Chevalier. I did meet him, though. Macdermott was enormous, Chevalier small and electric. He did coster songs and wore pearlies. He had a song, which I *can't* sing—it would be an injustice to him—called "You Can't Get a Roise Out o' Oi". But I'll try two lines from another.'

Max sang:

> 'It isn't so much what 'e sez,
> It's the nahsty way 'e sez it.'

'Chevalier's songs,' he went on, 'always had a clear form. They were well constructed. I knew them all by heart once. I got into his mind, don't you know, and, emboldened by this, I ventured to construct a song that, it seemed to me, he might have written himself. It tells about an old barman whom Chevalier had known and loved and who was dead and whose pub was now being run by his son. The song I wrote was called "But 'E'll Never Be the Man 'Is Father Woz", and the chorus went like this.' Max treated me to a private performance of the song, which he had also sung on his broadcast:

> 'I drops in to see young Ben
> In 'is tap-room now an' then,
> And I likes to see 'im gettin' on becoz
>   'E's got pluck and 'e's got brains,
>   And 'e takes no end o' pains,
> But—'e'll never be the man 'is Father woz.'

On the B.B.C., Max told his audience why he had never submitted the song to Chevalier. 'Nothing so irks a creative artist as to be offered an idea, good or bad,' he said. 'And I did not irk Chevalier.'

But Max's special affection, in the teeming past that so

crowded his present, went out to two Lilliputians who were giants of the old music halls—Little Tich and Dan Leno. These two were friends of his. 'Little Tich!' Max said. 'He *was* tiny. I felt gross beside him, and yet, you know, I couldn't have been *so* much larger, because I remember the time I was asked to appear and speak at some charity or other organized by the Playgoers' Club. The presiding officer was just about to call on me when some bigwig, some Eminence or other, made his sudden appearance. The chairman was so bowled over by this irruption that he quite lost his head. With a wave towards me, he said, "And now I have the honour to announce Sir Tich!" It made it easy for me to speak, you know. I apologized, I believe, for having forgotten my great boots. He used to slosh about—Little Tich—in great boots. They were as long as himself. He had them specially made, and the walk he managed in them was—well, incommunicably funny. It was . . .' Max's feet did a slosh on the carpet. 'No, it cannot be imitated. He had a sad face. So did Dan Leno—the saddest face, I believe, I have ever known. Little Tich told me this story himself. When his son was born, he was in a state of great anxiety, and he was sitting on the stairs, with his head bowed in his hands and wondering how everything was going, and presently the doctor came along and comforted him. "It's all right, my little man," he said. "You've got a baby brother." When the baby brother grew up, Little Tich worried dreadfully about him. He wanted his son to take holy orders. I met him one night in a pub near His Majesty's and found the dear man in a state of particular depression. "Oh!" he said. "My boy! I don't know what will become of him. He is not serious. He is not religious. I am afraid he hasn't a vocation. Instead of studying, he prefers to hang around your brother's theatre. He's probably in there right this minute. If he can't get a seat, he stands at the back of the stalls!" He was a marvellous mime, Little Tich. He was a *succès fou* in Paris—even more than in London. But Dan Leno was a great artist, the greatest artist of them all.'

Not having to worry about boots, Max was able to imitate Dan Leno. He did it with his fingers. 'The greatest thing he ever did—at least, to my taste—was a scene in a shoeshop. He made you *see* everything. He wrote his patter himself, and it was trenchant and shattering. Well, in the shoeshop, a mother comes in with a little boy. Dan skips over to her.' Max did the skip with his hands, in miniature staccato jumps. 'He asks the mother how old the little boy is. Three. *Three!* Leno is lost in admiration. He can't repress his amazement and wonder, don't you know, that a little boy of three could be so precocious, so mature, so altogether delectable. Then he skips up the step-ladder.' Max's fleet fingers skipped up the stepladder. 'And he rummages around for the shoes. Red boots with white buttons she wanted. While he's up there, on top of the stepladder, he keeps looking down at the boy, as if he had never before seen such a cynosure. But he can't find the proper shoes. He rum-mages around with increasing desperation among the boxes.' Now both of Max's hands were rummaging around wildly and helplessly among the shoe-boxes. 'He produces a multitude of shoes, but the mother won't accept them. By this time, his attitude towards the little boy has changed, don't you know. He becomes somewhat critical of the little boy—even homi-cidal. Oh, it was wonderful, but it is impossible to describe,' said Max as he finished describing it.

Max continued to talk about Dan Leno. 'You know, Con-stance Collier—she was a member of Herbert's company at His Majesty's—once told me an extraordinary story about Leno. She came home late one evening, after her performance —it was very late; she had been out to supper, I imagine—to her flat, in Shaftesbury Avenue. She noticed a brougham before her door as she went in. There in her sitting-room was Dan Leno. He had been there for hours. Constance had never met him, but, of course, she was thrilled to see him. What do you suppose he wanted? Now, mind you, you must remember that at this very moment Dan Leno was the idol of England; he could do no wrong with his public, which adored him. Well, he wanted to play Shakespeare. That is why he had waited, and kept a brougham with a coachman on the seat waiting— because he wanted to enlist Constance's sympathy for his ambition to play Shakespeare. He wanted to meet my brother. Constance arranged it. She brought Dan Leno to Herbert.

But nothing came of it. Why wouldn't Herbert employ him?
He would have been wonderful—Dan—as one of Shakespeare's
clowns. I didn't know about it or I should have pleaded with
Herbert.'

Max looked at me sorrowfully. 'He was a sad man, Dan Leno.
Wildly generous. Surrounded always, don't you know, by a
crowd of hangers-on and sycophants, to whom he gave freely
whatever they asked.' In *Around Theatres* Max pays a more
formal tribute to Dan Leno. He writes his obituary notice,
and he is not buoyant, as he was when he performed the same
office for Ibsen. Leno died in 1904, at the age of forty-five.
Max writes:

> So little and frail a lantern could not long harbour so big
> a flame. Dan Leno was more a spirit than a man. It was
> inevitable that he, cast into a life so urgent as is the life of a
> music-hall artist, should die untimely. Before his memory fades
> into legend, let us try to evaluate his genius. For mourners
> there is ever a solace in determining what, precisely, they have
> lost. . . . Well, where lay the secret of that genius? How came
> we to be spell-bound? . . . In every art personality is the
> paramount thing, and without it artistry goes for little.
> Especially is this so in the art of acting, where the appeal of
> personality is so direct. . . . Dan Leno's was not one of those
> personalities which dominate us by awe, subjugating us against
> our will. He was of that other, finer kind: the lovable kind.
> He had, in a higher degree than any other actor that I have
> ever seen, the indefinable quality of being sympathetic. I defy
> any one not to have loved Dan Leno at first sight. The moment
> he capered on, with that air of wild determination, squirming
> in every limb with some deep grievance, that must be out-
> poured, all hearts were his. That face puckered with cares . . .
> yet ever liable to relax its mouth into a sudden wide grin
> and to screw up its eyes to vanishing point over some little
> triumph wrested from Fate, the tyrant; that poor little battered
> personage, so 'put upon', yet so plucky with his squeaking voice
> and his sweeping gestures; bent but not broken; faint but
> pursuing; incarnate of the will to live in a world not at all worth
> living in—surely all hearts went always out to Dan Leno,
> with warm corners in them reserved to him for ever and ever.

Max spoke of the years between 1898 and 1910, when he
was drama critic of the *Saturday Review*. 'Most of the plays

then,' Max told me, remembering them in tranquillity, 'were written by either Naomi Greckle or Mr. Tompkins'—generic names he had invented for indistinguishable playwrights. Max had suffered much from Naomis and Tompkinses at Herbert's house, long before he became a drama critic. Managers, especially actor-managers, didn't take kindly to reading; they preferred to have plays read aloud to them. Herbert would invite Naomis to his house and have them read their plays to him and his wife in the drawing-room when he came back from his own performances. Often, Max was invited to listen, and shared his sister-in-law's agonies. Max used to dread these readings. He would watch a Naomi turn the reluctant pages of her typescript, and he would become involved in a breathless computation—comparing the number of pages that *had* been turned to the number that were still virginal. He would begin to 'work out little sums in rule of three, with an eye on the clock. Disheartening little sums!' He learned to cultivate an expression, during these readings, of 'animated receptivity'. He also practised occasional murmurs and ejaculations of a kind that had an ambiguous neutrality and that Naomi could interpret, hopefully, as expressions of pleasure.

Now, as Max and I talked, all that he remembered of these plays was that they had screens in them. The first stage direction usually read, 'A Drawing-Room in Mayfair. At back, right, a large Chinese screen'. The nationality of the screens might vary but not their presence. The moment you heard that stage direction, you knew that someone, ultimately, was going to hide behind the screen and overhear something disastrous. Max used to wait for the moment when someone got behind the screen, and once that had happened, he knew he could revert to his private thoughts. Naturally, as the younger brother of the great Herbert Beerbohm Tree, he kept meeting Naomi Greckle and Mr. Tompkins all the time. He also met all the leading and lesser mimes. (Max almost invariably referred to actors as mimes.) This intensive acquaintance in the theatrical world added to Max's self-disqualification for the job he took in 1898. In his introductory article, 'Why I Ought Not to Have Become a Dramatic Critic', he argued it eloquently as part of his own brief for the prosecution, though without effect:

> Of the literary quality in any play, I shall perhaps be able to say something, but I shall be hopelessly out of my depth in criticising the play itself. The mere notion of criticising the players simply terrifies me, not because I know (as, indeed, I do) nothing about the art of acting, but because I have the pleasure of personal acquaintance with so many players. One well-known player and manager is my near relative. Who will not smile if I praise him? How could I possibly disparage him? Will it not be hard for me to praise his rivals? If I do anything but praise them, what will become of the purity of the Press? Most of the elder actors have patted me on the head and given me sixpence when I was 'only *so* high'. Even if, with an air of incorruptibility, I now return them their sixpences, they will yet expect me to pat *them* on the head in the *Saturday Review*. Many of the younger actors were at school with me. They will expect me to criticise them as an old playmate should. . . . My whole position is unfortunate. I have the satiric temperament: when I am laughing at any one, I am generally rather amusing, but when I am praising any one, I am always deadly dull. Now, such is the weakness of my character that I cannot say in print anything against a personal acquaintance. I think I have met all the habitual playwrights in my time. . . .

He disqualifies himself even further. He disqualifies himself ultimately:

> I will not raise in my readers hopes which I cannot realise for them. It is best to be quite frank. Frankly, I have none of that instinctive love for the theatre which is the first step towards good criticism of drama. I am not fond of the theatre. Dramatic art interests and moves me less than any of the other arts. I am happy among pictures, and, being a constant intruder into studios, have learnt enough to know that I know nothing whatever about painting—knowledge which, had I taken to what is called 'art-criticism', would have set me head-and-shoulders above the great majority of my colleagues. Of music I have a genuine, though quite unenlightened, love. Literature I love best of all, and I have some knowledge of its technicalities. I can talk intelligently about it. I have my little theories about it. But in drama I take, unfortunately, neither emotional nor intellectual pleasure.

Having cleared his soul in full confession, Max trots off

blithely to review *The Beauty Stone* of which he writes, 'I am
sorry that I have not found much to praise in *The Beauty Stone*.
I should like it to have a long run, though I would rather not
be invited to the hundredth night.' He trotted for twelve years.

In spite of the myriad disqualifications and formidable
handicaps, Max's drama criticisms, some of which, like his
caricatures, he signed 'Max', can still be read with delight.
Because they convey his own personality and his own attitude
towards life, they have an extraordinary vivacity and con-
temporaneity. As most of Naomi's product was instantly
dismissible, Max was able to devote the rest of his articles to
himself. Though the plays and the players are gone, Max's
criticisms are very much left. The animating spirit of all Max's
criticism—as, indeed, of all his writing—is a cultivated common
sense. His congenital inability to like what he should like when
it happens that he doesn't like it is everywhere manifest. He
refuses, for example, to be knocked over by Eleonora Duse,
who acted in Italian, for the bizarre reason that he doesn't
know what she was talking about. He starts a review of her
performance as Hedda Gabler, in Italian, as follows: 'Eecoss-
toetchiayoomahnioeevahrachellopestibahntamahntafahnta . . .
shall I go on?' He does go on to explain that that is what
the whole thing sounded like to him. The article is headed
'An Hypocrisy in Playgoing', and he apologizes for his
brutality on the ground that 'only by brutal means can
humbug be combated, and there seems to me no form of
humbug sillier and more annoying than the habit of attending
plays that are acted in a language whereof one cannot make
head or tail.' In an earlier piece on Duse—she played Gioconda
—he has a good time envying the other drama critics. Since
they have praised Duse so immoderately—her every nuance,
her every intonation—he assumes that, of course, they all know
Italian as well as they know English, and he envies them their
bilinguality. He is disrespectful, too, about Sarah Bernhardt,
whom he saw play Hamlet: 'The only compliment one can
conscientiously pay her is that her Hamlet was, from first to
last, *très grande dame*.' That piece is called 'Hamlet, Princess of
Denmark'. 'The Tame Eaglet' tells about Sarah as the young

Duc de Reichstadt in Rostand's *L'Aiglon*. Max finds the play an interminable bore; 'the trouble' with Sarah's performance, he says, 'is that to every one she looks like a woman, walks like one, talks like one, *is* one.' He continues, 'That primary fact upsets the whole effort, mars all illusion. As the part would be tedious even if it were played by a man, I may seem captious in grumbling that it is played by a woman. My displeasure, however, is not that the eaglet is played by Mme Bernhardt, but that she plays the eaglet.' Next time he sees Sarah, she is playing a woman, the title role in *La Sorcière*; by this time Sarah herself is an old lady. Max is gallant; he recognizes the occasion as a last chance and thinks of the time he saw the aged Queen Victoria, in an old-fashioned barouche, on her way to Paddington Station. When he saw the Sovereign driving by, he remembered the phantoms of the past—Melbourne and the Duke, Louis Philippe, Palmerston, Peel, Disraeli. Now he thinks of Sarah:

> My imagination roved back to lose itself in the golden haze of the Second Empire. My imagination roved back to reel at the number of plays that had been written, the number of players whose stars had risen and set, the number of theatres that had been built and theatres that had been demolished, since Sarah's début. The theatrical history of more than forty years lay strewn in the train of that bowing and bright-eyed lady. The applause of innumerable thousands of men and women, now laid in their graves, was still echoing around her. And still she was bowing, bright-eyed, to fresh applause. . . . For all the gamut of her experience, she is still lightly triumphant over time. . . . Hers is the head upon which all the ends of the world are come, and the eyelids are not at all weary.

But the next day, at a matinée, Sarah reverted to type and played Pelléas in Maeterlinck's *Pelléas et Mélisande*. Mrs. Campbell played Mélisande—in French. Max didn't go. He stayed away on the assumption that Mrs. Campbell spoke French as exquisitely as she did English and that Sarah's Pelléas was 'not, like her Hamlet and her Duc de Reichstadt, merely ladylike'. But he wouldn't risk these illusions by having a look. It is one of the most interesting reviews ever written by a critic who hadn't seen the show.

Max was not a balletomane. Even though he was enchanted by the Danish ballerina Adeline Genée, whom he described as 'light and liberal as foam', he had certain objections to the art form as a whole. Max was a word-lover, and he didn't see why ballet shouldn't, like opera, employ words, to give him a hint as to what was going on. 'When a ballerina lays the palms of her hands against her left cheek, and then, snatching them away, regards them with an air of mild astonishment, and then, swaying slightly backwards, touches her forehead with her finger-tips, and then suddenly extends both arms above her head,' he writes in one article, 'I ought of course to be privy to her innermost meaning.' But he isn't. He doesn't know what the palms of her hands are saying. He doesn't know whether she is happy or unhappy. He begins to suspect that she isn't thinking anything, that 'such power of thought as she may once have had was long since absorbed into her toes'.

Reviewing *Andromache*, by the revered Gilbert Murray, Max admits that the Regius Professor of Greek at Oxford can translate but he wishes that he could also write. For Max, Gorki's *The Lower Depths* 'is no "slice" [of life]. It is chunks, hunks, shreds and gobbets, clawed off anyhow, chucked at us anyhow. . . . Mere gall is no better than mere sugar. It is worse.' Max didn't think that writers become artists merely by choosing depressing subjects. In forgiveness of the lapses of Dan Leno, he writes, 'Only mediocrity can be trusted to be always at its best.' Of William Gillette in *Clarice*, by William Gillette: 'Mimes ought never to write plays.' Mr. W. S. Gilbert 'for all his metrical skill is as unpoetical as any man who ever lived.' On soliloquies in drama: 'Talking to oneself has this obvious advantage over any other form of oratory or gossip: one is assured of a sympathetic audience. But it has also this peculiar drawback: it is supposed to be one of the early symptoms of insanity.' On *Peter Pan*: 'To remain, like Mr. Kipling, a boy, is not at all uncommon. But I know not anyone who remains, like Mr. Barrie, a child.' On honour among drama critics: 'We dramatic critics are, like the Metropolitan Police Force, a very fine body of men.' He is sent two volumes by Clement Scott, *The Drama of Yesterday and Today*, to review. The mere sight of them makes his heart sink: 'If I'm not very careful, I shall soon have that deadliest of all assets, a theatrical library.' His review of Henry James's *The High Bid* is a masterpiece of devoted evasion. He concentrates on six words of the dialogue: ' "What are you exactly?" asks Captain Yule of the aged and shabby butler who is in charge of the house; "I mean, to whom do you beautifully *belong*?" There, in those six last words, is the quintessence of Mr. James; and the sound of them sent innumerable little vibrations through the heart of every good Jacobite in the audience.' Max turns the rest of his review into a tribute to James as a literary artist. At the very end, he remembers that he is reviewing his play, which he has so far scarcely mentioned, and apologizes: 'My excuse must be that of all that I love in Mr. James' mind so very little can be translated into the sphere of drama.'

One day that winter, Miss Jungmann amused Max and me by recalling the time she saw Oscar Wilde's *The Importance of Being Earnest* in Genoa, played there under the title *L'Importanza di Essere Serio*. It led Max into a discussion of the play. He thought it a masterpiece. 'The scene in the last act—Miss Prism and the luggage left in the cloakroom at Victoria Station, and the intrusion of that innocuous drink—surely that is one of the funniest scenes ever written.' When Max reviewed a revival of the play in 1902, he wrote:

> Last week, at the St. James's, was revived *The Importance of Being Earnest*, after an abeyance of exactly seven years—those seven years which, according to scientists, change every molecule in the human body, leaving nothing of what was there before. And yet to me the play came out fresh and exquisite as ever, and over the whole house almost every line was sending ripples of laughter—cumulative ripples that became waves, and receded only for fear of drowning the next line. In kind the play always was unlike any other, and in its kind it still seems perfect. I do not wonder that now the critics boldly call it a classic, and predict immortality. And (timorous though I am apt to be in prophecy) I join gladly in their chorus.

I reminded Max that Shaw had panned the play when it was first presented, seven years earlier; he had seen nothing

funny in it. Max, who admired Shaw's drama criticism more
than almost anything else of his, was impressed by Shaw's
ability to resist it. 'Perhaps while the play was going on,' he
said, 'he was improving his theory of rent.' Max then went on
to talk about the ideas in Shaw's plays. 'Shaw's judgments were
often scatterbrained,' he said, 'but at least he had brains to
scatter.' When Max was a drama critic, he devoted an immense
amount of ambivalent attention to Shaw. As he himself said in
a dedicatory letter to Gordon Craig, written as a preface to
Around Theatres:

> One thing I never could, from first to last, make up my mind
> about; and that thing was the most salient phenomenon
> 'around theatres' in my day: 'G.B.S.' Did I love his genius or
> hate it? You, of course, survey it from the firm rock of your
> ideals. I wish I had had a rock of some sort. I went wavering
> hither and thither in the strangest fashion, now frankly
> indignant, now full of enthusiasm, now piling reservation on
> reservation, and then again frankly indignant. My vicissitudes
> in the matter of G.B.S. were lamentable.

Even before he took over Shaw's post, he had written articles
about Shaw in the *Saturday*. A series of two articles was called
'Mr. Shaw's Profession', and was inspired by Mrs. Warren's.
Shaw's great gift, Max said in one of them, lay in his wild and
irresponsible Irish humour. Max loved the comic plays, *Arms
and the Man* and *You Never Can Tell*; the serious plays, like
Mrs. Warren's Profession and *Widowers' Houses*, he questioned.
He reproached William Archer for taking Shaw's serious plays
seriously. 'Archer,' he said, 'would rather see a man trying to
be serious than succeeding in being funny.' As for Shaw's
'philosophy', he said that it rested, 'like Plato's *Republic*, on a
profound ignorance of human nature.' In Shaw's serious plays,
he wrote, 'the men are all disputative machines, ingeniously
constructed, and the women, who almost without exception
belong to the strange cult of the fountain-pen, are, if anything,
rather more self-conscious than the men.' He went on:

> Mr. Shaw's penetrating eye is of great use to him in satire
> or in criticism. He is one of those gifted observers who can
> always see through a brick wall. But the very fact that a man

can see through a brick wall means that he cannot see the brick wall. It is because flesh and blood make no impression on the X-rays that Herr Röntgen is able to show us our bones and any latchkeys that may have entered into our hands. Flesh and blood are quite invisible to Mr. Shaw. He thinks that because he cannot see them they do not exist, and that he is to be accepted as a realist. I need hardly point out to my readers that he is mistaken.

In 1900, reviewing *You Never Can Tell*, Max commented on '[the] author's peculiar temperament and attitude, of which the manifold contradictions are so infinitely more delightful, even when they make us very angry, than the smooth, intelligible consistency of you or me.' In 1901, he wrote, 'Assuming that Mr. Shaw will live to the age of ninety (and such is the world's delight in him that even then his death will seem premature), I find that he has already fulfilled one half of his life span . . . but as a personality he is immortal.' In 1902, again discussing *Mrs. Warren's Profession*, he wrote, 'having see it acted, I am confirmed in my heresy that it is, as a work of art, a failure. But the failure of such a man as "G.B.S." is of more value than a score of ordinary men's neat and cheap successes. . . . *Mrs. Warren* is a powerful and stimulating, even an ennobling, piece of work—a great failure, if you like, but also a failure with elements of greatness in it.' In 1904, he was saying, 'Of all our playwrights Mr. Shaw is by far the most richly gifted with this [dramatic] humour.'

Max was all on the side of the New Movement in the theatre of his time, particularly as represented by the repertory experiment at the Court Theatre, where some of Shaw's early plays were produced by Harley Granville-Barker. The business manager was J. E. Vedrenne. Max thought that a performance of *The Devil's Disciple*, in which Barker played General Burgoyne, was so bad that in his review he insists that Vedrenne not only cast and stage-managed the production but played Burgoyne as well. He heads the review 'Mr. Vedrenne', and begs the latter not to imitate so sedulously Barker's stage mannerisms. In other Shaw reviews he heaps scorn on the West End managers, who will not give Shaw a chance in the commercial theatre, on the theory that the public goes to the theatre just to be amused. Writing about Shaw's *John Bull's Other Island*, Max repeats their stale phrase: ' "Just to be amused." There is much besides amusement to be got out of this play (a fact which would, I suppose, form the manager's silly excuse for not producing it).'

It was not the *esprit de corps* which sometimes makes drama critics tolerant when one of them writes a play that made Max do battle for the plays of his predecessor on the *Saturday*. He knew at once that they were something new, removed by light-years from the works of Naomi Greckle—'brewed', as he said, 'of skimmed milk and stale water'—to which he was subjected in the commercial theatre. Moreover, he knew that Shaw's plays would be, once they got their proper hearing and the slow public got used to them, what the commercial managers claimed they could never be—commercial. When *You Never Can Tell* was put on for six matinées, Max protested. He wrote:

> Six *matinées*! Why are the commercial speculators who control theatres so obtuse as not to run Mr. Bernard Shaw for all he is worth? I assure them that he would be worth a very great deal to them. In the course of the next decade or two, they will begin to have some glimmerings of this fact. Meanwhile, they shake their heads and purse their lips at the sound of his name. 'Very clever, no doubt,' they pronounce him; 'much too clever; over the heads of the public.' Of course his head is over the heads of the public; but I protest that he is no mere cherub, that his feet are set solidly on the ground, and that his body is in touch with the crowd. Even had I not already witnessed Kennington's enthusiasm for *The Devil's Disciple*, my visit to the Strand Theatre would have convinced me that Mr. Shaw, as he stands, is a man who might save many managers the trouble of going bankrupt over the kind of plays in which they see 'money'. I have never fallen into the error of overrating the public, but I take this opportunity of insinuating to purveyors of farce and melodrama that the public's stupidity has its limits. Several farces and melodramas have been withdrawn lately after the shortest runs, for the simple reason that they were not good enough for the public. To provide something beneath the public is quite as disastrous as to provide something above it. In the latter case, moreover, disaster is no ignominy. Might it not, sometimes, be courted? Even had it not already been proved that some of Mr. Shaw's plays have qualities which delight

the public, it would still be surprising that no manager hastens
to give them a fair chance.

But nothing that Max could do towards selling his predecessor's plays could alter the fact that the reigning playwright of
his years on the *Saturday* was not Shaw but the author of
The Second Mrs. Tanqueray, Arthur Wing Pinero. Not only was
he the reigning playwright but he was considered to be the
master of a polished literary style. Max took care of *that*. He
polished off Pinero's style—analysed it, parodied it, revealed it
for what it was. Pinero had had the misfortune to write a
successful play called *Letty*. Max generously allows Pinero to
speak for himself:

> A visitor to Mr. Letchmere's flat complains of the heat. 'My
> man,' says the host, 'has been neglecting to lower the sun-
> blinds.' What a ghastly equivalent for 'my man hasn't pulled
> down the blinds'! He complains to the valet: 'This room is as
> hot as Hell.' 'Not quite so hot as that, I think, Sir.' 'We will not
> discuss that now. You will have ample opportunity for testing
> the truth of that simile at some future date.' Mr. Letchmere,
> sending the valet to bed: 'I shall require nothing further."
> Invited to join a supper party: 'let no one be incommoded.'
> Reassuring a lady who overhears a quarrel: 'These little dif-
> ferences are invariably settled amicably.' Very angry: 'The
> result, now that I view it closely, is none the more palatable.' . . .
> I wish to be quite just to Mr. Pinero. But I think I have quoted
> enough to show that no tempering with mercy, however
> gently rain-like and thrice blest, could prevent justice from
> condemning him to perpetual banishment among the penny-a-
> liners from whom his style is borrowed. Nay, these penny-a-liners
> have an excuse that cannot be pleaded by him. They are paid
> by the line. They live by the length and number of their
> words, whose quality matters not at all. Mr. Pinero just receives
> a 'royalty' for every performance of his play. His style is,
> therefore, penny-a-lining for penny-a-lining's sake.

In Rapallo, Max told me he thought that perhaps he had *not*
been just to Pinero. 'After all,' Max said, 'he *could* write a last
act.'

'Pinero's appearance was extraordinary,' St. John Ervine
has written. 'Except for very heavy black eyebrows, he was
almost hairless.' His appearance is even more extraordinary

in one of Max's caricatures: the eyebrows look like horizontal railings set to delimit the prairie of baldness; you feel that Pinero, if he needed exercise, could chin himself on them. Of these eyebrows, Max once made the mild observation that they were like 'the skins of some small mammal, don't you know—just not large enough to be used as mats.'

On the *Saturday*, Max took up a surprising cause. He constantly implored playwrights to write a play about servants. Henry Arthur Jones almost wrote one in *The Lackey's Carnival*. Max welcomed it, because it was partly about servants, but he wasn't entirely satisfied, because it wasn't all about servants. The servant problem was always on his mind, and in 1918 he wrote a profound and prophetic essay about it. But even in 1900, while reviewing Jones's play, he wrote:

> In all times, of course, domestic service has been a demoralizing state of existence. To belong to one class and to live in close contact with another, to 'live hardly' in contemplation of more or less luxury and idleness, to dissimulate all your natural feelings because you are forbidden to have them, and to simulate other feelings because they are expected of you—this has always been an unnatural life, breeding always the same bad qualities. . . . We, during the last thirty years, have been smiling over the blessings of universal education, and we are just beginning to realize, with horror, that we ought to have postponed that system until all menial duties could be performed by machinery.

In 1902, when Charles Frohman produced Barrie's *The Admirable Crichton*, Max was delighted: 'Keen, then, is my gladness that Mr. Barrie has broken triumphantly, in the eyes of all men, the very ground whose infinite possibilities I have in these columns boomed so long and wistfully.' He praised Barrie for having the courage to show 'that servility is merely a matter of environment, and that the most servile of slaves may become, in a place where there is free competition, the most masterly of masters, and *vice versa*. This may not strike you as in itself a startlingly new idea. But it is startlingly new for the theatre.'

In his 1918 essay, Max comes to grips with the whole problem. He takes the trouble to go to the British Museum and look up the Webbs' *History of Trade Unionism*, to find out whether servants have ever been unionized. He finds out that they haven't. And yet the conditions of domestic service have been ameliorated. The servants have accomplished this by themselves, just by quitting for other jobs, without benefit of unionization:

> I should like to think this melioration came through our sense of justice, but I cannot claim that it did. Somehow, our sense of justice never turns in its sleep till long after the sense of injustice in others has been thoroughly aroused; nor is it ever up and doing till those others have begun to make themselves thoroughly disagreeable, and not even then will it be up and doing more than is urgently required of it by our convenience at the moment. For the improvement in their lot, servants must, I am afraid, be allowed to thank themselves rather than their employers. . . . When I was a king in Babylon and you were a Christian slave, I promptly freed you.
>
> Anarchistic? Yes; and I have no defence to offer, except the rather lame one that I am a Tory Anarchist. I should like every one to go about doing just as he pleased—short of altering any of the things to which I have grown accustomed. Domestic service is not one of those things, and I should be glad were there no more of it.

Sometimes, in the course of his reviewing, little extra pleasures came Max's way—the earned increment of dispraise. In 1903, he was barred by a prominent actor-playwright-manager-husband, Arthur Bourchier, from his theatre, the Garrick. Mr. Bourchier was married to a famous actress, Miss Violet Vanbrugh, and had written a comedy for her that Max did not admire. When husbands write plays for their wives, Max calls it 'hymeneal dramaturgy'. He says:

> The public has a kindness for domesticity in theatrical art, or, indeed, in any kind of public work. Political economy is not a showily engaging science, and the books written about it do not fatten their publishers. But there is, I am told, an exception. The books written by Mr. and Mrs. Sidney Webb sell really well. . . . The 'and Mrs.' opens all hearts, and through that breach dash the battalions of dry facts and deductions to the storming of all brains. Even more potent is domesticity in the theatre than in the study.

But he is glad, on the whole, that Shakespeare was not half

of a husband-and-wife team. He feels that Anne Hathaway would have run him into sad courses, for she is said to have been a woman of commanding, even shrewish, temperament. He would have had to write *The Taming of the Shrew* for her without Katherine's conversion to docility, a mood that would have been outside Anne's acting range. *Hamlet* would have fared even worse; Ophelia's would naturally have been the leading part. Max imagines the effect of this uxoriousness on Cleopatra and Rosalind, and points out that since Anne Hathaway did not indulge in sentimental nonsense, Cordelia would have been merciless to her stricken father, and Juliet, on the balcony, would have fumed and raged—all because a dutiful husband-playwright writing for his wife must give her the opportunity to do in public what she is habituated to doing in private.

When the doors of Bourchier's theatre were shut on Max, he took it without dolour. 'Yet, cast thus into outer darkness, I uttered no cry of anguish,' he wrote. 'In the language of our police force, I "went quiet".' Mr. Bourchier kept up his proscription for a long time. It was still in operation four years later, and it yielded Max a new experience. For the first time in his life, he saw a show from the pit. He had borne his exclusion with equanimity except when there was a play at Mr. Bourchier's theatre that he particularly wanted to see. The playwright, Alfred Sutro, was a great friend of Max's, and there was a play of his running at the Garrick. Max insinuated himself into the Garrick by the surprising device of going to the box office and buying himself a ticket, but, 'suffering under the disability common to lads who are going to carve out a future in this great metropolis,' he found that he didn't have enough to pay for a stall. Max met the crisis as courageously as he had met Bourchier's expulsion. Infinitely resourceful, he bought an admission to the pit:

> I had no misgivings. Though I had never happened to see a play from the pit, and my heart was leaping with the sense of adventure, I knew no fear. How often, passing this or that theatre, hours before the performance, had I seen a serried row of men and women doggedly waiting outside the door that led

to the pit! Was it likely that they would spend their valuable time thus if there were not a great treat in store for them? The Pit! There was a certain traditional magic in the sound. There was some secret of joy that I had often wished to elucidate. . . . It was with a glad heart that I bounded down the stone steps.

The glad heart was saddened, the adventurer deflated. Still, like other men with warm and kindly natures who have suffered disenchantment, Max emerged from the experience not embittered but with an expanded tolerance. He could neither see the actors nor hear them. Across the intergalactic distance Max saw an infinitesimal miniature: a lady who crossed the stage and laid her hand on another miniature, also female, whereupon from the first puppet emanated the sound 'Want—pew.' Max had read the daily notices of the play, and now, feverishly piecing together all the bits of circumstantial evidence that abounded in his well-informed brain, he deduced that the first puppet was Miss Vanbrugh and that she had just said to the second, 'I want to help you.' Max felt that he was beginning to learn from his experience in the pit. Here he was, accustomed to sitting in a comfortable stall, and, moreover, to being paid for it, while surrounded by people who were sitting as he was sitting now and who, moreover, did it voluntarily and were not being paid for it. And there was no outcry, no rebellion. It was phenomenal. From where he now sat, the actors looked like performing fleas. As performing fleas, they were remarkable. And here he had been, all these years on the *Saturday*, sitting in the stalls, from which the actors looked like men and women and were instantly recognisable as such, and unreasonably expecting recognisable human conduct from them. His presumption overcame him. The majority of the audience— perhaps three-fourths—was watching fleas. A great light burst upon him:

If I went to criticise a troupe of performing fleas, I should not write and attack their trainer because the performance had not closely tallied with my experience of human beings. I should not go to be instructed. I should go to be amused. It is in this spirit, necessarily, that the majority of people go to the play. They know that they cannot see anything that will

remind them of actual life. What matter, then, how great be
the degree of remoteness from reality? The marvel to me, since
my visit to the pit of the Garrick, is not that the public cares so
little for dramatic truth, but that it can sometimes tolerate a
play which is not either the wildest melodrama or the wildest
farce. Where low tones and fine shades are practically invisible,
one would expect an exclusive insistence on splodges of garish
colour. . . . I shall in future be less hard on the public than has
been my wont.

Though in the first article Max wrote as drama critic he had
said that 'in drama I take, unfortunately, neither emotional nor
intellectual pleasure,' this could no longer have been entirely
true when he went, in February of 1908, to a tiny, unfashionable
theatre, Terry's, to see Ibsen's *Rosmersholm*. Shortly before, he
had met an American actress, Florence Kahn, who had brought
a letter to him from a friend at home who thought it might be
useful to Miss Kahn to meet the important critic of the important *Saturday*. Florence Kahn came from Memphis, Tennessee.
In 1900, at the age of twenty-four, she had become a star overnight, at the Carnegie Lyceum in New York. In 1901, she was
Richard Mansfield's leading woman. Mansfield, it has been
reported, found the audience reaction to Miss Kahn somewhat
irritating; he considered it uncritically enthusiastic. He
managed to break his contract with her, on the soothing ground
that she was capable of heading her own company. He did
not wish, evidently, for Miss Kahn to head his own. By 1904,
she was playing Rebecca West in *Rosmersholm* with the Century
Players at the Princess Theatre. She became known as an Ibsen
specialist, and it was this that accounted for her trip to
England to play in *Rosmersholm* at Terry's. Max must have
gone to Terry's that night, in the line of duty, with some
emotional expectancy.

Max gave Miss Kahn a rave notice. His piece is headed 'A
Memorable Performance', and he describes the performance
at length:

> It is difficult to write about Miss Florence Kahn's impersona-
> tion of Rebecca; for it is never easy to analyse the merits
> of great acting. . . . The part is a very subtle and difficult

one, a convoluted one, needing an intellect to grasp it, and
extreme skill to express it. Such skill would not, however,
suffice. Forthright emotion on the stage can often be expressed
merely by artificial means. But secret emotion can be suggested
only through a genuine emotion that is in the player. In the rare
moments when Rebecca breaks through her reserve, Miss Kahn
betrays the fact that she has a voice of great power and
resonance, and a face that will eloquently express the soul. . . .
In its appeal to the emotions, Miss Kahn's acting is not more
remarkable than in its appeal to the sense of beauty. Throughout the play, not a tone is inharmonious, not a movement
without grace.

An actress cannot easily refuse a man who writes about her
like that, and Miss Kahn did not refuse Max. After a two-year
courtship, they were married at the Register Office, Paddington, on May 4, 1910. Max took his bride to Italy for a honey-
moon. A friend of both of them has described Mrs. Beerbohm's
drawling, Southern voice as having the quality of 'cream-
coloured tussore'. One admirer said her voice had a 'stained-
glass quality'. She was lithe, thin, frail, with an aureole of
auburn hair—two aureoles, according to Arnold Bennett.
Reginald Pound, in his biography of Bennett, quotes Bennett's
description of the bride:

> She was of course preceded by the legend of extreme youth
> and beauty. Reddish hair, divided into two mops of unequal
> size, hanging loosely down in a shock on either side. Over this
> a black hat with a feather sticking out backwards from the
> left side. Very fair. Very thin. Very unassumingly dressed in
> black. Gloves ditto. Refined and rather worn features. About
> 35. Refined voice. Seriously interested in, and proud of, Max.
> Wondered whether his recent parodies of me and others not
> *too* good for a creative artist to do. On the whole, a shade too
> serious, and fairly precious. Deferential. Constantly stopping,
> with a grave air, when we began a sentence simultaneously,
> and making way for me—and then going on. But agreeable,
> intelligent (perhaps too!) and with a fundamental decency.
> She thought London the most beautiful city in the world, etc.
> But she preferred to live among Italian peasants.

To William Rothenstein, Miss Kahn was the reincarnation
of Elizabeth Siddal. He describes his first meeting with her:

> Then I met a girlish figure with red hair, looking, I thought,

like Miss Siddal, but so shy and with a beauty so elusive that I
wondered how she could dominate a stage. But my doubt was
shortlived, for when I saw her as Rebecca West in *Rosmersholm*, there was no shyness; the elusiveness remained, but her
voice and her presence filled the stage, and so human, yet so
spiritual was her acting, and so lovely her presence, that I
thought it was indeed Miss Siddal come to life again, to act
instead of to paint.

Perhaps Max saw Florence as Miss Siddal also, and perhaps
that is why he was always drawing Miss Siddal.

While Max and Florence were honeymooning, they found, in
Rapallo, the house in which they were to spend the rest of their
lives. In Portofino, close by, were his friends the William
Nicholsons and Elizabeth Russell, of *Elizabeth and Her German
Garden*, whose novels Max greatly enjoyed. Once, Sir Carol
Reed, the film director, asked Max, in Rapallo, how he could
have borne to leave the city he loved, full of people who adored
him, at a moment so vibrant with possibilities. Max turned on
Sir Carol his innocent look. 'How many people were there in
London? Eight million? Nine million?' he said. 'Well—I knew
them *all*!' When I asked him the same question, he said, quite
simply, 'I wanted to be alone with Florence.'

To be the wife of a great talker when you are yourself something of a talker is not easy. If you express yourself, you may
get the reputation of interrupting the great talker, or even of
blanketing him. If you say nothing at all, it may be assumed
that you are unresponsive or even bored at the discovery that
you have married a great talker. On this point, judgments of
Florence, among Max's friends who knew them both, varied
widely. Some said that Florence, having given up her stage
career to marry Max, tried incessantly to keep it alive by
talking about it. These say that she was a blanketer. Others,
less severe, say that she was an interrupter. Still a third group
say that she was an adroit stage manager, with a developed
technique for inciting Max to tell his best stories. In any case,
Max and Florence were, it appears, idyllically happy. They
were able to live in Rapallo very inexpensively, and, removed
from the distractions of life in London, Max was able to devote
himself to his writing, to his drawing, and to Florence. Max was

Ashmolean Museum

MR. HENRY JAMES

The name of Dan[te]
Gabriel Rossetti [is]
heard for the fir[st]
time in the Unit[ed]
States of Americ[a.]
Time : 1881.
Lecturer : Mr.
Oscar Wilde

Mr. Rudyard Kipling takes a bloomin'
day aht, on the blasted 'eath, along
with Britannia, 'is gurl

happy—though he watched minutely for a warning sign—that never at any time could he detect in Florence any trace whatever of Anne Hathaway, his model, evidently, of everything a literary man's wife ought not to be. They made trips—he took her to Venice and Florence, neither of which she had ever seen. He applied to her a medley of nicknames: the Pittsburgh Virago (though she was born in Memphis); the Houri-Housewife; the Gazy-Bo Girl; Graminivorous Gertie. Once, after a tremor of dispute between them, he did a drawing—Florence in a vaporous huff, himself penitently imploring and promising, although he did not know what he had done, not to do it again.

I had fallen into the habit of teasing Max, pretending that I knew more about his life than he did, in the months since I had read a book on him, *Sir Max Beerbohm, Man and Writer*, by the Dutch scholar J. G. Riewald, which was published in The Hague in 1953. Max himself said of Riewald, 'He knows much more about me than I do myself.' Dr. Riewald had embarked on this venture without any help from Max; Max had tried to discourage him, as he had tried to discourage Bohun Lynch thirty years before. But you can't discourage a biographer. The bibliography in the Riewald book is a phenomenon; it runs to a hundred and thirty pages. Max himself was astonished; in a short letter he wrote to Dr. Riewald after the book was finished, he said, 'I marvel at your multiscience. You know very much more about my writings than I could ever have remembered.' To bibliograph the conscientiously random writings and drawings produced by Max throughout his long lifetime was surely something of a job, but Professor Riewald seems to have accomplished it. That the little niche Max set out to find for himself, and found, should have inspired such exhaustive archaeology astonished him. When he was asked anything by curious visitors about his writings or his caricatures or his migrations, he would say, 'You will find it in Riewald.' It left him free to talk to his visitors about other things.

Dr. Riewald was not the only bibliographer to devote himself to Max. The first was John Lane, of the Bodley Head, who

6

brought out, when Max was twenty-three, his first published volume, *The Works of Max Beerbohm*. In his mock-pompous 'Preface to the Bibliography'—printed at the end of the little book, right after 'Diminuendo', the essay in which Max says that he is already outmoded and belongs to the Beardsley period—Lane writes about the retired author with nostalgic veneration, as if he were an august Grand Old Man of Literature being trundled off to the Poets' Corner in Westminster Abbey. Max went to Oxford, Lane says, to apply himself 'to the task he had set before him, namely, a gallery of portraits of the Dons', and to America with the more modest aim of establishing a monarchy there. In the traditional vein of biographers, Lane searches for momentous events contemporary with the birth of his subject on August 24, 1872:

> There was only one worth recording. On the day upon which Mr. Beerbohm was born, there appeared, in the first column of *The Times*, this announcement:
> On [Wednesday] the 21st August, at Brighton, the wife of V. P. Beardsley, Esq., of a son.

He notes the coincidence with breathless wonder:

> That the same week should have seen the advent in this world of two such notable reformers as Aubrey Beardsley and Max Beerbohm is a coincidence to which no antiquary has previously drawn attention. Is it possible to over-estimate the influence of these two men in the art and literature of the century?

In some of his essays, Max took up, autobiographically, where Lane left off. In 'The Boat Race', an essay written when he was twenty-four, he says that the earliest recollection of his life was of toddling beside his nurse along the Thames on the day of the Oxford–Cambridge boat race. They encountered another nurse, escorting another toddler. 'What are you?' inquired Max's nurse. The second nurse said, 'I am Cambridge.' 'Oh,' rejoined Max's nurse, with a fine show of forehanded loyalty, 'I am Oxford.'

Max had told me that when he was a child he was half asleep, but there were certainly, as 'The Boat Race' reveals, some clearly defined images in the somnolence. He was, he goes on to write, drawing and redrawing at eight, just as he was, I found, at eighty. He used to watch 'with emotion' the sentries pacing outside Kensington Palace, and his first ambition was one day to be one of them. 'Meanwhile I made many feeble little drawings of them, which I coloured strongly,' he continues. 'But somehow, mysteriously, when I was eight years old or so, the soldiery was eclipsed for me by the constabulary.' He quit drawing Guards and drew policemen:

> The dark lantern was the truly great, the irresistible thing about them. More than once, from the window of my night-nursery, I had seen that lantern flashed at opposite front doors and through area-railings. My paintings of policemen were mostly nocturnes—a dim, helmeted figure with a long white ray of light. Although I possessed, of course, a dark lantern of my own, and used it much, I preferred my occasional glimpses of the genuine article, and looked forward impatiently to being a member of the Force. But the young are faithless. By the time I was eleven years old I despised the Force. I was interested only in politicians—in Statesmen, as they were called at that time.

When Max was twelve, he had a great thrill. He actually saw, in the flesh, Eardley Childers. Mr. Childers was Chancellor of the Exchequer. In later years, Max was not enthralled by practitioners of economics, or what he called 'the bleak science', but when he was twelve the sight of Mr. Childers ravished him. He ran home and drew and redrew him. The sartorial eccentricities of the Statesmen, and the immense variety of their beards and moustaches, endlessly fascinated him, and he recorded them with pen and pencil and coloured chalks. The boy haunted No. 10 Downing Street (hoping for a glimpse of Gladstone) and the House of Commons. At Rapallo, Max told me how he recalled being present in the House when Coningsby Disraeli, Dizzy's nephew, made his maiden speech. Max recalled the tremor that was audible in the House when the Speaker announced that a Disraeli was about to speak. The nephew made a pretty good maiden speech, Max said, and much was expected of him, but the expectations were not fulfilled. Max's own disappointment was discernible as he told me this, for Dizzy was a pet of his. A mountebank who persisted in his mountebankery right up to the end was a diverting spectacle for Max. He adored Dizzy because, he said, you couldn't respect him, you could only enjoy him.

When the drowsy Max was nine years old, he was awakened by his parents and sent to Mr. Wilkinson's School, in Orme Square. Upon hearing, nearly forty years later, that Sir William Rothenstein was sending his youngest boy there, he was delighted. He wrote to Rothenstein:

> I am thrilled when you say that the last named is going to a school in Orme Square—Mr. Wilkinson's. As if I didn't know that school! I was there, as a new boy, just 39 years ago! I was there from '81 to '85, and I am greatly glad that Billie is going to follow in those obliterated old footsteps of mine. I wonder if the school has quite all the charm it had in my time. There were only 15 or 20 boys in my time. 16 or 21, counting Mr. Wilkinson, who was just one of us. . . . He is by far the best teacher I ever had; wonderfully understanding and 'enthusing'. He did—and I am sure still does—so sympathise with the mind of a small boy. It was he that first taught me Latin, and gave me a love of Latin, and thereby enabled me to write English *well*. . . . Mrs. Wilkinson, in those days, used to teach drawing to the boys. Hers were the only lessons I ever had. . . . And what a trial I must have been to Mrs. Wilkinson! But perhaps in those days my work showed more promise than it seems to show just now.

From Mr. Wilkinson's, Max went on to Charterhouse. Addison and Steele and Thackeray had preceded him there. 'I was,' he says in his essay 'Old Carthusian Memories', 'a queer child. I didn't care a brass farthing for games. What I liked was Latin prose, Latin verse, and drawing caricatures.' Mr. and Mrs. Wilkinson and the beards and moustaches of the Statesmen had done their dread work. Max is not sentimental about Charterhouse; he is not of the 'straitest sect', which 'simply can't bear the thought of having left Charterhouse,' and for which 'after-life . . . is one long anticlimax.' He adds 'My delight in having been at Charterhouse was far greater than had been my delight in being there.' At Charterhouse, Max became what would nowadays be called 'a controversial figure'. Addressing Max, in Rapallo, in a tribute broadcast from London over the B.B.C. on his eightieth birthday, Robert

Graves, who went to Charterhouse in 1909, was perfectly frank about it. He said to Max, 'You were a name about which there was a great deal of pro and con in the school. The older and stuffier members of the staff frowned when it came up; but the youngest and brightest . . . lent me all the books you had hitherto published and soon you were one of my heroes.'

While the other boys were playing games, Max did a complete set of irreverent caricatures of the masters and his schoolfellows. Between 1888 and 1890, the *Greyfriar*, a school periodical, published some of these drawings, under various heads: 'Humours of School Life', 'The Exeat Sketches', and 'Charterhouse Types'. The influence of Mr. Wilkinson remained strong also. Max wrote Latin verses, but in one instance, at least—his most ambitious effort—he infused into them an element that he hadn't got from Mr. Wilkinson. This was the Latin poem headed:

CARMEN BECCERIENSE
CUM PROLEGOMENIS ET
COMMENTARIO CRITICO
EDIDIT H.M.B.

Beccerius Naso Pianonicus, whom Max invented, was his first sketch for his later imaginary men of letters—Enoch Soames, Maltby and Braxton, Savonarola Brown. Max's notes on the song of Beccerius Naso Pianonicus are helpful to non-Latinists who might have difficulty reading them in the original. A few random ones follow:

A poem of singular power and beauty, and of the utmost historical value. Its authorship has been and still is disputed; so, in order to set all doubts at rest, I may at once state that I attribute it to the pen of Lucretius. I say this mainly because my old and valued friend Professor Mayor is convinced that it was written by Juvenal.

1. *Beccerius.* Of Beccerius Naso Pianonicus little is known; save from the famous hexameter of Ennius: 'Ingenui voltus et spectaculatus ocellos.'

2. *Concertum*, late, very late, Latin. Our word 'concert' is said to be derived from the same root, and indeed the etymology seems not unlikely. See also my old friend and schoolfellow Professor Madvig's most learned note on 'Entertainments'.

Dabat. Fine word; note too the desponding use of the imperfect. A less skilful poet would have 'dedit', but not so Lucretius.

6. *Innumeras k.t.λ.* Needless difficulties have been made over this line. Some suggest to take it thus: 'he scatters up and down his unnumbered hands.' But seeing that this theory depends upon the absurd supposition that Beccerius possesses more hands than other people, I dismiss it instantly. By far the simplest and most straightforward way of rendering it is 'he shakes on every side innumerable hands', i.e., he shakes hands all round. Cf. the custom among pugilists of shaking hands before an encounter.

By the sudden and unusual transition of sense at the end of the pentameter the poet evidently suggests something or other; what, we are not quite sure, but the idea is none the less skilfully suggested.

At Oxford, Max continued the tradition, established at Charterhouse, of plunging boldly into scholarly controversy, no matter how formidable his opponent. Having said his say to the great Juvenal authority Professor John Eyton Bickersteth Mayor, he took on, in Oxford, the great Shakespeare authority Professor Frederick James Furnivall. There had been some discussion in a learned journal about the meaning of certain difficult phrases in Shakespeare: Professor Furnivall had offered his interpretations, but without dogmatism; other authorities had opposed theirs; the debate went on unresolved. Max, who loved order, stepped in to resolve it. He wrote a letter to the *Saturday Review* in which he stated bluntly that the meaning of the phrases could be understood only by recourse to sixteenth-century heraldry. He was specific; he divulged a very rare heraldic term, and declared that a close analysis of this, which, he modestly admitted, he was not himself equipped to make, would shaft the revealing light on the obscure phrases. Hot on the scent of a new clue, Professor Furnivall repaired to the British Museum and began tracing down heraldic devices. Had it not been for the intervention of a traitor, who told him that the heraldic device he was looking for had been invented by Max, Professor Furnivall might have sat in the British Museum as long as Karl Marx.

It was inevitable that the boy who could pull off stunts like these in his adolescence would one day bring about one of the most fascinating controversial correspondences in literary history. In a review of P. H. Newby's *Picnic at Sakkara* in the *Listener* for April 28, 1955, Hilary Corke wrote, 'It was, oddly enough, a President of the United States who invented the world's best book review: "Those who like this sort of thing will find this the sort of thing they like." Lincoln's formula . . .' In a letter to the *Listener* the next week, Rose Macaulay wrote, 'Was Abraham Lincoln really, as Mr. Hilary Corke says, the first to make the incontrovertible statement that if one likes that kind of thing, that is the kind of thing one likes? It seems more familiar in Greek [she here gives the phrase in Greek]— whoever finds pleasure in this kind of thing, this is the kind of thing he finds pleasure in—but can any well-informed classic supply the author of this? If I ever knew, I have forgotten. And did Lincoln know this tag?' Miss Macaulay had consulted Gilbert Murray, who 'remembered nothing of this kind in any Greek writer'. So Miss Macaulay concluded that 'President Lincoln must be credited with this admirably incontrovertible remark, the hard core of reviewing.' The fact is that Lincoln was innocent. It was Max who was guilty. He invented it, both in Greek and in translation; it came off the point of his pen in the blue study when he was finishing *Zuleika Dobson*. He wrote a confessional letter to Miss Macaulay, cutting short all fascinating speculation. I bitterly reprimanded Max for his vandalism. Had he allowed this correspondence to go on, I explained, the attribution of the source of 'the world's best book review' might have been distributed among all the American Presidents, with the possible exception of Calvin Coolidge, who seldom expressed himself in Greek, or even in English.

On still another day that winter, when Max and I were settled down traditionally in front of the fireplace in his tiny living-room, I said, 'Max, what were you doing on the afternoon of February 19, 1923?'

'Look it up in Riewald,' said Max.

'This,' I said with quiet menace, 'is not in Riewald.'

Max played along with me. He passed his hand over his forehead in anxiety. 'Oh dear!' he said. 'I do hope that I killed no one on that day. If I did, I have no recollection of it.'

'No, Max,' I said. 'You didn't kill anyone, but you did take a married woman to lunch under the misapprehension that her husband was busy. You were even so shameless that you wrote a poem about it!'

Max's tension relaxed. 'Oh, yes,' he said. 'Of course. I do remember. Oh dear—I *was* terrified! Mrs. Harley Granville-Barker. Helen Huntington she was. Harley had only recently married her. But how ever did you come upon that poem?'

'I have my sources,' I said.

'But Harley *did* come to lunch,' he said, in pitiful self-defence.

'I know,' I said severely, 'but you didn't *know* that he was coming.'

'But,' said Max evenly, finally refusing to be bullied, 'what evidently you don't know is that my wife Florence was with us! But where did you get that poem? I have no idea where it is or how you could have come upon it.'

I explained everything. I had copied out the poem, which I had found, in Max's own handwriting, in the Gallatin Collection, in the Houghton Library, at Harvard. I gave my copy to Max, and he read it aloud to me:

'Triolets—composed on a day when I thought (from what he had said on a previous day) that Harley wouldn't turn up for luncheon.

> 'Harley's doing Cymbeline;
>   Helen takes a car.
> Behind yon castellated screen
> Harley's doing Cymbeline.
> Beetle-browed, athletic, lean,
>   Aloof, alone, afar,
> Harley's doing Cymbeline . . .
>   Helen takes a car.
>
> 'Helen eats and drinks with us;
>   Harley plies his quill.
> Gracious, fair, diaphanous

Helen eats and drinks with us . . .
Utterly oblivious
    Of Stratford's clever Will
Helen eats and drinks with us;
    Harley plies his quill.

'Helen's way is right;
    Harley's way is wrong.
As 'twere a swallow's flight,
Helen's way is right,—
To flit, to swoop, to alight
    And gladden us with song!
Helen's way is right.
    Harley's way is wrong.

'(Supplementary triolet composed at luncheon)

'Oh, bother and damn!
    These verses won't do!
How unlucky I am!
Oh bother and damn!
Harley, that sham,
    Has alighted here too!
Oh bother and damn!
    These verses won't do!

'P.S. Feb. 27
'Still, here they are,
    With my love to you both.
From perfect they're far,—
Still, here they are.
They're away below par,
    And to *write* them I'm loth.
Still, here they are,
    With my love to you both.'

Max settled down, with great animation, to talk about
Barker. He asked me to find Miss Jungmann and tell her,
please, to bring him the series of illustrations he had done for
Barker's book *The Exemplary Theatre*. That was a job after Max's
own heart—five drawings, and two copies of each in existence.
One set he had sent to Barker and the other was in his lap now.
Barker had had a scintillating career in the London theatre.
At the Court Theatre, under the management of Vedrenne,

6*

he had produced not only Shaw's first plays but his own. I had seen two of his productions when I was an undergraduate, *Androcles and the Lion* and *The Man Who Married a Dumb Wife*. He was considered a genius and one of the leading dramatists of the era. Shaw looked upon him as a son. Barker was married to Lillah McCarthy, a leading lady of great beauty. On one of his American visits, he met Mrs. Archer Huntington—the wife of the son of Collis P. Huntington, one of the Big Four of American railway finance. After obtaining divorces, Barker and Mrs. Huntington got married. Helen Huntington was a versifier and occasional novelist. She couldn't abide Shaw, and Barker gave up Shaw. Mrs. Huntington didn't like actors, either, and wouldn't allow them in the various establishments she set up for Barker. She tolerated another close friend of Barker's, Gilbert Murray, because of his academic connection, but only just. With a great stretch of tolerance, she barely admitted J. M. Barrie. The fact seems to have been that Helen Huntington simply didn't like show business. Barker, who had already been disappointed in the theatre, gave it up and turned to scholarship. He wrote several volumes of *Prefaces to Shakespeare*, and *The Exemplary Theatre*, privately illustrated by Max.

Max took a very poor view of Barker's abdication from the theatre, and of books like *The Exemplary Theatre*. The illustrations he showed me represent the kind of characters he imagined an exemplary theatre would produce. These people are exemplary, all right, but etiolated by earnest endeavour; you feel that their red corpuscles are white with aspiration. The first illustration bears the legend, 'The Managing Director addressing the cast on the prime importance of civic conscience.' He wears three pairs of glasses—two on his nose, and a spare on his forehead. He, as well as the characters called 'The Front of the House' and 'The Call-Boy', looks under-nourished and dehydrated. So do the actors. In one drawing, Orlando, played by 'Ex-Seminarist Smith', and Rosalind, played by 'Ex-Seminarist Robinson', are on the verge of holding hands, but you get the feeling that that's just where they will stay. The last drawing, called 'The Public', presents Max's notion of the audience that the Exemplary Theatre would attract. The drawing is a grey, and utter, blank.

Barker ended his days with a sense of failure. In a way, he was, like the characters in Max's drawings, enervated by aspiration. In his aloofness from the rough-and-tumble of the theatrical world, he resembled Gordon Craig. Of Craig, Max said to me, 'In a gregarious profession he wouldn't gregar.' Max had once brought Craig to C. B. Cochran, who was eager to enlist Craig's genius. But Craig's demands were impossible. 'Craig had no notion of expense, don't you know,' Max told me. 'His productions might cost anything, and his flats went way up into the heavens—he used no sky cloths. The actors were apt to be dwarfed.' On another occasion, Max, joining forces with his sister Constance, who adored Craig, prevailed upon their brother Herbert to engage Craig to do a production of *Macbeth* at His Majesty's. They were both overjoyed, feeling that at last Craig would be able to demonstrate his full genius in the English theatre. Craig's drawings turned out to be beautiful. Everything looked rosy, and Max and Constance congratulated each other. But there was a hitch; Sir Herbert, since it was his theatre as well as His Majesty's, kept dropping in to see how things were going. Craig suggested to Sir Herbert that he leave London. The suggestion came at a moment when Sir Herbert didn't feel at all like leaving London; London had never seemed more cosy to him. The result was that it was Craig who left London; he went to Moscow to produce *Hamlet*.

Max said that in his day the two most influential drama critics were probably A. B. Walkley and William Archer. Of Barker's play *The Voysey Inheritance*, Walkley wrote, '*Triple extrait de* Shaw.' Walkley may have been influential, but he couldn't have been very discerning. Barker was a Fabian—at one time he was a member of the Society's executive—and *The Voysey Inheritance* is a Fabian tract, but a dreary one, without a trace of Shaw's invention and exuberance and incandescence. Except in theory, it is as far away from Shaw as possible. '*The Voysey Inheritance*,' Max said, 'is Barker at his worst. The characters aren't in the least interested in each other—only in their ideas. I went to see a revival of it with Lady de Grey. When the final curtain fell, she said, "Everything will be all right if we all go on the London County Council." '

In a vain effort to dissuade Barker from quitting the sickroom of the Fabulous Invalid, Max wrote a poem 'To H.G.B.':

> The Theatre's in a parlous state,
>   I readily admit;
> It almost is exanimate—
>   But then, when *wasn't* it?
> It always *was*, will always be;
>   God has decreed it so.
> Canst thou rescind His grim decree?
>   O, my dear Harley, No!
>
> In Shakespeare's and in Marlowe's day,
>   In Congreve's, in Racine's
> The wretched Theatre murmured 'I'm
>   One of the Might-Have-Beens!'
> 'O May-Be-Yet!' the critics cried.
>   'We'll teach you how to grow!'
> And were their fond hopes gratified?
>   O, my dear Harley, No!
>
> The Theatre is Exemplary,
>   Now as in other ages,
> Of all a Theatre shouldn't be—
>   Of all that most enrages
> Right-thinking men like you and me
>   And plunges us in woe . . .
> Mightn't perhaps the L.C.C.—
>   O, my dear Harley, No!
>
> Shall cubits come by taking thought,
>   And Drama gain her soul
> By learning what she doubtless ought
>   From dear old Mr. Poel?
> Shall syllabi and seminars
>   And blackboards all in a row
> Somehow uplift us to the stars?
>   O, my dear Harley, No!

After he had written this, Max discovered that he had been guilty of a lapsed rhyme in the second stanza. He did his best to make amends:

I'd meant to write in my MS.
  'Time,' and wrote 'day,' it seems.
This error fills me with distress
  And haunts me in my dreams.
A lover I'm of chime of rhyme
  And to vers libre a foe—
Shall such a man rhyme 'day' with 'I'm'?
  O, my dear Harley, No!

Max said that he and his mother and sisters, when he was living on the top floor of his mother's house in London, had a game that became a lifetime habit with them. It was imagining and predicting what people would say, especially if you hadn't been seeing them frequently. Max taught this game to Florence. The Barkers once invited Max and Florence to spend a week-end with them at their country house. It had been some time since the two couples had met, and on the way down, Max played the game. 'Helen will say, "As Max and Florence are here, we'll have to have champagne tonight!",' he predicted. 'This,' he went on, 'will also apprise us that we won't get it every night.' Mrs. Barker said it, and they didn't, after the first evening get it.

For a time, the Barkers settled in Italy, not far from Rapallo, and Max described for me a joint expedition to San Fruttuoso. Barker decided to walk and tried to persuade Max to join him—an effort that failed, since Max didn't believe in walking. Max described the wonderful equipment Barker had for his walk. 'He wore knickerbockers and the most wonderful high laced boots. He must have been most painfully fitted for them in one of those little streets off Jermyn Street, and they were in the best and most intricate tradition of British cobblership. Why did he insist on making that painful walk? I suppose he felt he had to live up to those knickerbockers and those boots. Anyway, while Florence and Helen and I arrived fresh and rested by motorboat—the sea was like a carpet— Barker arrived absolutely done in, pale and exhausted. He had to lie down; he couldn't join us for lunch. While he lay prostrate, the *padrone* stood staring at him. His lips murmured sympathy but his eyes were riveted to those boots; he had manifestly never seen such boots, and his eyes were famished

with envy, with despair, because he knew that no fortune could
befall him so fabulous that he could ever own a pair of boots
like that. At other times, Harley would wear a sombrero and an
Inverness cape. I never knew why.'

Max sighed. 'Poor Harley,' he said. And then his light manner changed. 'When he left Lillah McCarthy,' Max said, 'he
wrote her a long letter telling her that he no longer cared to live
with her, that he had fallen in love with Mrs. Huntington,
though he hazarded the doubt that he didn't know how long
that would last, either. The letter was in the best tradition of the
Fabians, and of both Shaw and Marx. They would both have
written like that.' Max, I could see, was appalled; he sat back in
his chair thinking about it, as if he had just read Barker's letter,
as if the enormity had just happened. 'It isn't only the in-
sensitiveness,' he went on. 'It is the *anaemia*, don't you know.
Isn't it of the essence of being in love—and we must charitably
assume that Harley *was* in love with Helen—isn't it of the
essence of being in love that when it happens, while the rapture
is upon you, you cannot imagine its ever ceasing? But Granville-
Barker could, and he wrote such a letter as would have pleased
his master Shaw and would have been understandable to the
Fabians, and would even have got an approving nod from
Marx himself.'

Max, whose life at Rapallo was a long evocation, in memory,
of the people he had known, of their foibles and mistakes and of
their enchantment when they were at their best, found less
understandable than anything else about Shaw his remark
when he was asked whether he missed any of his contemporaries
who had died. 'No,' said Shaw. 'I miss only the man I was.'
Max's comment on this was 'When I think of the gay and
delightful people he knew . . .' He shook his head in bewilderment. Prophets with idiosyncrasies like Shaw's couldn't, for
Max, prophesy anything good.

Several years before, I had met Bernard Berenson in Venice,
and he had asked me, if I ever found myself in Italy again, to let
him know and he would invite me to visit him at his home—
I Tatti, outside Florence. During this stay in Rapallo, I had

written to him, and now came a letter from Miss Elizabetta (Nicky) Mariano—the chatelaine of I Tatti, as Miss Jungmann was of the Villino Chiaro—inviting me to come for the week-end. I wrote to her, accepting, and, having done so, I felt a certain trepidation. Suddenly, the idea of the trip to Florence loomed as formidable, like an excursion from a secluded island into a seething world.

Some years later, Christopher Sykes told me the following story. Sykes had been staying with Harold Acton in Florence and had been taken by him to call on Berenson at I Tatti. On the way back to London, he stopped off in Rapallo to call on Max. He said to Max that he had just seen Berenson, and described his visit.

Max said, 'And now, I suppose, you are going to Cap Ferrat to see Maugham.'

'No,' said Sykes, 'I am not. As a matter of fact, I don't know Maugham.'

Max was puzzled. 'But you *must* be going to see Maugham!'

Sykes asked why this was inevitable.

'Because,' said Max, with the air of a savant rigidly expounding the second law of thermodynamics, 'people come to see me either on the way *from* Maugham *to* Berenson or on the way *to* Maugham *from* Berenson. I am a wayside station.'

Sykes assured him that for himself Max was a terminal.

'Do you mean to say,' Max said, 'that you have come here just to see *me*?' He turned to Florence, manifestly delighted by Sykes's eccentricity. 'Imagine, Mr. Sykes has journeyed here,' he said, 'just to see *me*!'

Had I known this story on the day I told Max and Miss Jungmann, at tea in the living-room, about my impending week-end, I might have pointed out that I was even more eccentric than Sykes, since Max was my point of departure. But the best I could do that day was to make the unembellished announcement.

'Well, you can get warm at Berenson's,' Max said. 'Desmond MacCarthy used to tell me how warm it was there even in the worst weather.'

Miss Jungmann was full of curiosity about Miss Mariano. I

told her that I had seen Miss Mariano, too, in Venice, and that she was one of the most enchanting people I had ever met. Miss Jungmann said she so wished she could meet her.

'Come along,' I said. 'You and Max both come. I am sure B.B. would be overjoyed to have you. I have never been there, and it would make it easier for me.'

For a minute or so we revelled in the delicious contemplation of an impossible journey. Miss Jungmann insisted on knowing more about Miss Mariano; she evidently looked on Miss Mariano as, in a sense, her opposite number, for she was inquisitive about the minutiae of her devotion to B.B.

'They say,' said Miss Jungmann, 'that she warms his wristwatch for him!'

I said that I had never seen Miss Mariano do this but that I would be on the look-out.

'Max hasn't got a wristwatch,' said Miss Jungmann. It was clear that if he had, it would have undergone conditioning.

Max did not exactly change the subject, but he deflected it. 'My brother Herbert never knew what time it was,' he said. 'He was always late, therefore, for appointments. He was vague. Oh, he had a watch and he often looked at it, but he never seemed to draw any deductions from it.'

I asked Max whether he knew B.B.

'Oh, it is many years since I have seen him,' Max said. 'The last time was with Sibyl Colefax. Sibyl was in a nursing-home, and I went to see her, and Mr. Berenson was there.'

'Tell him Florence's story,' said Miss Jungmann.

Max turned to her, inquiring. 'Which story?'

'You remember, Max. About the Berensons' visit to the Villino.'

Max remembered. 'Oh, yes,' he said. 'It was curious. I have never understood it. The Berensons were passing through Rapallo, and Mary Berenson telephoned. I was in London at the time, on some business or other—I don't remember what— and Florence told Mrs. Berenson this and asked them if they wouldn't come to lunch anyway, and they did. They had lunch here, in this room, and after lunch Florence took them into *that* room.' Max pointed to the little library. 'As they walked in,

Mary said, "Oh, Florence, how wonderful it must be for you to live with absolutely *nothing*!" '

Miss Jungmann giggled.

Max was anxious for me not to be under a misapprehension. 'But you know, Elisabeth, Florence also said—she made it clear —that Mary Berenson's remark was not meant invidiously. Not at all. She *meant* it. The Villa I Tatti is a very grand place, and she was weary of running it. Desmond MacCarthy used to tell me how grand it is. Oh, no, Mary really *envied* Florence, I believe.'

'I'm sure she did!' said Miss Jungmann.

Max turned to me. 'But the curious thing was this,' he said. 'I have never understood it, but I have been told this by so many people that it must be true. You know, Berenson didn't believe I was in London. He believed that I was in the house the whole time and that I didn't wish to see him, or was afraid to see him—I don't know what. He is convinced I was here— hiding under a bed, I imagine! Do give him my affectionate and admiring greetings, and if it should come up, please assure him that, had I been here, I should have been most happy to see him.'

I promised to do this. I asked permission to take with me Max's illustrations for Granville-Barker's book; I thought they might amuse B.B. Max gladly gave them to me.

'And my greetings to Miss Mariano,' said Miss Jungmann.

In Florence, I was met at the station by Berenson's Welsh chauffeur, who had been with him for about forty years. He drove me to the great house, where Miss Mariano greeted me.

The suite into which I was shown was one that not long before had been occupied by the King of Sweden, who was one of Berenson's annual visitors. Its chandeliered, damasked drawing- room was hung with Old Masters. On the mantelshelf was a large leather folder; within, under cellophane, were printed— one side in Italian, the other in English—the names of the pictures that hung in the room and of the artists, with their dates. I walked around the room with this guide in my hand, checking to see if the pictures were all there (they were), and put the card back on the mantelshelf for ready reference.

The four days I spent at I Tatti were a joy. Miss Mariano said that there were three performances a day—lunch, tea, and dinner. These consisted mainly of the prolonged chamber music of conversation, with B.B. playing first violin, and visiting virtuosi playing their appropriate instruments and changing at each meal: Harold Acton, Peter Viereck, Mrs. Ralph Pulitzer, Richard Offner. Walter Lippmann had just left; Judge Learned Hand was coming.

I had recently read an interview with Berenson in which he singled out Max as perhaps the most exquisite writer of his time, and also expressed immense admiration for his caricatures. In one of my talks with Berenson, I referred to this interview. 'I have been propagandizing for Max for fifty years,' he said.

Another guest repeated to Berenson a remark that had been made to him by a very famous and very successful and very old friend of Max's, to the effect that it was no wonder he was poor, since he had done no work for thirty years.

'That is a piggish remark,' Berenson said quickly. 'Whatever Max has done is exquisite; he has done enough, he has done more than enough. We are all his debtors.'

I showed Berenson the illustrations for the Barker book. He was enchanted. He handed them round to other guests. 'They're as good as Goya,' he said, with the authority of one who can say things like that. 'Max is the English Goya.'

Berenson wanted to hear as much news as possible about Max. As he did not bring up the history of the lunch he and his wife had had at the Villino, I brought it up. The result was curious.

'Max told me that you think he was there the whole time,' I said.

'He *was* there,' said Berenson quietly.

'But why shouldn't he have greeted you if he were there?' I said. 'What reason would he have had for avoiding you?'

'That is what I don't know,' said Berenson. 'That is what mystifies me. Because Max hasn't a warmer admirer in the world than I am.'

I gave Berenson Max's message, but I soon saw that nothing

in the world would persuade Berenson that Max had not been
in the house that day.

On the morning I left, I did something I had never done
before. I stole. I stole the picture guide from my suite, because
I thought it might amuse Max.

On the train back to Rapallo, as I thought over the pleasures
of my visit, a riddle obtruded—bafflement over the story of
B.B.'s visit to the Villino Chiaro. I knew that Max was telling
the truth; I knew him well enough to know that he would have
been incapable of avoiding Berenson by stooping to a ruse. I
knew also that Berenson was convinced that *he* was telling the
truth. I wondered. Why should Berenson have somehow,
obscurely, wished to be the victim of a snub from Max? It led
me into psychological speculations that I had no confidence in.
But this much I did see: that Max's relations with other people
were simpler, often, than theirs with him. He had many friends
—Desmond McCarthy, for example—who took him as he was,
with sheer delight in his mere existence. But there were others
in whom the delight was mottled with some nagging resentment
of Max's non-competitiveness, of his indifference to the glories
of careerism. Year after year, he sat in the Merton chair in his
little living-room, summoning up and reanimating the past,
or in his blue study off the terrace, polishing his small output of
prose, drawing caricatures, devoting himself to exiguous tasks
in order to amuse one friend—a year to re-do Archibald
Henderson's *George Bernard Shaw* to amuse William Archer,
weeks to turn out several exemplary Goyas to amuse Granville-
Barker. As far as he was concerned, there was, in his relations
with everybody, no sparring for position. He liked the one he
had, he did not wish to alter it; it fitted him. He was, as the
cartoonist David Low once wrote of him, 'free of envy'. When a
great royal honour was conferred on a writing friend and contemporary, Max was clearly happy about it. He wished only
that it had been conferred earlier, so that his friend might have
enjoyed it longer. When this honour was announced in the
papers and we sat in the study discussing it, Miss Jungmann, out
of loyalty, couldn't resist saying, 'Max gets nothing!' But Max
didn't want anything beyond what he had, and somehow this

absence of ambition, which rendered him immune from envy, sent ripples of unease through the consciousnesses of some of his unswervingly successful friends, who might have enjoyed, just here and there, just occasionally, being envied.

On my return, Miss Jungmann and Max were agog to hear about my visit. I told them everything. I was happy to be able to report that I had not seen Miss Mariano warm Berenson's wristwatch. 'If she did it,' I said, 'she must have done it behind my back.' Max listened to my account as if he were listening to the story of a novel; he kept laughing at this and that. I told him about my succeeding to the suite of the King of Sweden, and he was amused when I repeated to him a story told me by an intimate friend of Berenson's who had been invited to tea on one of the King of Sweden's visits. The house, he said, was surrounded by police on motor cycles and by security officers. The tea party was very pleasant, and the King very personable. At one point, though, he ventured an opinion on some aesthetic matter which Berenson thought was a bit out of line. Berenson at once clipped the budding generalization. He waved an admonitory forefinger at the King: 'Now, look here, my boy . . .' The King humbly resumed his proper place in line.

Max and Miss Jungmann—especially Miss Jungmann—were greatly interested when I told them that Berenson, who was eight years Max's senior, walked every day; that, in fact, he wore me out walking. I also told them that Berenson was even then planning a journey to Tripoli to see some excavations. 'I should think,' said Max, 'that, at our age, an excavation would be the last thing one would care to see—too suggestive, don't you know.'

Miss Jungmann took courage from my account of Berenson's feats, and was sure that if Max willed it he could partly emulate them.

'Not to Tripoli,' said Max. 'No, I don't think I can undertake Tripoli. But I will essay the terrace.'

I told Miss Jungmann that we would both have to treat Max with more veneration henceforth, because B.B. had said that he was the English Goya.

'I shall wear Spanish costume,' said Max. But he was pleased at Berenson's praise of his drawings, and he made no effort to conceal it. 'I have, you know, a picture hanging in a museum in Florence,' he said. 'Did you know that?'

'In the Uffizi?' I asked.

Max laughed. 'In the Museo Horne. Herbert Horne was the biographer of Botticelli, you know, and gave his art collection to Florence.' Max became very impressive. 'I hang there,' he said, puffing his cheeks out a bit to give the effect of pomposity. '*I am hung!*' His voice rose. 'Who knows? Who knows? The art historians of the future may call me the English Botticelli.' Suddenly he collapsed the pumped-up pose of inflation. 'I don't think so, though, do you? I haven't the air of Primavera about me—not quite—do you think so?'

I whipped out the stolen catalogue.

'I stole for you, Max,' I said. 'This was in my room. This was how I lived. Those pictures were all in my salon!'

Miss Jungmann and Max stared at the card.

'Why,' said Max, in rapture, 'it's a *menu*!' He pronounced it in French, with the accent on the 'u'.

VI

THE EXECUTIVE FOREFINGER

BEFORE going to Rapallo in June of 1954, I carried on a brisk correspondence with Max and Miss Jungmann about projects for a film version of Max's novel *Zuleika Dobson*. It all began because Miss Audrey Hepburn had expressed an 'interest' in playing Zuleika. When a fabled young woman like Miss Hepburn expresses an interest in anything filmable or dramatizable, it is exactly as if Juno, on the summit of Olympus, had lightly pressed a push-button; earthlings go scurrying. It has the instant effect of lifting a work of literature to the status of a 'property'. Other people had taken an interest in *Zuleika Dobson* long before Miss Hepburn. From a popular point of view, it has survived better than anything else Max wrote; if people know nothing else of Max's, they do know *Zuleika*. It has been a success as a Penguin book and in the Modern Library in America. Among its eminent admirers have been Lord David Cecil, who has said that it distils the quintessence of Oxford; William Empson, who has said, in praise, that it ranks Max among the 'ambiguous' poets; and E. M. Forster, who has said that it has a 'beauty unattainable by serious literature . . . it is so funny and charming, so iridescent, yet so profound.' But the combined interest of these distinguished men did not have the galvanizing effect of Miss Hepburn's gentle coo. Miss Hepburn may have liked it because all the undergraduates kill themselves for Zuleika. Actresses love to be loved—especially in public—and you can't ask for a greater tribute than to have an entire university jump into a river for love of you.

I had myself had a long flirtation with Zuleika, thirty years before I met Max, having done some exploratory work on a musical version with George and Ira Gershwin. She eluded us. With a view to dramatizing the novel, Wolcott Gibbs, an unregistered Maximilian, had held an option on it for years, but he had been stymied, as I had been, by the problem of how to get Max's delicious side-remarks into a dramatic frame.

While the activity set off by Miss Hepburn was bubbling, Max wrote various letters to me on the subject. In one, he said:

> I do not at the moment know just how Zuleika stands since the retirement of Wolcott Gibbs. Two or three suitors have forthcome, and I have left all negotiations in the hands of my brother-in-law and of an English friend, Selwyn Jepson, the novelist. . . . I have never in my brightest youth or my noblest prime been able to deal with any matter involving the simplest sum in arithmetic. I shall soon, I expect, know what has been happening and whether Zuleika is still—as it were—unmarried.
> Longing to see you in humdrum Rap,
>
> > Devotedly,
> >
> > > MAX.

When I arrived in Rapallo that June, I was met at the station by Miss Jungmann. After I had got installed at the Excelsior, we drove to the Villino. On the way, Miss Jungmann said breathlessly, 'I wonder how you will find him! I'm worried about his health. He's so frail.' The winter had been a hard one in northern Italy, and Max had suffered from various minor ailments. Besides, his heart was not strong. Miss Jungmann told me with pride that although the house had been very cold, she could assure me that Max himself had never felt cold. 'Sometimes, when he is sitting there in his chair, and I am trying to make him comfortable,' she said, 'he will take my hand and press it without saying anything. It makes up for everything.' I could believe it. Miss Jungmann's devotion to Max's well-being and comfort was the animating principle of her existence; it was unremitting. Her life, however, was far from easy. She had a twenty-four-hour-a-day job; she slept listening, and when she heard Max moan in the night she would go to see what was wrong. Usually it was only that he was suffering what he called 'the stringencies of a nightmare'. From the beginning, Miss Jungmann had felt about my visits that they were 'good for Max'; the word she sometimes applied to them was 'therapeutic', and in this, I felt, there was a quality of desperation. Miss Jungmann hadn't been away from the Villino overnight since 1952, when she made a journey to London to arrange for an exhibition of Max's drawings at the Leicester Galleries. Even when she went to Rapallo to shop, she was haunted by anxiety.

I could see that Miss Jungmann couldn't wait to get back to the Villino. I had wired her from Paris not to meet me, but Max, she told me, had insisted. 'I left him happily doing *The Times* crossword puzzle,' she said, as we approached the Villino. 'Last night, we had such a delightful evening. He read me a most beautiful passage from Henry James's *Partial Portraits*. As a special celebration for your arrival, we are going to have lunch on the terrace.'

At the Villino, Miss Jungmann made for the kitchen and I went through the house and climbed the outer staircase to the terrace. Max was sitting under the umbrella by the little table, with his straw hat on, reading *The Times*. He was wearing his shade-of-primrose suit, with black patent-leather pumps and white socks. He stood up to greet me. By now he was almost eighty-two, but I thought he looked better than I had ever seen him before. We walked, as of habit, across the parti-coloured flagstones to the parapet, and stood looking out across the Gulf of Genoa and at the backward-leaning, Swinburnean tree, now in full leaf and flourishing.

At the Excelsior, Turco had told me that during the summer months there was to be inaugurated a three-times-a-week aeroplane service between London and Rapallo. I ventured into a fantasy with Max on this. 'Tell you what, Max,' I said. 'You and I will take the Friday plane. It will bring us into London at about five, in good time for dinner. Where would you like to have dinner? Then we'll go to a play—and you won't have to review it! Won't it be nice for you to see a play without antagonizing the author? Then we'll go to the Savoy Grill for supper. For once, Max, shake off this pose of valetudinarianism and give yourself a time!'

Miss Jungmann joined us.

'Max and I are going to London,' I said. 'Friday's plane.'

Miss Jungmann demanded to be taken along.

'Shall we take Miss Jungmann?' I asked Max.

Max suggested that she be given the option.

A new Italian servant, a girl of about twenty, brought out apéritifs. We sat down under the umbrella and began sipping them. I told Miss Jungmann that I thought Max was looking better than I had ever seen him, and this made her happy. I teased her. 'Tell me, Elisabeth,' I said. 'After working for so many years for a really great man, the successor of Goethe, a writer on the heroic scale, like Gerhart Hauptmann, isn't Max, with his little effusions, something of a comedown?'

'Gerhart adored Max,' said Miss Jungmann. 'He told me. "Elisabeth," he said, "Mr. Beerbohm is special." Oh, yes, though they couldn't converse, he *understood* Max. He *knew*. So did Margarete. So did Benvenuto.'

I found out that these were Hauptmann's wife and son. I asked about Benvenuto and what he was up to.

'He is a contemporary,' said Miss Jungmann definitively.

Max leaned forward in his chair. 'It's true,' he said. 'I couldn't speak a word of German, and Herr Hauptmann didn't know a word of English. Florence adored him, and he adored her, too. I did a caricature of Hauptmann. . . .'

I knew this caricature: Hauptmann, Goethe in plus-fours, doing a metronomic walk along the shingle at Rapallo, his handsome, noble face uplifted to let the wind blow through his hair.

'Oh, he loved your caricature, Max,' said Miss Jungmann.

'Well,' Max said, 'when Hauptmann was living in Rapallo, he used to give these wonderful dinner parties. He was lavishly hospitable. I used to come with Florence. There were great crowds of celebrities always, mostly visiting Germans. To them, Hauptmann wasn't just a writer, you know, he was a kind of god. And, of course, being a god, he was omniscient, and, since he was omniscient, there was no question he could not answer. He was asked all sorts of things by his worshippers, covering a limitless range, and I never knew him not to answer, with amplitude. Thomas Mann used to come. He used to call Hauptmann "The President of the Republic of Letters". That's how Hauptmann was regarded, and that is how he regarded himself. Elisabeth once told me that an unpleasantness occurred between Mann and Hauptmann. Mann published *The Magic Mountain*, and the character of Peeperkorn—Have you read *The Magic Mountain*?'

I said that I had, and that I remembered vaguely that the character of Peeperkorn, if I was not mistaken, was something of a windbag.

'That's what Hauptmann thought,' said Max, smiling. 'And he had a strong feeling that he *was* Peeperkorn, though Mann denied it.'

It had been a happy inspiration on the part of William Rothenstein to introduce the Beerbohms to the Hauptmanns, in 1926. Hauptmann was a perfect host, Max a congenial guest. The fact that Hauptmann couldn't speak English and that Max couldn't understand much German was an advantage; it gave Max ample opportunity, while Hauptmann was expounding, to ruminate privately in English, which he did understand. Florence Beerbohm felt for Hauptmann the adoration of an actress for a playwright, which can be intense—at least before she appears in one of his plays. In his memoirs, Rothenstein records Hauptmann's notion of how a writer should live:

> Hauptmann's views on life were large and generous. Artists, he held, should live proudly, as Dürer and the great German craftsmen had lived, putting on fur-lined gowns and gold chains as it were at the end of each day's labour. We had neither fur-lined gowns nor gold chains; but every day we sat down to a table glistening with silver and glass. We drank choice Rhenish and Mosel wines out of great Venetian glasses; huge salmon were handed round, boar's head or saddle of veal, dish following dish. . . . Never before had we fared so richly.

Max had an equally clearly defined notion of how a guest should live; he has told about it in one of the best known of his essays, 'Hosts and Guests', and it can have been seldom that two men held views so ideally complementary as Max and

Hauptmann. 'In every human being,' Max writes, 'one or the other of these two instincts is predominant: the active or positive instinct to offer hospitality, the negative or passive instinct to accept it. And either of these instincts is so significant of character that one might well say that mankind is divisible into two great classes: hosts and guests.'

Having established this great human division, Max goes on to substantiate it. 'Lions do not ask one another to their lairs,' he says, 'nor do birds keep open nest.' He traces from prehistoric and Biblical times the history of hospitality. He gets to the Borgias, in Italy, and to the Macbeths, in Scotland:

> I maintain that though you would often in the fifteenth century have heard the snobbish Roman say, in a would-be off-hand tone, 'I am dining with the Borgias to-night,' no Roman ever was able to say 'I dined last night with the Borgias'.
>
> To mankind in general Macbeth and Lady Macbeth stand out as the supreme type of all that a host and hostess should not be. Hence the marked coolness of Scotsmen towards Shakespeare, hence the untiring efforts of that proud and sensitive race to set up Burns in his stead.

After a scholarly historical survey, Max gets down, as he always does, to himself. He himself was a born guest, and he has the courage to tell an embarrassing story to prove it:

> In my school, as in most others, we received now and again 'hampers' from home. At the mid-day dinner, in every house, we all ate together; but at breakfast and supper we ate in four or five separate 'messes'. It was customary for the receiver of a hamper to share the contents with his mess-mates. On one occasion I received, instead of the usual variegated hamper, a box containing twelve sausage-rolls. It happened that when this box arrived and was opened by me there was no one around. Of sausage-rolls I was particularly fond. I am sorry to say that I carried the box up to my cubicle, and, having eaten two of the sausage-rolls, said nothing to my friends, that day, about the other ten, nor anything about them when, three days later, I had eaten them all—all, up there, alone.
>
> Thirty years have elapsed, my school-fellows are scattered far and wide, the chance that this page may meet the eyes of some of them does not much dismay me; but I am glad there was no collective and contemporary judgment by them on my

strange exploit. What defence could I have offered? Suppose I had said 'You see, I am so essentially a guest,' the plea would have carried little weight. And yet it would not have been a worthless plea. On receipt of a hamper, a boy did rise, always, in the esteem of his mess-mates. His sardines, his marmalade, his potted meat, at any rate while they lasted, did make us think that his parents 'must be awfully decent' and that he was a not unworthy son. He had become our central figure, we expected him to lead the conversation, we liked listening to him, his jokes were good. With those twelve sausage-rolls I could have dominated my fellows for a while. But I had not a dominant nature. I never trusted myself as a leader. Leading abashed me. I was happiest in the comity of the crowd. Having received a hamper, I was always glad when it was finished, glad to fall back into the ranks. Humility is a virtue, and it is a virtue innate in guests.

Of course, Max goes on to say, a guest has sometimes, out of sheer pride, to assume the role of host, and, equally, a host must on occasion be a guest. The trouble with this is that a born host doesn't like to be a guest. It doesn't suit him; it makes him uncomfortable:

> He does not adjust himself. He forgets his place. He leads the conversation. He tries genially to draw you out. He never comments on the goodness of the food or wine. He looks at his watch abruptly and says he must be off. He doesn't say he has had a delightful time. In fact, his place is at the head of his own table.

That is the place that, in those expansive Hauptmann days, Max allowed the latter-day Goethe to occupy. Of course, Hauptmann came occasionally to the Villino. Florence understood German and translated their guest's gravest remarks, so that Max could ponder them. But what Max enjoyed most was the lavish Hauptmann dinners, where the food and wines were wonderful, where German worshippers asked questions that required interminable answers, and where Max could be, at last and luxuriously, a sheer guest.

It was a happy lunch on the terrace that day. Max was in wonderful form, and kept telling story after story. 'You have told me you were a friend of Sibyl Colefax,' he said to me. 'Well, she was a very dear friend of mine for a great many years. She kept writing to me that I must see a friend of hers who wished to call upon me here in Rapallo, a countryman of yours, Mr. James Hazen Hyde. He had a house in Paris, and Sibyl kept writing to me how beautiful this house was. She was ecstatic about the wonders of this house. She wrote to me—you remember how indecipherable her handwriting was?—about the miscellaneous works of art Mr. James Hazen Hyde's Paris house contained: Japanese wallpapers, paintings, ormolus, jades. Well, I do not consider myself a fancier in such matters, but since Sibyl was so eager that I receive him, I wrote to her and said that I would. Something over ten years ago, the day came! Mr. James Hazen Hyde was in Rapallo, and an appointment was made. It was a winter's day, I remember, and at the destined hour I tiptoed to the window to observe the arrival of Mr. James Hazen Hyde. He came in the shiniest and most ambitious motor-car I have ever seen. From it emerged a footman who was sitting beside the chauffeur, beyond a glass barrier, and he was magnificently dressed. He opened the door of the saloon, and from it emerged Mr. James Hazen Hyde himself. He was encircled in a great-coat with a tremendous wide collar of astrakhan. I was dazzled. I thought, Oh dear, how can I receive a magnifico like this in my poor little house? Why did Sibyl do this? I watched. The footman, preceding Mr. James Hazen Hyde, walked up the steps and pressed the doorbell. Luisa, who served us then, opened the door. Then I observed something that faintly disconcerted me. Luisa began to help Mr. James Hazen Hyde off with his coat, as was her custom, but Mr. James Hazen Hyde's footman quickly intervened. *He* helped Mr. James Hazen Hyde remove his coat. Moreover, once it was removed, Mr. James Hazen Hyde did not give it to Luisa, who was waiting to receive it; he gave it to his footman to hold, as if Luisa were not worthy to be custodian, however briefly, of so regal a garment. I *felt* for Luisa, who was left with nothing to do. I crept back to my chair to receive, as well as I could, Mr. James Hazen Hyde. He entered. I rose to greet him. He sailed at once, as if he had prepared them, into his introductory remarks, calculated to put me at my ease. He said'—Max's voice rose into what was, for him, a kind of bellow, to approximate the American resonance—' "Sir Max, I have in my life had five valets. One was Italian, one was French, one was Japanese, one was Malayan—but, Sir Max, the BEST valet I have ever had WAS AN ENGLISHMAN!" His manner of conveying to me that I need not feel inferior just because I was English rather put me off, don't you know, and from that high summit the rest of our interview was, I am afraid, a declension.'

I had noticed before that Max wore a handsome scarab ring. I now asked him about it.

He extended his hand so that I could have a better look at it. 'It *is* pretty, isn't it?' he said. 'My friend Reggie Turner brought it back to me from Egypt. Scarabs! There was a man in London, a clergyman, the Reverend W. J. Loftie, who wrote a book about scarabs—two books, I believe . . .'

I could see that Max was wound up for a clerical recollection. He was, I knew, sympathetic to clergymen.

'He was a great authority on gravel,' Max went on. 'He liked scarabs, but his great passion was gravel. He was a chaplain somewhere, but he lived for gravel. He was constantly excavating the substrata of old buildings and old churches to find out what was beneath them. He was on the *Saturday Review* for a while. He published articles, and even, I believe, a book, about gravel. But there was a still greater authority in London on gravel even than the Reverend W. J. Loftie. He was the acknowledged master of gravel, and Loftie knew, as everyone interested in gravel knew, that his great work was coming from the publishers soon. For this the Reverend W. J. Loftie waited, hoping, praying that his own more modest endeavours would be noticed in it. One day the book arrived. Loftie was knee-deep in an excavation beneath some church, but he had arranged that the Master's book be delivered to him, no matter where. He opened the volume, with trembling hands, at the index.' Max's hand riffled feverishly through the index. 'There it was, his name—"Loftie, the Rev. W. J." His heart leapt—and then sank. Because after his name was written, in smaller type, "Strange error of . . ." He looked up the page where his name appeared in the body of the book, and found that, according to the author, he had made a wrong deduction from certain of his observations about London gravel. At the Savile Club, of which he and I were both members, there was nothing we could do to alleviate this disaster to his pride.'

Max stopped for a moment. Disappointments of this sort always moved him. He went on, 'And, do you know, I wonder whether the rest of Loftie's career, its deterioration, did not stem from this disappointment. Years passed. One day, the Savile Club reverberated with scandal. What do you think had happened?' Max asked me this question as if I were a member of the Savile and would share the incredulity of the other members. 'The Reverend W. J. Loftie had been diverted from gravel long enough to seduce a parlourmaid, and he had found it expedient to give up the Church. He was left alone with his major passion. Aleck Ross came into the club and was told the shattering news. "Oh," he said. "Poor Loftie, W. J.—the strange error of." '

From the Savile Club, Max took me to dinner with him at Bernard Shaw's flat, in Adelphi Terrace. 'G.B.S., you know, loved prizefighters,' he said. 'He had a deep regard for prizefighters. One night, he invited me to Adelphi Terrace to meet a great countryman of yours in that field—Mr. Tunney. Charming man, delightful man. Not at all what you would have expected. I mean, you would never have guessed his profession from his conversation. It was so literary, you know. The windows of G.B.S.'s flat looked out over the river, and the sun was setting. Do you know'—Max leaned forward—'Mr. Tunney took me by the arm and led me to the windows and compelled my attention to the beauties of the sunset? I had never—no, I think I had *never* before met anyone so militantly aesthetic. I felt I could not reach his level, I could not match his appreciation. When he left, I felt he must have an impression of me as somewhat soulless.'

Max didn't want me to have this impression. He leaned forward just a little more and made a confidential comment to me on the incident. When Max reached the climax of a story, the little pauses, the little intakes of breath, were not hesitations, they were the beautifully timed dynamics of crescendo. 'You know,' he said, 'I cannot be considered a coarse person ... and yet ... you know ... I had to strain every nerve ... to meet ... *that* sensitivity!'

Miss Jungmann said that Max must take his nap, and suggested that I take a nap, too. She said she would make me comfortable in the Casetta—a tiny guesthouse on the hillside behind the Villino. Being less interested in naps than Miss Jungmann was, Max asked her to bring me—against the possibility that I might want to read in the Casetta—a two-volume book he had himself greatly enjoyed, *Monckton Milnes*, by James Pope-Hennessy. He opened the first volume at the description of a meeting between Henry Adams and Swinburne (Adams was sure he had met a new type) and waited while I read it, chuckling in anticipation because he knew I would find it funny. He was not disappointed. He leafed through the second volume. He began to ruminate on the footnotes. 'The footnotes!' he said. 'How swift mortality is in footnotes; in them mortality hurtles by, don't you know. People are born, live their lives, and die in a footnote.' He glanced up at me from the page with his innocent, inquiring look. 'Did you know that J. A. Roebuck, the radical M.P. 1801–79 ... But there! He's gone! In footnotes the hearses are always at the double trot, aren't they?' He reached for a pencil and quickly sketched a rocking hearse, drawn by horses racing at breakneck speed. 'Poor Roebuck,' he murmured to himself while he was sketching. 'So unseemly to rush him off like that.'

Then, at Miss Jungmann's prodding, Max and I walked through the cool sunshine to the pair of staircases at the edge of the terrace. I was to go up; Max was to go down. Max was still so buoyant that he stopped at the parting of the ways. 'You know,' he said, 'when Florence was alive, the Casetta was her domain. She did it up and used it for a study, and she abdicated it when we had guests. Desmond MacCarthy used to stay in the Casetta. Once I prepared a little surprise for him.' Max paused a moment to give me time to adjust myself for the surprise. 'We had a friend, a poet and playwright named Herbert Trench. He managed the Haymarket Theatre for a while. He

MR. BERNARD SHAW

Mild surprise of one who, revisiting England after long absence, finds that the dear fellow has not moved

Mr. Thomas Hardy composing a lyric

MR. ARTHUR WING PINERO

wrote some charming lyrics, but sometimes he over-extended himself. He wrote a long poem called "Apollo and the Sea-man". When I was reading it, I found myself—I don't know how or why—mentally converting it into Cockney. Later, I actually *did* convert it into Cockney; I had to put "h's" before vowels, and it meant also excising a great many "h's". It re-quired great manual dexterity and manual skill.' It was the only time I ever heard Max boast. 'It took a long time, but I did it and left it on Desmond's bed table in there.' Max smiled in recollection. Here was a job of work that suited Max perfectly, since it was arduous and time-consuming and had as its objective the entertainment of one person—Max's notion of a sizeable public. 'Desmond was quite taken aback, don't you know. He came to me with the book, wondering what had happened to our friend Trench. He understood the Seaman, all right, but Apollo's speech seemed to him strange.' Elated by a sense of achievement, Max smiled and started downstairs.

I walked up to the Casetta and went in. It consisted of a large, dark sitting-room, with a kitchen and a bedroom and a bath off it. I walked across the sitting-room to a door on the opposite side and, with some difficulty, opened it. I stepped out on to a farm track. A farmer was walking a donkey hitched to a haycart past the house. He nodded and smiled at me, and I smiled back. The difference between this road and the Via Aurelia, below, was the difference between the eighteenth and the twentieth centuries. This was a road, Max had told me, that Byron and Shelley and, before them, the travelling English milords of the eighteenth century had used on their way to the sea. From it, Max said, one could see the same sights they saw; Shelley, driving down it for the last time, could see the bay in which he drowned. The road was drowsing there, unaware of having moved into another epoch, and its spell was such that I found it difficult to believe that motor-cars existed at all. I could not resist taking a walk on it, and had just started when I heard Miss Jungmann calling me from the doorway. I returned. In her hand she was holding an immense volume magnificently bound in red morocco.

7

'What is that little brochure?' I asked.

'Wait,' she said. 'I'll show you. But first let me make you comfortable.'

She led me to the sitting-room sofa, made me lie on it, and then fetched a blanket and covered me with it. 'The Casetta is chilly,' she said. 'Yes, there is no use pretending. It *is* chilly. But I think you'll be warm enough with this.' She put the great book next to *Monckton Milnes* on a table beside me. 'I thought you might want to look at this—the *Festschrift* volume of tributes given to Max by his friends and admirers to commemorate his eightieth birthday. I think you will enjoy it. But first you must take a nap. First you must rest.'

I said I would try.

'I'll call you for tea,' she said.

Miss Jungmann was gone. I *was* tired. I stretched out on the sofa, but I found I couldn't sleep. I opened the great *Festschrift* volume. The first thing that greeted my eye was a superb full-page coloured drawing of Max by Ronald Searle. It shows Max in a toga, with a laurel wreath on his head, at a rakish angle—the same angle at which he habitually set his straw hat. Max was the only man in the world, I thought, who could look rakish in a laurel wreath, and Ronald Searle perhaps the only man who could make him do it. Max's arms are bare, and, anachronistically, he is smoking a cigarette in a long holder. He looks infinitely bored, presumably at the echoing plaudits that, around the civilized world, greeted his eightieth birthday. The caption beneath the drawing reads, 'Max Accepts with Resignation His Place Among the Classics'.

I turned the vellum pages covered with tributes, in verse and prose, from the most distinguished stars in the British literary firmament. I couldn't, after that, settle down for a nap. I got up and made a tour of the little house. I sat at the desk, which was between the sofa and the window. I opened a drawer. It was full of letters addressed to Lady Beerbohm. I closed the drawer. In one of the pigeonholes was a photograph. I took it out and looked at it. The photograph was by Sarony, of New York. It was the picture of an extraordinarily lovely girl, dressed in the fashion of the nineties. I turned it over. On the back was written, in pen, in a flowing hand, 'Kilseen Conover'. I looked at the girl again. So this was Kilseen Conover! I stared at Kilseen, the young actress Max had fallen in love with sixty years back. One could easily see why Max had felt as he had about Kilseen. He had written rapturously from America about her to Reginald Turner, who was his closest friend. Max and Turner carried on a steady correspondence from 1892, when they met at Merton, until Turner's death in 1938.

My thoughts travelled back, by way of association, from Kilseen and Turner to a caricature bearing the legend 'Are We As Welcome As Ever?' Max drew it in 1911. It shows five men, one of them Turner's father, entering Buckingham Palace, in full evening dress. Four of the men are grotesquely convex and one quite attenuated even, as far as his stomach is concerned, concave. Their expressions are frowning, apprehensive, saturnine. As this was the year in which the House of Lords was gelded of its power, through the passage of the Parliament Bill, an American interpreter of Max said the caricature represented five disgruntled members of the Lords burdened by their sense of loss of power. Once, I had mentioned this interpretation to Max, who took a certain pleasure in being misunderstood, and he had chuckled. At the time, he was holding the volume in which this caricature appears, *Fifty Caricatures*, on his knees.

'Not at all,' said Max. 'It was indeed in 1911 that the House of Lords had to endure a curtailment of prerogative. But also this was not long after George the Fifth replaced King Edward the Seventh as the chief tenant of the Palace. These five men, all of them Jewish financiers, are friends of Edward coming for the first time to see the new King George the Fifth, and being somewhat apprehensive, don't you know.' Well they might have been! King Edward, like some other very rich men, was always in need of money. He liked financiers because they made it possible for him not to think about money. He spent a great deal of time abroad, in Paris and Biarritz, and particularly in Marienbad, his favourite haunt, and he was charged, not unnaturally, a king's ransom for his accommodation. While the King was abroad, his expenses at home did not diminish; his palaces had to be staffed as if he were in residence, and he was in no position to let them. The first of the apprehensive figures in Max's caricature is Sir Ernest Cassel, who advised the King on investments. The advice he gave must have been very costly to the giver, because, in spite of it, the King owed Sir Ernest a vast sum of money when he died. There was no one who saw more of the King or was closer to him than Sir Ernest Cassel. The Marquis de Soveral, the witty diplomat from Portugal whom Max often caricatured, and who was so ugly that he was known as the Black Monkey, was asked by the King whether he had yet seen *The Importance of Being Earnest*. 'No, Sir,' said the Black Monkey, 'but I do know the Importance of Being Sir Ernest Cassel.'

In Max's drawing, when these five men, with Sir Ernest in the lead—the four others are two Rothschilds, Lord Burnham, and the Baron Maurice de Hirsch—make their doleful way into Buckingham Palace to pay their respects to the new monarch, they know in advance that they are migrating from the Gulf Stream into Baffin Bay. The new monarch made no pretence of cosmopolitanism and did not need money. He was severely English; he stayed at home; he lived within his means. Max's 1911 caricature conveys in advance the gelid reception the quintet will get as the little cortège passes the candelabraed mirrors in the Buckingham Palace vestibule. In their minds, they are as doleful as when they were walking behind the coffin containing the remains of their dead friend, the great *bon vivant*.

The most convex of the five men is Turner's father, Lord Burnham. He was the proprietor of the *Daily Telegraph* and a great pioneer in English journalism. He also owned the Gaiety Theatre. He was one of the celebrated men of his time. Edward VII, when Prince of Wales, visited him every year at Hall Barn, his country place near Beaconsfield. Burnham was born Levy. He later changed his name, first to Levy-Lawson, and then to Lawson. The family was of obscure origin. The elder Lawson, Max told me, was very clever and made a great fortune. Turner was an illegitimate son. It is not known who his mother was. He became very curious about his mother's identity, and he was about to engage in research on the subject when he was gently advised by his solicitor not to try to find out anything about her. Max's affection and tenderness for his own mother were intense, and years after Turner's death he reflected sadly on the tragedy of a man whose mother couldn't be inquired about.

Though Turner's maternal origin is subject to dispute, there is one fact about him that is indisputable; he was regarded by all who knew him as the most engaging companion in the world, and the most loyal friend. Max pays tribute to him in his essay called 'Laughter'. 'His face,' says Max, 'is a great part of his equipment.' It became part of Max's equipment, too, for he drew countless caricatures of Turner. He drew countless ones of Lord Burnham also.

In Max's bedroom in the Villino, there was a little mural he had painted; in it, among others, were King Edward the Seventh, Winston Churchill, Kipling, Pinero, Lord Burnham, Reggie Turner, all mysteriously walking in the same direction. The caricatures of the last two run to noses: Reggie's bulbous, dispersed, as wide, almost, as his generosity; Lord Burnham's capable of serving, by itself, as the figurehead of a Roman galley, sharp, finlike, and, to use one of Max's favourite words about strenuous people, 'propulsive'.

Until Turner inherited money, he was rather meagrely provided for, but he was generous to others even when he couldn't afford it. Later, when he did come into money, he was generous even though he could afford it. He was one of those rather rare well-to-do men who do not plead poverty when you happen to mention that you are hard up; he had money, wasn't in the least ashamed of it, and was glad of the opportunity to be liberal to his friends—an opportunity that was seldom denied him. He was constantly giving presents: not only books, cuff-links, handkerchiefs (some of these were so lovely that, Max said, they made him long for a cold in the head so that he could flourish them), field-glasses, travelling cases, chocolates, eau-de-Cologne, umbrellas, and shirts, but even, when his imagination failed, just plain money—simple, unaffected cheques. When Max got married, Turner sent him a staggering cheque; at least, Max and his bride were staggered by it. The amount is not specified in Max's rhapsodic letter of thanks, but the young couple were bowled over.

Though Turner was an incessant novelist, nothing at all would be known about him today were it not for the fact that he exists in Max's caricatures and in the memoirs of the famous people he enchanted in his lifetime. Arnold Bennett and H. G. Wells were devoted to him. In *The Vagrant Mood*, Somerset Maugham, who has all his life been a connoisseur of amusing people, says flatly, 'Reggie Turner was on the whole the most amusing man I have known.' 'His wit had the lightest butterfly touch,' says Harold Acton, 'and fluttered its wings from what he left unsaid as well as from what he said. . . . He was one of the kindest and wittiest of men.' He is the character Algy in D. H. Lawrence's novel *Aaron's Rod*. Turner was one of the few of Oscar Wilde's friends who saw him through to the end; he was with Oscar when he died. A *mot* of his had cheered Wilde up a few days before his death. Reggie had come in on the dying man to find him terribly depressed. Oscar described a dream he had just had: 'I dreamt that I had died and that I was supping with the dead.' 'I am sure,' said Turner, 'that you must have been the life and soul of the party.'

Like many people who make a pastime of gaiety, Turner was a sad man, with a deeply tragic personal life. He was possessed of one of the most engaging of social gifts; he was a marvellous mimic. He did Gladstone, Henry Irving, Walter Pater, Lord Morley, and English clergymen in Italian railway compartments. He made rather a speciality of ecclesiastics, lawyers, and poets, with a leaning towards poetasters. Max describes his rare faculty in 'Laughter':

> His voice, while he develops an idea or conjures up a scene, takes on a peculiar richness and unction. If he be describing an actual scene, voice and face are adaptable to those of the actual persons therein. But it is not in such mimicry that he excels. As a reporter he has rivals. For the most part, he moves on a higher plane [than] that of mere fact: he imagines, he creates, giving you not a person, but a type, a synthesis, and not what anywhere has been, but what anywhere might be—what, as one feels, for all the absurdity of it, just would be. He knows his world well, and nothing human is alien to him, but certain

skeins of life have a special hold on him, and he on them. In his youth he wished to be a clergyman; and over the clergy of all grades and denominations his genius hovers and swoops and ranges with a special mastery. Lawyers he loves less; yet the legal mind seems to lie almost as wide-open to him as the sacerdotal; and the legal manner in all its phases he can unerringly burlesque. . . . Nor are his improvisations limited by prose. If a theme call for nobler treatment, he becomes an unflagging fountain of ludicrously adequate blank-verse. . . . Nothing can stop him when once he is in the vein. No appeals move him. He goes from strength to strength while his audience is more and more piteously debilitated. . . .

You would never, everyone agrees, want to stop Reggie once he got going. What did stop him was his own writing, yet he kept writing. He was one of those men who talk like angels and write like pedestrians. He turned out one novel after another, year in and year out. He was rueful about their failure. 'With most novelists,' he said, 'it's their first edition that is valuable, but with mine it's the second. It doesn't exist.' Some of his titles were: *Imperial Brown of Brixton*, *The Steeple*, *Samson Unshorn*, *Count Florio and Phyllis K.*, and *Cynthia's Damages*. Though these books never succeeded with the public, they certainly succeeded with Max. 'Usually,' Max has written, 'the good talker is a dead failure when he tries to express himself in writing.' Max himself was an exception, and he fondly thought that Turner was, too. Max is always inquiring how Reggie is getting on with his current novel, is sure that it's much better than Reggie thinks it is, and, when it arrives and he has read it, is always delighted. Reggie's anxiety about Max's verdict on his books was so acute that he couldn't settle down to anything till he'd heard from Max. Turner realized very early that Max himself was a unique and an exquisite artist in prose, so he kept mailing his packages, endured agonies of waiting until he had heard the verdict, and, when it came, and it was favourable (it was never not favourable), retired to his room and wept. It was Turner in whom Max confided about his love affairs. Turner saw him through his earliest romance, with Cissie Loftus, the first of four actresses with whom Max was, at various periods, to fall in love.

Vaudeville addicts in America in the opening decades of the century, those fanatics who would never miss a Monday afternoon at the Palace in New York or at The Keith's of Boston and Philadelphia, had their counterparts in the music-hall devotees of London. The English music halls were less formal, more relaxed, than our vaudeville houses. Through the famous promenade at the back of the stalls at the Empire strolled the daughters of joy, and you could relax with them from a too tense study of the artists on the stage. William Rothenstein, in his memoirs, tells about meeting the poet Richard Le Gallienne in the promenade at the Empire just after Le Gallienne had published a book, which irritated many of his contemporaries, called *The Religion of a Literary Man*. (Max quoted to me a reviewer who said of this book that the style was 'a curious blend of the New Testament and the *Daily Telegraph*.' 'Why,' inquired Max, 'does the man's very name sound ungrammatical?') Evidently, the price of admission to the English music halls gave you the privilege of walking around, glass in hand, and getting chummy with the artists.

Max did a drawing of Richard Le Gallienne, with an immense mop of hair, like a seventeenth-century wig, smelling a rose and standing near the footlights looking up at one of the divas. He seems to be considering whether it's worth while to throw the rose. Beside him is a table with a brandy bottle on it, and behind him are two ladies who look very much as if they had followed him from the promenade. Max has caught them all: the two uncertain ladies, with hard, computing faces; the actress, her hands somewhat defiantly on her hips, as if challenging the poet to action. But Le Gallienne just goes on smelling his rose and perhaps adding to his concept of the religion of a literary man. Le Gallienne, says Rothenstein, was 'a little self-conscious at being found in this equivocal haunt, and explained he had rather be lying on his back in an orchard, looking up at the sky through blossoming trees.' Why he did not indulge his preference, he did not say; he merely stated it.

The English music halls attracted a more literary and artistic crowd than did American vaudeville houses; Arthur Symons,

Ernest Dowson, Herbert Horne (who was not only the biographer of Botticelli but the architect of the Savoy Hotel), Oscar
Wilde, Selwyn Image, Walter Sickert, and Max were habitués.
It was at one of the famous English halls, the Tivoli, that Max
first saw, and fell in love with, 'the mimetic marvel', as she was
billed in the advertisements, Cissie Ooftus. When Max encountered Cissie, she was a little girl of sixteen, who had made
a sensation singing songs and doing imitations.

The griefs and ecstasies of Max's love affair are recorded in a
long series of letters he wrote to Turner. As Cissie was a mere
child, though already famous when Max first saw her, he
constantly refers to her in these letters as Mistress Mere. In the
fantasy he wrote later, *The Happy Hypocrite*, the heroine with
whom Lord George Hell falls in love is also a music-hall artist,
and her name is Jenny Mere. The White Child and Small Saint
are other pseudonyms Max provides for Cissie. Max had many
chances to meet Cissie and talk with her, but for a very long
time he was too shy; he risked it only after he had gone through
agonies of pain and foreboding. Night after night, Max went
'*au Tivoli*' to see Cissie, building up the minutiae of memory
to last him until her next appearance. Max permits himself, in
the privacy of his correspondence with Turner, to indulge in all
sorts of fantasies about Cissie. She imitated, with exquisite
delicacy, popular singers of indelicate songs; Max is riven by
the thought of these ribaldries emerging from the lips of
innocence. Max's passion for Cissie was epistolary; it was
sincere and deep, and Max was absorbed in it, but it is evident
that he extracted from the letters he wrote to Turner the
vicarious delights of a rendezvous. How long this passion would
have lasted without Turner to write to about it, one cannot tell.
But Turner was also a writer, and would appreciate the chimes
and changes of the serial novel Max was spinning for him about
Mistress Mere. He kept up the correspondence that kept up
Max. Max got, as he always got from Turner, many more
than the few words of sympathy he asked for, and went to the
Tivoli to indulge again in the pleasures of self-laceration. Max
finds the crowds' adulation of his sweetheart unbearable; he
wishes she could perform just for him, and he is exacerbated by

7*

the suspicion that possibly Mistress Mere understands the suggestive references in the songs she is singing.

Herbert's invitation to Max to come with him to America gave him a chance to forget Cissie Loftus and to acquire a new passion to write to Turner about. That was Kilseen Conover. Max returned to London before Herbert did; Kilseen came back with the company in May of 1897, and Max picked up where he had left off with her. For a while, everything was promising. Then Kilseen went on tour. She and Max corresponded steadily, and Max missed her frightfully, and she missed him frightfully. But as the tour lengthened, the correspondence waned, and the love affair with Kilseen expired of inanition.

Max then fell in love with a member of Herbert's company who was playing in London, a stellar member this time—Constance Collier. In her autobiography, *Harlequinade*, Miss Collier tells of her first sight of Max. It was at one of Herbert Beerbohm Tree's famous supper parties in the Dome of Her Majesty's, the Dome being an enormous dining-room Herbert built under the eaves to entertain his friends and some of the more distinguished members of his audience after the performance of a play. Max was there, 'smiling that insidious smile of his, bowing gently to his partner while his great eyes stared dreamily ahead.' Constance Collier was tall, one of the most beautiful women in the English theatre, and a superb actress, and is supposed to have been the model for Zuleika Dobson. I asked Max about this, and he told me she was not; the actual model was a girl he had known who died of consumption. But Max, fearful that I would go back to New York, where Constance Collier was then living, and destroy this myth, implored me, 'Please, don't say anything about this. Let her think that she was!' I promised. To her dying day, Constance Collier thought that she was the model for Zuleika.

At first, Max's courtship of Constance seemed to go swimmingly. Max's mother and sisters adored her, and she adored them. Max and Constance were ideally happy. They became engaged. And then Constance, too, went on tour—Max's girls were always going on tour—and the engagement was broken. I met Miss Collier once in London after my first visit to Max in Rapallo. Miss Collier was full of curiosity and asked me all sorts of questions about him. I teased her. 'How could you have been engaged to an exquisite man like Max and broken off your engagement?' I asked. Her eyes looked far off into the past. 'Well, you know,' she said, 'Herbert sent me on tour. The leading man was tall and very handsome. We got to Manchester, and—well, you know how things are on tour.' But the breaking of his engagement with Constance really devastated Max. He didn't at all blame Constance; in fact, he thought that she was right, since he lacked a driving ambition and was therefore futureless. And then, after all these failures, he met the fourth actress, Florence Kahn. Miss Kahn did not go on tour. Max knew then that all his stumblings through the forest of romance had been providentially designed to give him the ultimate happiness that he found with Florence and that he shared with her till her death.

Sitting in the diminishing light of the Casetta—I had long since given up the pretence of trying to take a nap—I wondered how often Max still thought of Cissie and Kilseen and Constance. From what I knew of Max, I suspected that they strolled through his thoughts very often. I went back to the desk and took out Kilseen's photograph again. I was staring at it when I heard Miss Jungmann's step on the flags outside. I put Kilseen hastily back in her pigeonhole.

Miss Jungmann came in. 'Did you have a good nap?' she asked.

'Let's just say I feel rested,' I answered.

'Good!' she said. 'Poor Max! He couldn't sleep, and he's hurt his hand again. Come. We'll have tea.'

I found Max in the Merton chair, in the living-room, staring at his left hand. There was a purplish discoloration on it. It often happened to him that if he struck his hand while he was reaching for a book on the tea-table beside his chair, a bruise would appear. Miss Jungmann had put pads on the edges of his armchair, but they did not help much. Max kept looking at the bruise—it seemed to be spreading while he looked at it—as if in self-reproach for having added to the ugliness in the world. He glanced up at me almost apologetically. 'No matter what I do, if my hand strikes anything at all, these bruises come,' he said.

I made light of it, of course.

'Hasn't Max got beautiful hands?' asked Miss Jungmann.

They were beautiful—the fingers strong, and square at the tips. I said as much. Max looked at his unbruised right hand; he extended the spatulate forefinger. 'That,' he said, 'is the executive forefinger. It had to be strong or I should have been unable to draw all those caricatures, don't you know.' Max spoke of his forefinger as if it were a faithful assistant who had never let him down.

'It used to be much more of a temptation to draw caricatures in the world I knew and which has now gone,' Max said. 'There was so much more variety in the appearances of people. They walked, and they walked slowly, so you could observe them. There were whiskers without moustaches and moustaches without whiskers, and there were so many amusing things moustaches could do and did do. Men wore beards of different shapes and different cuts; they wore their hair in varied styles; and they took much more care about their dress, and there were so many *ways* of dressing, which expressed individuality. Elisabeth, will you be so good—could I just have the 1907 volume, the Methuen? I had it by me just before. What have I done with it?'

Miss Jungmann explained that since it was so large, she had put it away. She now fetched it and put it on Max's knees. I sat down beside him.

I told Max that this volume, called *A Book of Caricatures* and published by Methuen in 1907, was the only book of his caricatures I did not own—that I had been unable to obtain it in America. I knew that, with the possible exception of *Rossetti and His Circle*, it was considered by art critics to contain the cream of his work in the field of caricature. I noticed that his copy had on the flyleaf the inscription, in pen: 'To Mama, with love, Max, 1907.' It is a large book; the drawings are beautifully reproduced on stiff paper, with wide margins, and interleaved with guard-sheets bearing the titles in Max's hand-writing. He stopped at the first drawing, 'Mr. Sargent at Work'. It shows the huge figure of John Singer Sargent, in evening dress, rushing violently, with a dripping paintbrush in each hand, at an ermined model. In the foreground, three musicians—a violinist, a violist, and a cellist—are supplying mood music. Max called my attention to the hirsute variations among the three musicians.

He looked up from the drawing to talk about Sargent. 'You know, he and Henry James were alike in this when they talked,' he said. 'They seemed to chop the sentences out of themselves, with a great preliminary spouting, as of whales.' Max began to heave and spout. 'And when you met them at dinner parties, you felt an air of embarrassment about both of them, as if they'd never been out of an evening. And they dined out every night. Whenever I went out, there they were. One night, I was sitting across the table from James; my parody of him in *A Christmas Garland* had just appeared. The lady at James's right asked for his opinion on something or other. He pointed straight at me. 'Ask that young man,' he said. 'He is in full possession of my innermost thoughts.' But James was always gentle to me; he was very nice about that parody. Edmund Gosse wrote me a charming letter about it.' The letter is quoted in Evan Charteris's *Life and Letters of Sir Edmund Gosse*:

Henry James has been eating his Christmas dinner here with us, and I am anxious to let you know that he started the subject of your *Christmas Garland*, and discussed it with the most extra-ordinary vivacity and appreciation. He was full of admiration. I told him that you had a certain nervousness about his acceptance of your parody of him, and he desired me to let you know at once that no one can have read it with more wonder and delight than he. He expressed himself in superlatives. He called the book 'the most intelligent that has been produced in England for many a long day'. But he says you have destroyed the trade of writing. No one, now, can write without incurring the reproach of somewhat ineffectively imitating—*you*! What could be more handsome? And alas! my dear Max [and here Gosse must have sighed, remembering Max's parody of himself in that same volume], what can be more true?

Max continued, 'But Sargent! One night, at some dinner, he was asked about portrait-painting. He began to heave and pant, but he did get out an amusing definition. "Oh— Portraits—A portrait-painting——" ' Max finally gasped it out: ' "A portrait is a painting where there's always something not quite right about the mouth." '

Max turned the page, to a caricature of Lord Althorp: a tremendous orb of a cravat, like a great pearl eardrop; above the vast cushion of the cravat a tall cylinder of stiff collar, with Lord Althorp's moustache resting on it; and then a residue consisting of a sublimely supercilious head.

I remarked on the beautiful shape of Mount Cravat.

'People of that class dressed that way in those days,' said Max. 'Lord Chesterfield, for example—he wore a cravat like that. In both cases, I drew the cravat first—it was the salient thing—and the rest of the caricature exhaled corollarily from it.'

He next stared at Lord Ribblesdale, and Lord Ribblesdale displeased him. 'Oh dear,' he said, 'oh dear.' He reached for a pencil. He began to redraw Lord Ribblesdale. 'Lower part of the face utterly incorrect—nose wrong, too. . . .' He changed pencils to get a finer point, and performed a delicate operation on Lord Ribblesdale's nose. His irritation with himself increased. 'Eyelids also . . . the eyelids . . . they weren't . . .' He again changed pencils to get a finer point, and did a delicate operation on Lord Ribblesdale's eyelids. He stared at the result. He took comfort. 'And yet, you know, on the whole— though the drawing here and there is wrong, it is, on the whole, a good spiritual likeness.'

At Winston Churchill he stared in desolation. 'Very poor drawing,' he said. 'Beyond redemption. I drew him again a few years later. That was even worse. No, I never succeeded with Winston.'

Signor Tosti showed up, the composer of 'Good-Bye'—a very funny little grey-haired, grey-bearded man in a billycock hat, who had great, protuberant eyes and was grinning amiably. 'Not good,' Max said. 'I did him well afterwards. He was Queen Victoria's favourite composer, you know.'

Max wasn't happy, either, when he came to Count Bencken-dorff, the Russian Ambassador to London, though I laughed aloud at my first meeting with this distinguished diplomat. Count Benckendorff, if you get to know him better, might entertain you in other ways, but when you first meet him, suddenly, this way, through Max's eyes, he is simply funny. 'His chin should recede more,' said Max, and with his pencil he somewhat unceremoniously forced the Count's chin into recession.

At Professor Ray Lankester, Max stared with affection and contrition. He forgot me and expressed a belated apology to Ray. 'Dear Ray,' he said, looking at the strangely disordered expanse of face, the cheeks like protoplasm in an unsettled state. 'Dear Ray. He was rather hurt by this. And good heavens, I don't wonder. I only wonder that he so quickly forgave me. I wish he were alive. He was one of the most delightful men I have ever known.'

He turned the page, and there was one of the oldest and dearest friends of his youth, the painter William Nicholson. When Max was in London, he was always dropping into Nicholson's studio, in Appletree Yard. Max used to leave his silk hat there, and Nicholson stacked his paintbrushes in Max's silk hat. Robert Graves, who became Nicholson's son-in-law, told, in his eightieth-birthday tribute to Max over the B.B.C., of looking at a collection of discarded hats in his father-in-law's studio and coming upon Max's. 'It was a certain superbly glossy top hat,' Graves said. 'I had the curiosity to look at the lining. Inside was your visiting card. It commemorated your abandon-ment of London club life when you went to live in Italy. You had written:

> 'Once I used to perch on Max Beerbohm's pate,
> But now he's become Italianate;
> So here in contempt and disregard
> I moulder for ever at Appletree Yard.'

Now, in the Nicholson caricature, we were confronted by a gloved, wasp-waisted, dour character in a choker collar that made his eyes pop out, so that he looked like some strange fish in a suddenly electrified aquarium. Max looked lovingly at this odd creature. I said that Nicholson had done better by him than Max had done by Nicholson. Nicholson painted a portrait of Max when Max was a young man; it is a study in beauteous elegance—*jeunesse dorée* in full fig. Max did not defend himself. 'Mrs. Nicholson used to say,' he told me, ' "Oh, Max, you're so good on my husband—at his worst!" I remember when this volume arrived. I was in Portofino, and the Baroness von Hutten came with her little boy. The child recognized the Baroness's friend Nicholson. *"Kann man sehen,"* he said, *"dass die Karikatur auch Kunst ist!"* '

Only one drawing gave Max complete satisfaction, and that was of Lord Tweedmouth. 'This is the best drawing in the book,' said Max, looking happy. He did nothing to improve the drawing of Lord Tweedmouth. And, indeed, though I hadn't the faintest idea who he was or what he did (he had, I later learned, a long, imposing political career), I instantly experienced a warm feeling towards Lord Tweedmouth.

The great promontory of Reginald Turner's nose jutted suddenly before us. I have never seen such a nose; it was bigger than Lord Althorp's cravat, and not so shapely.

'How did your friend Turner feel about *that*?' I asked.

'Oh, well, you know,' said Max, 'when you exaggerate as much as that, there can be no offence in it.'

We then came upon H. G. Wells—'prophet and idealist, conjuring up the darling Future.' Wells, all head and eyes, is talking to himself, zoning Utopia, but his remarks are being overheard by an unattractive female with glasses, holding a mathematical symbol in one hand and a baby in the other. The baby is wearing glasses, too, and is evidently to be consigned to a day nursery in Utopia, where he, or she, will be given a number.

Max kept looking at Wells and remembering him. 'I walked into the Savile Club one day and saw H. G. lunching alone in the bow window,' he said. 'I had just finished reading *Love and Mr. Lewisham*, and I had been so taken by it that I felt that I must speak to H.G. about it. I went up to him and told him—"The quarrel of the young couple," I remember saying to him, "I thought exquisite." Do you know . . . Do you know

THE OLD AND
THE YOUNG SELF

Mr. Arnold Bennett

OLD SELF : 'All gone
according
to plan,
you see.'

YOUNG SELF : '*My* plan,
you know.'

THE OLD AND
THE YOUNG SELF

Mr. George Moore

YOUNG SELF : 'And have
there been
any pain-
ters since
Manet?'

OLD SELF : 'None.'

YOUNG SELF : 'Have there
been any
composers
since Wag-
ner?'

OLD SELF : 'None.'

YOUNG SELF : 'Any nove-
lists since
Balzac?'

OLD SELF : 'One.'

Max accepting with resignation his place among the classics

From the drawing by Ronald Searle in the commemorative volume
presented to Max Beerbohm on his eightieth birthday

... H. G.'s eyes filled with tears. People used to say to me that H. G. was vindictive. I never saw that. He was always extraordinarily nice to me, perhaps because of that encounter in the bow window of the Savile.'

A caricature captioned 'Sir William Eden Revisiting Paris' somewhat mystified me. Sir William is about twelve feet tall, and he is staring, with angry defiance, at a gnomelike figure who is floating in a miasmic cloud and reaching out a clawlike hand to tear at him. 'Oh,' said Max. 'The gnome is Whistler. Whistler did a portrait of Lady Eden. Sir William didn't like it and wouldn't pay. Whistler sued him. We were all on Whistler's side, because we knew that Sir William was very rich and we felt that he could pay without feeling it and then give the portrait, don't you know, to somebody he didn't like for a wedding present. But Whistler lost the suit.'

When Max's hero and friend Sem, the French caricaturist, came along, Max was as pleased as if Sem had just come into the room. 'Oh, Sem!' said Max in welcome. Sem has a very elegant little figure, with an enormous head. His eyes, though shut, are penetrating; he is drawing caricatures inside his head. Max began to talk about Sem with joy. Max's hands became very active in order to convey Sem's volatility, his mercurial gift, in life and as an artist. 'My figures were all done from memory, jellied in memory, but not Sem's,' Max said. 'He did everything from life. He was always taking notes on people.' Max's hand scribbled imaginary notes in the great white margin of his own book. 'At the race track, on the beach at Dieppe, in the theatre, anywhere—a nose, the back of a neck, a forehead, an eye, the hunch of a shoulder. I never could remotely do what Sem did—*instantaneous* caricatures of living, moving people. There was tremendous *movement* in everything Sem did. And he was so funny, so amusing! We used to meet always in Dieppe. Coquelin also came every summer to Dieppe. Coquelin always had the same rooms, of course—the grandest rooms, the best vantage for seeing the fireworks. But the proprietor, M. Bloch, was a friend of ours, and as Coquelin was late one summer, and partly to share the joke and see the effect, don't you know, he consented, to coincide with Coquelin's arrival, to give us his rooms, just for a day—we couldn't possibly have afforded them. We knew how it would irritate Coquelin. Well, the great man came, and Sem and I were in a position to make Coquelin a generous gesture. We invited him to see the fireworks from our rooms, because, as we modestly said, our vantage was, for once, better than his. Coquelin was so furious that he did not even answer our kind invitation. Oh, Sem used to do wonderful imitations of Coquelin. Coquelin had a reverberant voice, don't you know. Sem would start, as Coquelin would often start . . .' Max's voice became reverberant. He leaned forward over the barrier of the 1907 volume and enunciated in a slow bellow, ' "MOI, JE N'AIME PAS . . . PARLER DE MOI-MÊME . . . PARCE QUE—" And then, don't you know, from the safe platform of that "*parce que*", Coquelin would take a long dive into the wonders and intricacies and triumphs of his career; it might well go on for two hours. Fascinating, too, you know. And Sem did it marvellously. He even did it for Coquelin, at my urging, and Coquelin couldn't help but laugh. There was never anyone like Sem.'

Max turned a page. 'And here's Coquelin,' he said. 'Naturally, in Dieppe.' Coquelin is very fat and wears a cap and soft shoes, and his mouth is wide open in declamation.

'Is he explaining why he doesn't care to talk about himself?' I asked.

Max chuckled. 'Oh, no,' he said. 'He's merely learning a part. There's the script of the play in his hand.'

The Marquis de Soveral, the Black Monkey, is startling. He is in full evening dress, wearing white gloves with black stitching; he is monocled and carries a collapsed opera hat, and his eyebrows and mustachios (they are too grandiose for the ordinary designation) divide the great circumference of his face into three fleshy parts. The eyebrows and mustachios are waxed up in baroque spirals. With all his splendour, he needs a shave. I remarked upon this. 'Soveral always needed a shave,' Max said. 'His beard was so heavy that directly he had razored it, it looked as if he should have razored it. That is why he was called the Black Monkey. He was really ugly, and a great success—oh, a monumental success—with women. You know,

John Wilkes was very ugly and also a great success with
women. He was a great talker, and so was the Marquis. Wilkes
said, "I am only half an hour behind the handsomest man in
Europe." I would say that the Marquis wasn't behind at all.'

By this time, I could see that the people before Max in the
book were no longer caricature subjects for him. They were the
friends and acquaintances of his youth, returned to the Villino
for brief communion. So many dead people, I realized,
depended for their lives on Max. The room was thronged with
live ghosts, dressed, in the pages of the 1907 volume, in their
habits as they lived, and, in Max's evocations, speaking in
their natural voices, struggling with the devils who beset them
while they lived.

I stared at the vast figure of Mr. Henry Chaplin—the biggest
overcoat I had ever seen, with a fur collar and fur cuffs like
embankments. He is carrying a walking stick that looks short
in relation to him; he is holding it up—it could obviously never
reach the ground—and his face is compressed briefly but keenly
between the fur collar and a close-fitting hat of some kind.
'Chaplin,' Max said. 'He was very rich, you know. He won the
Derby with a hundred-to-one shot and made a great fortune on
that, but he already had a great fortune. But he spent and spent
and spent—he entertained in a royal manner, wouldn't go
anywhere without a special train—and finally he found himself
poor. Now you see him in his old age. He was pensioned off by
the Conservative Party, to which he had given great sums, and
for which he had performed great services. The Conservative
Party had a fund for such cases. It could only happen in
England, you know.'

I waited to hear what could only happen in England, but
Max was making the rim of Henry Chaplin's monocle a bit
firmer.

'He was a Member of Parliament, and he rose in debate on
an old-age-pension bill and made a vehement speech against it as
destroying initiative, incentive,' Max said. 'He denounced it as
paternalism, and whatnot. Now, everybody knew that he himself
was living on just such a pension, granted him by the Conservative Party. There were, even then, Socialists in the House, and

they were listening to this speech. Nobody smiled, no one in opposition rose to point this out. He had been too great a figure in his own way, too generous a figure. No, this could only happen in England.'

A man named Tommy Chaine came to life in the niche. It was probably the last time he would ever be heard of, except for those who might find him in Max's book and take the trouble to inquire about him. It was perhaps his last appearance even as a ghost. The drawing in which Tommy Chaine appears is called 'In Angel Court'. I asked what Angel Court was, and Max said it was the stock market. The drawing shows three men—a Mr. Benjamin, a Mr. Cohen, and Chaine. Benjamin is tiny, and looks depressed. Chaine is in the centre, wearing one of those cravats and smoking a cigar as big as a torpedo, uptilted like a lance, to do battle against hostile circumstance. Cohen is tall and lanky, and looks as depressed as Benjamin. Only Chaine is defiant. They all three wear silk hats. Max told the whole story of Tommy Chaine, which perhaps only he, in all the world, then remembered. 'He was vain and self-indulgent and extravagant and high-spirited,' Max said. 'His mother was lady-in-waiting to the Queen. The Queen, who always had an eye for a good-looking man, picked out Tommy's father as a good match for her lady-in-waiting, of whom she was fond. She got them married off. Tommy was born in Kensington Palace. He and his wife were a very popular couple; Tommy's wife was almost as popular as he was, and so was Tommy's mistress, who was a well-known and lovely London society woman. It was accepted then—perhaps it still is—that it was all right for a man to have a mistress as long as the mistress's husband had one also; it was all right to be a *mari complaisant* if your wife was involved with a *mari* equally *complaisant*. And how happily married and happily mistressed and gay and well off and popular Tommy Chaine was! So popular that he attracted the attention of Solly Joel, the great African diamond millionaire. Tommy was in a wonderful position. And then he did something that Solly Joel did not like, something obscurely dishonest, and was about to be sued by Solly Joel in the courts. Tommy used to come to Dieppe with Wilson Steer and myself.

Steer was very fond of him; he was so amusing and high-spirited you couldn't help being drawn to him. When he got into this trouble with Solly Joel and the threat of this suit hung over him and all sorts of unpleasant rumours were going on about him, he dropped out of sight and I didn't see him for a very long time. Then, one day, I came out into the street after lunch somewhere, and there, sitting in a hansom, was Tommy Chaine. I shall never forget that moment. He had changed so—his expression, I mean. He looked frightened. It was terrible to see a look of fright on a face that had always expressed such gaiety and confidence. And he conveyed a sense of being in a vacuum, of being frightened in a vacuum—a kind of general-ized fear, don't you know. I decided not to let Tommy see that I had seen him in this way, and I turned quickly away. But he had caught sight of me and he called to me. "We must see each other," he said. "You must lunch with me." We made a lunch appointment for the following week. The day before the appointment, I heard that he'd fled the country and was on the Continent. I never saw him again. When the 1914 war broke out, his friends got together and raised money, so that he could straighten out the off-colour transaction that had alienated Solly Joel. He came back to London. He had become enormously fat. He got a job in the Civil Defence. One day, at his duties, he dropped dead.'

Max took a last look at Tommy. I looked, too. With that cigar pointed defiantly at destiny, Tommy looked as if he could surmount anything. But the cigar was wrong.

Henry James rates two drawings in the 1907 volume, the only person so honoured, and Max's recollections of Henry James were gayer than those he had of poor Tommy Chaine. One of the drawings is titled 'Mr. Henry James (in London)'; the other, the last one in the book, 'Mr. Henry James Revisiting America'. It is only with the James drawings that Max indulges himself in luxuriant captions; he cannot resist imitating James's prose style. The first drawing shows James, silk-hatted and carrying an umbrella, groping through a London fog. He has his hand before his eyes, as if to be reassured by a familiar landmark. The caption, in Max's handwriting, reads:

> . . . It was, therefore, not without something of a shock that he, in this to him so very congenial atmosphere, now perceived that a vision of the hand which he had, at a venture, held up within an inch or so of his eyes was, with an almost awful clarity, being adumbrated . . .

In the American one, 'Mr. Henry James Revisiting America', Max shows the returned expatriate surrounded by various locals, whose reaction to him is mixed. A little girl is staring at the vast dome of his head, and exults, 'My! Ain't he cree-ative?' A Negro boy is doing a cakewalk in celebration of James's arrival; he is singing, 'We wants you mighty badly—Yas, we *doo*!' An Indian chief is impassive but pleased: 'Hail, great white novelist! Tuniyaba—the spinner of fine cobwebs!' A plainsman observes, 'Guess i ken shoot char'cter at sight!' A Negro mammy is ecstatic: 'Why, it's Masser Henry! Come to your old nurse's arms, honey!' A plump, effete Harvardian, gazing at him without enthusiasm, inquires, 'What's—the matter with—*James*?,' to which a Beacon Hill hostess answers languidly, '*He's*—all—right!' A Westerner with a down-tilted stogie in his mouth looks grim and says, '*Who's*—all—right?' To which an immense plutocrat, with his eyes shut, answers, '*James!*' James, not looking at anybody, lifts a deprecatory hand to still this polyphony of welcome; he is thinking (in an 'Extract from His Unspoken Thoughts'):

> . . . So that in fine, let, without further beating about the bush, me make to myself amazed acknowledgment that, but for the certificate of birth which I have—so quite indubitably—on me, I might, in regarding (and, as it somewhat were, overseeing) *à l'œil de voyageur* these dear good people, find hard to swallow, or even to take by subconscious injection, the great idea that I am—oh, ever so indigenously!—one of them . . .

Max then showed me another caricature of Henry James, in which Max has let his prose style alone. It is quite dumb but eloquent. James is shown kneeling in the corridor of a country house on a crowded week-end. It is very early in the morning. His eyes are beaded on two pairs of Edwardian shoes—a man's and a woman's. He has been staring at them for a long time; he will continue to do so. He will stare at those four shoes until they have yielded the last drop of their secret to him.

Miss Jungmann came in with tea. She took the 1907 volume carefully away, and then rejoined us. Max went on talking about Henry James.

'One day,' Max said, 'I was coming out of the Carlton Hotel after lunch. I had heard that there was a new story by Henry James in a review that had just been started, and I thought I would go to the Savile Club to read it. Just as I was going up the rise of Piccadilly'—Max's hand rose with Piccadilly—'I was hailed, I was hailed by the Master himself. A certain rumbling and circumlocutionizing emerged from him. He was a great hesitator, you know, the greatest of the hesitators. He would have been a great Parliamentarian, because in the House of Commons those who hesitate are greatly valued; a fluent speaker is apt to be considered superficial, while a hesitator, they think, is hesitating because he is deeply pondering the grave issues. Balfour was a great hesitator, and so is Winston. But that day in Piccadilly, James said he was a country cousin in town for the day and were there any exciting new pictures in any museum? I told him that indeed there was one—a new Augustus John in the Grafton Galleries. He asked me then if I couldn't take him along to see it. I don't know why, I shall never know why, but I feigned a previous engagement. Henry James walked on alone, and I made my way to the Savile to read his story. I preferred, somehow, to be with the Master's work rather than with the Master himself.'

Miss Jungmann and I thought that this was, in itself, a Henry James story. We urged Max to write it.

'I am beyond composition,' he said. Nevertheless, encouraged by us, he said he might.

'We will make a writer out of you yet, Max!' I said.

Max did write it. It was the next-to-last literary task he ever undertook. He called it 'An Incident', and it was published in the enlarged edition of *Mainly on the Air*.

Max went on talking about James. 'I had my difficulties with him,' Max said. 'He wrote in a deprecatory manner about Bennett's *Old Wives' Tale*. I think it the finest novel that has been produced in England in this century. I remember James's saying, when I expressed this opinion to him, "What's it all about?" ' At this enormity, Max put down his teacup. He resumed the argument with Henry James. ' "What's it about? What's it about?" Why, I told him, it's about the passing of time, about the stealthy merging of youth into age, the invisibility of the traps in our own characters into which we walk, unwary, unknowing. "WHAT'S IT ALL ABOUT?" !'

To soothe Max, I asked him about Arnold Bennett. I referred to an uncomplimentary remark he had made about Bennett. Bennett had made some *gaffe* about the hanging of a picture in the National Gallery to its director, which was a reckless thing to do. Someone said to Max, recounting it, 'A.B. made a fool of himself.' '*Made* a fool of himself?' said Max.

'Oh, well, you know,' Max replied, 'it's this same thing of having to know *everything*, of being omniscient, of being unable to say the simple words "I don't know". Arnold was a card, all right, but without guile. At his birth, his good fairy must have promised, "I will make him ill-favoured, crude, egotistical, but I will give him a stutter that will draw people to him, make them sympathetic to him, and listen to him." And he used the stutter marvellously, don't you know—with a great sense of timing. I believe it was Siegfried Sassoon who told me a story which illustrates this. He was at some party; I think he said Aldous Huxley was there, and Bennett, and there was great and acrid discussion about some vastly popular lady writer whose work they all despised. There was tremendous and profound discussion of her defects—on psychological grounds, on spiritual grounds, on the grounds of taste. When they were all done with their dissertations, Bennett said, "*I'll* tell you what's the trouble with that woman. She c-c-c-CAN'T WRITE!" ' '

By this time, Max had got over his difference with James, and he returned to him. 'James greatly wished to be a novelist, but he was not essentially a novelist, he was an evocative writer,' Max said. 'The Pagoda passage in *The Golden Bowl*, for example. No one in the world could have written that but James. Often what he called his *donnée* was a dubious gift, don't you know. Still, I return to him and return to him; I read him and read him. I find, don't you know, after I've read this one and that one, that I feel like reading James.'

I mentioned that Miss Jungmann had told me he had been reading to her from *Partial Portraits* the night before. What had he been reading?

The little book was by his side. He picked it up and opened it. As he leafed through the pages, he stopped, caught by a passage. 'This is touching,' he said. 'This always gives me a pang when I come upon it.'

I asked what it was.

'The end of James's essay on Daudet,' he said, and he read aloud:

> Daudet is bright, vivid, tender; he has an intense artistic life. And then he is so free. [Max emphasized the word and looked up at me to see whether it had registered.] For the spirit that moves slowly, going carefully from point to point, not sure whether this or that or the other will 'do', the sight of such freedom is delightful.

Max paused. He forgot that he had been looking for something else. He was lost for the moment in thought. 'Dear Henry James,' he said, as if sympathizing with his old friend for not feeling free.

To take his mind off it, Miss Jungmann said, 'But it was about Turgenev you were reading to me last night.'

'Oh, yes.' Max turned the pages, and quickly found the passage. Before he began to read, he addressed an explanatory remark to me. 'You know, James had just come from the service at the Gare du Nord when Turgenev's coffin was being sent to Russia. Renan and About had stood beside the train and delivered eulogies. James describes beautifully what Renan said about Turgenev, but what he has to say himself about Turgenev is equally beautiful.'

It had got dark in the room. Miss Jungmann turned on a lamp for Max. Holding the book under it, he began to read; he read exquisitely, quietly, without inflection, merely allowing James's words, as he had set them down, to make their effect:

> I shall never forget the impression he made upon me at that first interview. I found him adorable; I could scarcely believe that he would prove—that any man could prove—on nearer acquaintance so delightful as that. Nearer acquaintance

only confirmed my hope, and he remained the most approach-
able, the most practicable, the least unsafe a man of genius
it has been my fortune to meet. He was so simple, so natural,
so modest, so destitute of personal pretension and of what is
called the consciousness of powers, that one almost doubted
at moments whether he were a man of genius after all. Everything good and fruitful lay near to him; he was interested in
everything; and he was absolutely without that eagerness of
self-reference which sometimes accompanies great, and even
small, reputations. He had not a particle of vanity; nothing
whatever of the air of having a part to play or a reputation to
keep up. . . .

Max's voice went on reading, his head under the lamp.
Something made me look at Miss Jungmann. Her eyes were
full of pain. We were surely thinking the same thing.

VII

THE LAST CIVILIZED VOICE

IN JUNE of 1955, I visited Max Beerbohm in Rapallo for the last time. He was by then nearly eighty-three, and it was perhaps natural that on one of the afternoons when we sat talking together in the tiny living-room of the Villino he should bring up his series of caricatures called *The Young Self and the Old Self*, and that afterwards we should discuss them again and again. This series—one of the most striking and Maxian of Max's achievements as a caricaturist—shows his subjects simultaneously in youth and in age, the Young Self confronting the Old Self. They are like little novels, done in a single drawing and a line or two of dialogue—Max's convex mirror miniaturizing a lifetime. By collapsing time altogether, by wiping out the inconvenient gap between the present and the past, by bringing the Young Self and the Old on to the stage at the same moment and letting them exchange a few words, he was able to dramatize the passage of time and catch the essence of a man's character.

The Old Self of Arnold Bennett, in white tie, oozing affluence, immense of girth, toothy, a figure of dishevelled elegance, befobbed and wearing a pleated shirt, his pudgy hands clutching his white waistcoat, and his face bearing an expression of not entirely convinced complacency, is addressing his Young Self, a scrawny, stubborn yokel from Staffordshire:

OLD SELF: All gone according to plan, you see.
YOUNG SELF: *My* plan, you know.

The young Stanley Baldwin looks at his pipe-smoking elder

self, who has one of those consciously 'strong' faces with not much behind them, and is astonished that so much could have been accomplished by so little:

> Prime Minister? *You?* Good Lord!!

The young George Moore, rubbery, amorphous, stands obeisantly, silk hat in hand, before the old George, more rubbery still but sitting. This dialogue ensues between them:

> YOUNG SELF: And have there been any painters since Manet?
> OLD SELF: None.
> YOUNG SELF: Have there been any composers since Wagner?
> OLD SELF: None.
> YOUNG SELF: Any novelists since Balzac?
> OLD SELF: One.

The Old Self of Sir William Rothenstein is so offended by the materialization of the Young Self, bumptious and cravated and ugly (the two selves are actually very much alike), that, in front of a bevy of his students at the Royal Academy, he thunderously orders the unwelcome apparition to disappear:

> Take off your hat, Sir!—and leave the room!

The young Joseph Conrad bursts out in Polish—a gibberish invented by Max, but it certainly *looks* like Polish—and the old Conrad, splendid and goateed and monocled, replies to his Young Self's harangue:

> Mais oui, mon enfant—and what's more, I was a Master Mariner! And I've written some books, too . . . but you are hardly old enough to understand them.

The Young Self of H. G. Wells, a calmly impassioned zoologist, asks the Old Self of H. G. a purely scientific question:

> Did you ever manage to articulate the bones of that micro-glamaphoid lizard?

But the Old Self has soared into the empyrean; he rather brushes his Young Self off:

> I'm not sure. But I've articulated the whole past of mankind

on this planet—and the whole future, too. I don't think you know very much about the past, do you? It's all perfectly beastly, believe me. But the future's going to be all perfectly splendid . . . after a bit. And I must say I find the present very jolly.

In a drawing Max captioned 'A Momentary Vision That Once Befell Young Millais,' the ardent, idealistic young artist is appalled by what he is to become—a country squire, well fed, successful, very 'county', in shooting clothes, with a Sherlock Holmes cap. Max's awareness of the penalties exacted by success is acute. In one of his many caricatures of, or involving, Dante Gabriel Rossetti, he shows Lord Leighton, the president of the Royal Academy and the most successful painter of his time—a man who was himself eroded by the knowledge that he had made an easy compromise—haranguing Rossetti, urging him smoothly to do the right thing, get in the swim, join the swirling traffic of the drawing-rooms where commissions are bred. Of Rossetti, habitually recumbent, you see only his slippered feet, and these seem not to be listening. Of Leighton, you feel that his harangue is mechanical, that he has turned it on, it is his 'line', and, for all his look of success, you sense the wish that he him-self, as his Young Self, had not listened to it. Max, in his own volume of *Zuleika Dobson*, drew an impromptu caricature of an Old Self that never existed—Byron at sixty, plump, spectacled, with mutton-chop whiskers, respectable. He looks as if he were president of the Birmingham board of trade and were about to take the chair at a weekly meeting. The drawing is called 'But for Missolonghi'. Elsewhere, Max speculated about what would have happened to Byron if he had lived on; he would, Max said, have spent his time 'writing very long and able letters to *The Times* on the Corn Laws, and much exacerbated by Queen Victoria's refusal to sanction his appointment to a post in Lord John Russell's Government.'

As a youth, Arthur Balfour was persistently valetudinary. In the Young and Old series, Max shows the interminable elongation that was the young Balfour swooning, on the longest chaise longue in history. The dying swan looks up—it is, you feel, his last mortal effort—at the old Balfour, in flannels, with open-necked shirt and horn-rimmed glasses, and carrying a tennis racket. He just barely addresses him:

> YOUNG SELF (faintly): Who are you? You look rather like Uncle Salisbury, shaved. And what is that curious thing you're holding? And won't you catch cold, with so little on? But don't answer: I don't really care. And don't let me talk: I don't fancy I've long to live; and I want to devote the time to thinking—not that I suppose my thoughts to be of much value, but—oh, do, please, go away.

In reality, Balfour's Old Self refused to go away; he went on and on. The historian Oscar Browning, in his memoirs, remembers Balfour's telling him, when the future Prime Minister was twenty-two years old, that 'the doctors had assured him that he could not possibly live to the age of thirty, a fact of which I have now and again reminded him during his career.' With time, according to Max, the prolonged valetudinarianism became transformed into a passion for longevity. Having arranged for his funeral in his twenties, he postponed it long enough to become an aggressive Chief Secretary for Ireland. Stimulated by this unexpected show of strength, he became Prime Minister. As his friends, acquaintances, and colleagues died, he clocked them off—the milestones of his own survival. To Max, he was unbeguiling but fascinating, and Max never stopped drawing him. When he didn't formally draw him, he doodled him; the early manuscript of *Zuleika Dobson* is dappled with him. There is a remarkable difference in the physical appearance of the two drafts of *Zuleika Dobson*—the unfinished one written in London in 1898, and the one completed in Rapallo in 1911. Both drafts are owned by Mr. Robert H. Taylor, of Yonkers, who also owns the greatest collection of Trollope in the world. Max would have felt very cosy in the society of the Trollopes; there is surely no one in the world he would rather have had Zuleika marry than Anthony Trollope. The early manuscript is scraggly, written in random columns and riddled with doodles—of Balfour, Disraeli, Reginald Turner, Henry James, Oscar Wilde, Henry Irving, Lord Ribblesdale, Edward VII. Winston Churchill's perky nose keeps jutting inquisitively into the various scenes. The London manuscript is written in pencil, the Rapallo one in ink. There are no doodles in the Rapallo manuscript, but there are tremendous erasures, which Max made with a paint-brush; the pages present a decorative spectacle, covered with great solid promontories of black ink, with islets, peninsulas, and sometimes continents. In the earlier manuscript, however, you may watch the struggle between Max's dual careers. Often the graphic seems to gain the upper hand; several times, Max seems to have forgotten that he was writing a novel, and whole pages are devoted to drawings, some of them sketches for caricatures that later became famous. When *le mot juste* proved elusive, he doodled Balfour.

Max never did a drawing of his own Young Self and Old Self, but if he had done one, it might have resembled to some extent the drawing of Arnold Bennett. The Old Self might again have said, 'All gone according to plan, you see,' and the Young Self might have answered, '*My* plan, you know.' In the essay 'Diminuendo', written when Max was twenty-three and in Chicago with his brother Herbert, he not only said his farewell to literature but set down his vision of the life he was to lead, and to a large extent he did lead it. He would retire, he said, to the country and contemplate existence:

> I shall look forth from my window, the laburnum and the mountain-ash becoming mere silhouettes in the foreground of my vision. I shall look forth and, in my remoteness, appreciate the distant pageant of the world. Humanity will range itself in the columns of my morning paper. No pulse of life will escape me. . . . Tragedy, comedy, chivalry, philosophy will be mine. I shall listen to their music perpetually and their colours will dance before my eyes. . . . I shall have friends. . . . And I, who crave no knighthood, shall write no more.

'I shall have friends,' Max promised himself, and the promise was fulfilled. Max had friends, and his friends loved him. For forty-five years, they came in a stream to visit him in Rapallo. When they weren't visiting, they wrote to him. Even when, as he grew older, he didn't always keep up his end of the correspondence, they still wrote to him. When he went to London on visits from Rapallo, staying at the station hotels he so adored, his friends gobbled him up. Max inspired a peculiar devotion in people; his presence—his very existence—was a delight. It was not only that he was witty and that his speech was exquisite but also that he so evidently had, in social intercourse, no axe to grind. In 1932, Sir William Rothenstein, speaking, in his *Men and Memories*, of Max's talent for friendship, wrote:

> Indeed Max, of later years especially, shrinks from offending people; the once pitiless satirist has become the most human and understanding of men. I know so many with wandering eyes, who feel their time wasted with any but important persons. Max, who charms everyone, finds most people charming. And how quickly he discovers the essence of each personality.

Max's friends were aware of his habit of saying, in the voice of one asking for tutelage, 'Tell me,' to anybody he was talking to, as if only you in all the world could divulge the secret. He was leisured, he was in no hurry to express himself, he wanted to listen. The fact that there was not in him any trace of the impulse for self-aggrandisement made him eager to elicit the essential quality of his interlocutors. He could tell *you*, all right, and he did, but, equally, he wished to be told. To have dinner with Max, wrote Edith Wharton, 'was like suddenly growing wings.' From the diary kept by Elizabeth Russell during the time she lived in Portofino, her biographer Leslie de Charms quotes a passage showing what her talks with Max meant to her:

> December 31 Florence-Rapallo. Tea at Max Beerbohm's on way. . . . I was blissfully happy at hearing such delicious talk after the Cannes aridities. . . . They begged us to go again after supper, when the Granville-Barkers will be there and an Italian pair, but we don't want to spoil the perfect memory. A delightful finish to the year.

In Rapallo, Max was scarcely ever not anticipating some visitor—Arnold Bennett, Compton Mackenzie, Somerset Maugham, Constance Collier, Desmond MacCarthy, Osbert Sitwell, Reginald Turner, S. C. Roberts (Master of Pembroke, Cambridge), the Hamish Hamiltons, the Laurence Oliviers, the Selwyn Jepsons, the Christopher Sykeses, Gordon Craig, Ada Leverson, Siegfried Sassoon. His sisters and his nieces, the daughters of Herbert Tree, and their children came. One of those children was Ivan Moffat, the son of his favourite niece, Iris Tree. Ivan Moffat, a film writer, and his mother were both old friends of mine, and every time I visited Max he would ask whether I had seen them. From time to time, I could give him news of them. I once teased Max by saying Ivan had told me that his Great-Uncle Max had given him a bad moment on one of his family visits in London. 'In fact, Max,' I said, 'I am not sure you didn't, out of your goodness of heart, induce—to use a word you're not fond of—a trauma in Ivan.'

Max stroked his moustache tranquilly. 'Really!' he said. 'And how did I do that?'

I repeated for him Ivan's anecdote. Max's visits, were, of course, a great event in the Tree family. On this occasion, various grand-nieces and grand-nephews were assembled for Max's inspection. There were David, Dennys, Virginia, and Ivan, who was then fourteen. 'The others were all older and taller and more renowned than I was,' Moffat recalled. 'Their accomplishments were paraded for Max, in athletics and in scholarship.' Ivan kept his gaze fixed on the little figure at the head of the table, and saw Max's clear blue eyes reflecting wonderment at so much erudition, so many prowesses. Ivan became terribly self-conscious about his own anonymity in such a welter of celebrity. There was a bowl of English walnuts on the table, and to assuage his nervousness and self-consciousness he began cracking these walnuts and eating them without intermission. A nervous hunger assailed him, a compulsion to swallow. Nut followed nut. 'The crepitation was tremendous,' Moffat continued. 'I knew what a racket it was making, but I just couldn't stop. The babble went on, important and clever, and as every moment passed and I still hadn't made any contribution to it, I knew, with a sort of panic, that I could not and that I would not. Max took everything in, including my self-consciousness and my desperation. As the virtues and greatnesses of the others were paraded, Max, in turn, courteously saluted them. Suddenly there was a silence, and in that silence the nuts cracked like a fusillade. Max turned his mild glance on me; I became the centre of attention, because everyone's eyes followed Max's. "And you, Ivan—tell me—what about you?" Max said. "Are you a Great Nuttist?" '

Another of Max's promises to himself was fulfilled. 'I shall look forth,' Max promised at the age of twenty-three, in Chicago, 'and, in my remoteness, appreciate the distant pageant of the world.' He certainly did, and, sitting in his niche in Rapallo, he recorded that pageant in caricatures that cover, in their penetration and diversity, much of the vast range of human character. Even those vanished politicians and other celebrities that one has never heard of still stand out arrestingly as individual human beings—personalities. You want to know about them; you want to know *them*. In 1954, the eminent American critic Edmund Wilson paid a visit to Max at the Villino. As he and I sat in the Excelsior afterwards, he told me that he had just seen André Malraux in Paris, and that in both men—a startling juxtaposition, it seemed to me—he had been much impressed by their self-confidence and strength of character. 'He's quite sure of himself,' Wilson said of Max. 'He knows the value of what he has done, both as a writer and as an artist. He doesn't give a damn about having all his caricatures collected and published, as I suggested to him they ought to be. He doesn't even know where many of them are. He knows very well that somebody else will have to worry about all that some day.' In connection with the mural that Max had painted in his bedroom, Wilson was struck by the fact that he had brought to Rapallo with him all of his favourite characters: Balfour, of course, and G. K. Chesterton, George Moore, and so on. 'It is a kind of Divine Comedy that he has been working at all his life,' Wilson said. 'The celebrated men he has been caricaturing have come to play significant roles. There is a whole hierarchy of values: people like Joseph Conrad and Henry James, whom he both admires and likes; people like Bernard Shaw, whom he admires but doesn't like; people like some of the politicians—Lloyd George, for example—whom he neither admires nor likes.' He said that he thought Max was the greatest caricaturist of the kind—that is, portrayer of personalities—in the history of art.

For a time, Max was concerned lest his separation from the 'au-courantism' of London affect the veracity of his caricatures. He needn't have worried. Although Max lived the last forty-five years of his life in the remoteness of Rapallo, in spirit he lived in London, and he kept drawing and redrawing the important London figures. I have never met anyone more stubbornly English than Max. When he bitterly satirized England during the Boer War, it was because, as he has said, 'on se moque de ce qu'on aime'. The changes in London, its wanton deterioration, which he mourned in his moving B.B.C. broadcast 'London Revisited', were for him personal bereavements. The more he lived away from England, the more he became infatuated with her. England as an idea seemed to him unique in the world, and he was proud of her. In all the years Max lived in Italy, he never drew a caricature of an Italian. He was eternally drawing Balfour, Disraeli, Byron, George Moore, King Edward the Seventh. He couldn't even write about a foreign country. He could write only about England. It was because he couldn't bear to be out of England during the two world wars that he lived there through both of them. For a time during the Second World War, he lived in the country house of his friends the Sydney Schiffs, at Abinger. While he was there, he contributed some pieces to a local paper, the Abinger Chronicle, circulation three hundred, and he worked at them as carefully as if the Abinger Chronicle had had a circulation of a million.

Certain reproaches about not living up to the Chicago contract might have been levelled by the Young Max at the Old Max. As the Young Max didn't level them, I did. On my final visit to Rapallo, I pointed out to Max that he had not stuck to his promise not to achieve a knighthood, having received one in 1939. Max met the charge with good humour; he had done his best to prevent it, he said, since he had not spared the Royal Family when he was in the mood to lampoon it. He had not, I went on inexorably, stuck to his promise not to do any more writing. Here, too, Max defended himself, saying he had done pretty well, considering the importunities that were put upon him by magazine editors and publishers. A London publisher once invited Max to allow a famous essay of his to be included in an *Omnibus of Contemporary English Literature*. 'I do not care to be omnibussed,' he wrote to the publisher. The publisher then pointed out to him that as the anthology was to be edited by and have a preface by W. Somerset Maugham, it would probably bring him to the attention of three or four hundred thousand readers. That settled that. The prospect of such a crowd frightened Max. 'There are only fifteen hundred readers in England and one thousand in America who understand what I am about,' he wrote back. For the fifteen hundred readers in England and the thousand in America, Max went to enormous pains to make his meaning clear. He did everything for readers except get them.

I stubbed my own toe hard, once, against the bulwark of Max's fastidiousness. The National Broadcasting Company had begun a series of filmed television broadcasts, under the title 'Wisdom', by distinguished old men and women. The N.B.C. people wanted Max badly. They had sent their Italian representative, Miss Gioia Marconi, and an American representative, Mr. Davidson Taylor, to the Villino to sound him out, but he had not proved responsibe. An N.B.C. man who happened to be a friend of mine asked me if I would try to persuade Max. Knowing that Max needed money and that the network was willing to pay him three thousand dollars, I agreed. I thereupon wrote him a letter. I paraded the great names that N.B.C. had already signed—Bertrand Russell, Arnold Toynbee, Robert Frost, Pablo Casals—and urged Max to queue up to enter the geriatric pantheon. 'Now, dear Max,' I wrote, ' I hate to introduce a vulgar note, but they will pay three thousand dollars. They want to send their representative, who is a very nice man, to see you. . . . And, you know, they tell me you won't have to leave your niche, they'll do it all while you're sitting in the niche. It seems to me this is a lot of money to get for not leaving your room, as I've seen you not leave it so often for nothing.' The letter went, airmail. I waited. N.B.C. waited. Max's reply came very promptly. In his beautiful, crescent-paragraphed handwriting, he wrote, in pencil, as follows:

> I look forward to seeing your friend and communing with him, but I am, alas, quite incorrigibly opposed to any idea of

being televised. Mr. Davidson Taylor was here recently and wished me to revoke the unwillingness I had expressed last year to Miss Marconi even after she had shown me on the wall the immensely mobile features of Bertrand Russell amplifying the artful modulations of his voice.

This was a shocker. I had been so confident. But when I showed my friend Max's letter, he was not too badly let down. 'I am going there anyway,' he said. 'You can't do these things by letter.' His confidence restored mine. Later, I heard an account of what happened in Rapallo.

Max received the N.B.C. emissary cordially. The television man was admitted to the niche. He was smooth and ingratiating. 'You see, Sir Max,' he said, 'it will be very simple. Our people will come and arrange everything. You will sit, if you like, as you are sitting now. You will simply say, "My dear friends, I am very happy to be here addressing you." '

'Do you wish me,' asked Max courteously, 'to start with a lie?'

It had been a near thing, but Max won out. With that remark, the flood of affluence that had threatened to inundate him was dammed for ever.

When I saw Max again, he apologized for having snuffed out my effort, and went on to explain why he had done it. 'I could not but dash their hopes,' he said. 'Had I been televised, it would have been impossible for the viewers to concentrate on what I was saying. They would have concentrated on me. How fortunate, how very fortunate, that Goethe or Browning—whoever you like—was not televised in his old age. Now we can have our idea of them, our imagination of them, but had they been televised—No, television is not literature, it is actuality.' I asked Max why, when he had been so adamant in his refusal to be filmed for American television, he had been willing to do all those B.B.C. radio broadcasts during the Second World War. He replied that in written prose the sound was always important to him, that he laid great emphasis on the acoustics of prose, and that in radio broadcasting it was paramount. The human voice had always fascinated him. Even his caricatures, he said, had been influenced by the voices of his subjects; Balfour, for example, had a shrill, high-pitched, unmelodious

voice, and its vibration was always in his mind when he caricatured him.

It is odd that one of the least popular writers in the world
should have become, next to Winston Churchill, the most
popular broadcaster in England during the most critical
moment of its history. Max may have had few readers, but he
had millions of listeners. Of his B.B.C. broadcasts, Rebecca
West has written, 'I felt, when I was listening to them, that I
was listening to the voice of the last civilised man on earth,'
adding, 'Max's broadcasts justify the entire invention of broadcasting.'

In January of 1942, while London was blacked out, and
a vast number of its inhabitants were sleeping in the Under-
grounds and shelters, and the fires lit by incendiary bombs
furnished the only illumination, Max treated his listeners to the
broadcast called 'Music Halls of My Youth'. In a letter to
Sir Sydney Cockerell, Siegfried Sassoon wrote of this broadcast, 'Max's talk I listened to with delight. For me it was and
will be the only B.B.C. half-hour worth remembering in 1942.
No words can express what I feel about it. I laughed aloud—
but there were tears in my eyes too.'

It must have been a curious instinct of self-interest that had
caused me, in Rome in 1954, to send Max a little gramophone,
along with some recordings of his favourite composer, Puccini,
for now, one afternoon in June of 1955, sitting in Max's niche,
I was able to hear all his broadcasts, which had been recorded
on special discs and sent to him by the B.B.C. Max and Miss
Jungmann enjoyed the gramophone almost as much as I did.
It constituted a singular contemporary, mechanical intrusion
into the niche, which had theretofore been dominated by the
bronze girl with the averted head and by the pair of photographs on the mantelshelf. It was installed beside the Merton
chair. It played Puccini and Max. On this gramophone I now
listened to Max's music-hall broadcast. He delivered this one
when it was well past his own bedtime. He assumes, he says,
that most of his contemporaries are, as he should be, already
asleep, and that those of his listeners who are up and doing will
'know little of the subject on which I am going to dilate with

senile garrulity.' After talking about Dan Leno, Little Tich, Albert Chevalier, George Robey, Marie Lloyd, and others, Max ends with a few words to his listeners on how he had come to squander his youth drinking in the words and music of these vanished ghosts:

> Perhaps you will blame me for having spent so much of my time in Music Halls, so frivolously, when I should have been sticking to my books, burning the midnight oil and compassing the larger latitude. But I am impenitent. I am inclined to think, indeed I have always thought, that a young man who desires to know all that in all ages and in all lands has been thought by the best minds, and wishes to make a synthesis of all those thoughts for the future benefit of mankind, is laying up for himself a very miserable old age.
>
> *Good* night, childrenn . . . everywhhere.

Max's whispered voice dwindled away at the end. The broadcast was thrilling and funny and moving; I understood perfectly why Sassoon had written about it as he had. Max had a tremendous mastery of the dynamics of his own voice. He set his own threshold in decibels, rationing them shrewdly. His normal speaking voice was soft, small, infinitely courteous, and musical. By talking twice as loud, he gave the effect of shouting. Alan Dent, the drama and film critic, has written a description of Max's delivery on the air, in the album note for the gramophone record of 'London Revisited'. The Maximilian Society of London was Mr. Dent's idea. Founded on Max's seventieth birthday, it had seventy admirers of Max as members, including William Nicholson, Edwin Lutyens, William Rothenstein, Philip Guedalla, Robert Lynd, and Desmond MacCarthy. The idea was to add a member on each of Max's birthdays. Mr. Dent, animated by Max's constant reference to himself in his broadcasts as a Cockney, writes:

> It is *like him* to refer to his Cockney or low-London accent, even though his diction is so precise that he gives 'perambulator' five clear vowels, and bestows upon such a word as 'initiation'—which the vulgar, both rich and poor, slur into something like 'inishation'—its full consonantal complement. It is *like him* to reveal that this same sedulous care in speaking the English language can turn a word like 'poetry' into a poem.

One Sunday night in 1942, Max did a broadcast on 'Advertisements', and now Miss Jungmann put the record of that one
on the gramophone. In it, Max says he wishes that he were not
incurably ironic in his manner of expressing himself; he wishes
that, for once, he could be straightforward. But perhaps, he
reflects, it's as well that he can't, for on the subject of advertising
'my language might be overstrong for Sunday evening'. Max
doesn't mind want-ads. To 'these spontaneous cries from the
heart' he is sympathetic. What he can't abide are the 'you *do*
want, and woe betide if you don't get' ones. He remembers the
want-ads of his youth. He read them, when he was a child, with
fascination. He cherishes one that he read in the *Church Times*:
'Medical Man in Cheltenham can accommodate one female
resident patient. Epileptic Churchwoman preferred.' But
though he loved it, he has become, in retrospect, suspicious
even of that. Perhaps it was the thin edge of the wedge:

> Somewhat later, a wonderful soap swam into my ken. Sir
> John Millais had painted a great picture of a little boy with
> golden curls and a green velveteen suit, and upturned eyes,
> blowing bubbles; and this picture had been acquired by the
> vendor of the soap and widely reproduced on the soap's behalf.
> My elders, in those pre-historic days, wondered that Sir John
> should have authorised this use of his great gifts. And they were
> shocked, too, that the beautiful young Mrs. Langtry had for the
> soap's sake allowed engravings of a photograph of herself to be
> sown broadcast in the Press, with the admonition 'For look you,
> she is fair as a lily!' Mrs. Weldon, the famous litigant, had
> gone even further. Her portrait was subscribed by her, 'I am
> forty-seven, but my complexion is seventeen.' I wonder what
> my elders would think of those perfectly well-brought-up and
> non-litigious young ladies of rank and fashion who nowadays let
> their photographs be reproduced in favour of some unguent
> used by them and ecstatically praised by them, with an accom-
> panying diagram of their features and a laudatory description
> of each feature by the unguentarian?

An American driving along English roads is particularly
struck by the merciful fewness of road signs. But Max, without
benefit of the American standard, is irked by what has happened
in England:

> And now for a matter which agitates me far more than the

effect that advertisements have on newspapers. Though newspapers without advertisements could not nowadays survive, I
see no reason for believing that without this support the
streets and squares of our cities, and the roads and hills and
valleys of our countryside, would presently disappear. On the
contrary, they are rather by way of disappearing already behind
the insistences on what we ought to purchase. Beautiful archi-
tecture and beautiful scenery are things far more important to
the soul of man than even the best newspaper.

Max, in spite of all his protests, is himself not free from the
itch to advertise. He wishes he were rich, so that he could place
an ad. He is even more ambitious. He wants to start a whole
advertising campaign:

> Meanwhile, if I were endowed with wealth, I should start
> a great advertising campaign in all the principal newspapers.
> The advertisements would consist of one short sentence, printed
> in huge block letters—a sentence that I once heard spoken
> by a husband to a wife: 'My dear, nothing in this world is
> worth buying.'

As Max and I sat by the gramophone in the niche, Miss
Jungmann kept bringing in more discs. Max tried to restrain
her, on the ground that he did not wish to bore me, but Miss
Jungmann and I prevailed. He accepted our interest as a
compliment. 'The best compliment I have ever received,' he
said, 'was from the head waiter at the Berners Hotel, where I
was staying, after a B.B.C. broadcast. He came up to me and
said, "I congratulate you on your broadcast, sir. May I sy, you
speak such mervlus English!"'

We now listened to Max on George Moore. Max met George
Moore at Nevill Holt, the country home of Lady Cunard.
'There was something about Moore,' Lady Cunard said later,
'that evoked a fish, a large, distinguished carp.' Moore was a
natural for Max. Max immediately made a caricature of him,
showing him in the drawing-room at Nevill Holt—the first of
the many caricatures Max did of Moore. His broadcast on
Moore he had written in 1913, as a sketch for *The Mirror of the
Past*. It contains, besides much else, a description of Moore's face:

> His Parisianism, grafted upon an imperishable brogue, gave
> to his utterance a very curious charm. Aided by his face and

his gesture, this charm was irresistible. I say his 'gesture' advisedly; for he had but one. The finger-tips of his vague, small, inert, white hand continually approached his mouth and, rising thence, described an arc in the air—a sort of invisible suspension-bridge for the passage of his i-de-a to us. His face, too, while he talked, had but one expression—a faintly-illumined blank. Usually, when even the most phlegmatic of men is talking, you shall detect changes of expression. In Moore you never could. Usually the features of the most vivacious man's face retain the form that Nature assigned to them. But in Moore's face, immutable though the expression was, by some physical miracle the features were perpetually remoulding themselves. It was not merely that the chin receded and progressed, nor merely that the oval cheeks went rippling in capricious hollows and knolls: the contours of nose and brow, they too, had their vicissitudes. You think I exaggerate? Well, I myself, with Moore there before me, did sometimes doubt the evidence of my own eyes. It was possible that my eyes had been deceived. But the point then is that no face save Moore's ever deceived them in just this way.

I looked up at the small convex mirror on the wall—*the* mirror, of *The Mirror of the Past*—and said that it was a keen observer.

Max chuckled. He began to talk about Moore. Moore had no learning at all, Max said; for him everything was a sudden discovery, and Oscar Wilde had once complained to Max that 'George Moore is always conducting his education in public.' Max quoted Samuel Johnson on talkers—those who talk from a tank and those who talk from a stream. Irishmen, Max said, talk from a stream, Anglo-Saxons from a tank. Moore talked from a stream, and marvellously when he was in midstream, but he allowed himself to be diverted into backwaters that were sometimes muddy. Once he had got stuck in an inlet, he could not extricate himself. The thing in his conversation that Max liked best was his descriptions of scenery; Moore had an extra-ordinary feeling for natural scenery and an extraordinary gift for describing it. It irritated Max that invariably, when Moore was describing some field or wood or stream, he would bring into it a lady—met accidentally or by assignation—who swooned over him. In the years when Max was a drama critic, he developed a neat device for getting Moore on to the subject of scenery. Moore was a playwright, and he would ask Max what play he had been reviewing. Artfully, Max would say, 'Well, the play wasn't anything at all, but, really, never in my life have I seen such wonderful *scenery*.' This would ignite Moore, in a damp way: 'Ah, the scenery was wonderful, was it?' And off he would go, to Max's joy, on scenery—'perhaps some lovely vista in Ireland, don't you know, or in France, and it would be delightful. But after a time, inevitably, the shepherdesses would come in. Never was a man so importuned by imaginary women! I have never met a shepherdess. Have *you*? But Moore was always running into them—rather, they kept running into *him*. Evidently, they revived their craft just to conquer Moore. He was modest; they were not conquests *by* him, they were victories *over* him. In the same limp voice and Frenchified brogue, he would go on about it. He would have satisfied the democratic ideal, don't you know; he wasn't snobbish—barmaids, duchesses, waitresses, ladies of easy virtue, who forgot commerce, apparently, when they met *him*, and, in his idyllic moods, to which I often incited him, shepherdesses.'

Miss Jungmann brought in tea. Knowing that I was particularly interested in all those broadcasts that had been written thirty years before for *The Mirror of the Past*, she put on a record of one about H. B. Irving, the son of the great Henry. It turned out that H. B. Irving was the Oxford undergraduate who influenced Max more than anyone else there. Max describes the tremendous impact the young Irving had on Oxford. Max and I listened to a record of the broadcast. Irving, Max says, had the 'bent strut' of his father. He had a way of clapping you on the shoulder and saying "Ha!" at you that was stupefying. Max describes an undergraduate scene, a Sunday breakfast in one Bancroft's rooms:

> As he [Irving] crossed the threshold, he said in a deep voice, 'Ha!' He clapped a hand on Bancroft's shoulder, rather in the manner of a very eminent detective arresting a very unimportant thief. Then, with that hand still on that shoulder, he distributed nods and 'Ha!'s among the company—the company of 'supers'. His gaze alighted on *me*.

'This,' said Bancroft (with the pride of a 'super' who has a line to speak), 'is Mr. Beerbohm of Merton.'

'Ha!' He had a way of looking at one through his pince-nez, less intimidating only than a way he had of looking at one *over* his pince-nez. 'Ha!' he repeated. And then 'A brother of Beerbohm Tree, aren't you?'

'A half brother,' I said faintly.

'Ha!'

It was as though he had said 'That may or may not be an extenuating circumstance, I will consider it.'

Max doesn't remember much that Irving said during the breakfast, but he does remember that what Irving said 'had at the moment the effect of a Standard Work condensed by him for the occasion.' For the rest of that memorable Sunday, Max went around saying lightly to everyone he met, 'I met Young Irving at breakfast this morning.' There came a moment when Young Irving actually invited Max to lunch. 'I quaked,' Max recalls, 'as at the service of a writ, and was gratified as by a royal command.'

That lunch changed the whole course of Max's life. His brother Herbert had encouraged him to go in for either for diplomacy or for the Bar. Max, who knew that he had to go in for something, had rather decided on the Bar. To his horror, when he came to lunch he found himself alone with Young Irving. He was in a panic. To bolster his morale, he remembered a report that one of his masters at Charterhouse had written about him. ' "Has natural abilities of a rare order" —this phrase from a form-master's report came floating into my brain. Why should I not impress myself on Irving today as a man with abilities of a rare order?' But he couldn't. The pince-nez did him in. The 'Ha's' did him in. 'I felt,' says Max, 'I had no abilities of *any* order. That form-master had been a fool.' After lunch, there came a critical moment, a moment that Max had felt from the beginning would come—a question he dreaded.

'And what,' he [Irving] asked, 'are you going to do in after-life?'

'Well,' I said—and the poor monosyllable came out as a polysyllabical bet, 'we-e-e-e-ell,' after which the other poor

words came out in three separate gasps sped by a weak smile—
'as a matter of fact I'm—I'm thinking of—being called to the
Bar.'

And these words, at the very moment of utterance, became
untrue. I *had*, up to that moment, vaguely destined myself for
the Bar. But in expressing to Irving this ambition, I saw the
full absurdity of it and for good and all dropped it before he
had time to say (as he did with more than his usual gravity
say) 'Ha!'

Miss Jungmann next put on 'Nat Goodwin—and Another'.
Again, it had originally been written as a sketch for *The Mirror
of the Past*. The other was Hall Caine. Max tells how, in the
eighteen-nineties, he arrived at Jackwood, his brother Herbert's
country home, very late on a Saturday night. He was confronted
by an appalling sight: Hall Caine's hat was standing on an
oaken chest. Max felt terror at the imminence of confronting its
owner. Herbert was doing a play of Caine's, and the two of
them were upstairs in Herbert's study, conferring. Max had
never met Hall Caine, but this had not prevented him from
drawing widely publicized caricatures of him:

> I knew the hat. I had often caricatured it—it and its wearer.
> I knew them both well by sight. . . . With all the ribaldry of
> youth, I had persecuted Hall Caine. And here he was, under
> this roof. Here was his hat. . . . [One caricature] showed Hall
> Caine, with frenzied eyes and hair, bearing a sandwich-board
> on which his name was inscribed in lavish capitals. It had been
> reproduced on a small scale in one of the English papers. . . .
> He went to lecture in America, and, into whatsoever city he
> entered, always that presentment stared him in the face. It
> cropped up, with nerve-shattering iteration, in every local
> paper, often magnified to the scale of a full page.

Hall Caine was born, in 1853, with a great asset for success
in life—the total absence of a sense of humour. This enabled
him to turn out, with complete sincerity and in the conviction
of greatness, a series of novels and plays, which had tremendous
popularity. He wrote *The Deemster, The Christian* and *The
Eternal City*, the last of which Herbert Beerbohm Tree put on
at His Majesty's. It was *The Eternal City* that Caine and Herbert
were discussing upstairs while, below, Max was being pulverized by the author's hat. Seldom has a writer launched

himself on a fabulously successful career by the simple device of writing a fan letter, but that is what Caine did. He wrote such a letter, when he was working in an architect's office in Liverpool, to Dante Gabriel Rossetti. Rossetti answered; how could you not answer a letter full of such appreciation and detailing the efforts made by the writer to popularize his correspondent in Liverpool? One thing led to another, and the first thing Rossetti knew, Caine was staying with him, in his dishevelled house at 16 Cheyne Walk.

After we had listened to the Caine record, Max talked a bit about what is a perennial literary phenomenon—the vast discrepancy between writers who attain popular success and are anathema to the cognoscenti and those who are approved by the cognoscenti and have no public at all. In his youth, Max said, the great popular successes were Marie Corelli, Ouida, Mrs. Humphry Ward, and Hall Caine. At the parties he used to go to, he said, you could get a laugh just by *saying* 'Hall Caine'.

Max then went on to discuss other members of the Rossetti Circle. It was characteristic of Max that in speaking of the Rossetti Circle he should tell me he admired Dante Gabriel's sensible brother William Michael and, of the ladies—that is, the models employed by the Pre-Raphaelites—preferred the healthy Fanny Cornforth to the doomed Elizabeth Siddal. It must have been hard work for the Pre-Raphaelites to be constantly ethereal, and Miss Cornforth was bosomy and earthy. She afforded the Pre-Raphaelites a nice change from Pre-Raphaelitism; she was Rubensy. In the mid-thirties, Max had received from Sydney Cockerell several photographs of the Rossetti brothers, Swinburne, and Miss Cornforth. Cockerell had at that time just bought three drawings of Max's for the Fitzwilliam Museum, which he directed, and Max wrote, in acknowledgment of both benefactions:

DEAR MR. COCKERELL,
  It is a grand thing to be represented in the Fitzwilliam; and I am so glad that this honour is to befall me, and glad that I have been deemed worthy of it by you. . . .
  Meanwhile I return, with very many thanks for the joy they have given me, those wondrous little photographs. Miss

Cornforth is incredible. Credo accordingly—and indeed am but confirmed in a belief I already had—that she must have been just like that and almost like what (reading between the lines of D.G.R.'s presentments of her) I had made of her in one of those cartoons of which you were speaking in such kind terms the other day. William Michael is decidedly the most distinguished in aspect of the figures in that group of four. You and I were arguing, in Nicholson's studio, that William Michael had been underrated because he happened to be the one (superficially) dull man in a bevy of brilliant ones. Perhaps a time will come when he will be *over*-rated, as having been the one sane man among lunatics!—for there was, wasn't there? a silver thread of lunacy in the rich golden fabric of 16 Cheyne Walk.

In a drawing of Hall Caine in *Rossetti and His Circle*, Max represents the time when Caine was living with Rossetti. Theodore Watts-Dunton, the chronic caretaker of genius, is admonishing Caine, who is truculent. They are in the studio at 16 Cheyne Walk, Caine red-headed, red-moustached, red-goateed, and with a fanatical gleam in his eye—the gleam of a man who knows that he carries greatness in each hand, in the shape of two manuscripts of his own, which he is determined to read to Rossetti. He is, plainly, not going to take the advice that Watts-Dunton is offering him. Frederick Shields, a painter friend of Rossetti's, is standing near Watts-Dunton, backing him up. In the background, lying-sitting on a sofa, is Rossetti, corpulent, brooding, hearing the argument that concerns him but not listening. The caricature is called 'Quis Custodiet Ipsum Custodem?' and Max's caption reads:

THEODORE WATTS[-DUNTON]: Mr. Caine, a word with you! Shields and I have been talking matters over, and we are agreed that tonight and henceforth you *must* not and *shall* not read any more of your literary efforts to our friend. They are too—what shall I say?—too luridly arresting, and are the allies of insomnia.

In another caricature in *Rossetti and His Circle*, Max shows Rossetti embarked on an exciting project for a set of murals in the Oxford Union—'The Quest for the Holy Grail'. Rossetti, in brown smock and trousers, has one foot on a ladder, on his way to put the finishing touch on a symbolic Miss Siddal, who, with outstretched arms, is ready, presumably, to receive the find. Benjamin Jowett, a little man in a flat hat, is standing at the foot of the ladder. Max's caption is:

THE SOLE REMARK LIKELY TO HAVE BEEN MADE BY BENJAMIN JOWETT ABOUT THE MURAL PAINTINGS AT THE OXFORD UNION. 'And what were they going to do with the Grail when they found it, Mr. Rossetti?'

It was in the winter of 1917 that Max, re-creating a vanished *milieu* that he had never known first-hand, drew the caricatures for *Rossetti and His Circle*, while staying in a rented cottage at Far Oakridge, in Gloucestershire, near the home of William Rothenstein. The Beerbohms took their meals with the Rothensteins. To Rothenstein, who worshipped Giotto, Max once sent a sketch he had made of the Rothenstein family. He apologizes for what his sketch may make various members of the family suffer. 'But,' he goes on to say, 'there is in the whole design a sense of a *family*, I think—something spiritually real, though not up to the mark of our old friend Giotto—(I say *our* old friend, because I regard any friend of yours as a friend of mine).' Sir William describes in his memoirs how Max, wearing gloves and with a cane over one arm, used to walk over the snow carrying the Rossetti drawings carefully protected in a portfolio. 'No wonder Max was nervous of leaving his Rossetti caricatures in an empty cottage,' he writes, 'for they are now regarded as classics. What a remarkable reconstruction of a period! So intuitively truthful that one of William Michael's daughters wrote that no person living within their circle had given so accurate a picture of its physical and spiritual composition. Max, with his air of delicate sprightliness, is the profoundest critic of men I have known.'

As Max saw things, the silver thread of lunacy that wound through 16 Cheyne Walk also wound through the lives of many of his friends and acquaintances. From the Rossetti Circle, we went on to talk about D. H. Lawrence. Max leaned forward a bit in his chair. 'Oh, Lawrence,' he said. '*Poor* D. H. Lawrence!' The adjective was not uttered in condescension but in true sympathy for the afflicted. 'Poor D. H. Lawrence. He never realized, don't you know—he never suspected that to be stark, staring mad is somewhat of a handicap to a writer.'

I told Max that I had been tremendously moved by *Sons and Lovers* when I first read it, and that I had tried two later novels, which I couldn't read.

'Oh, of course,' Max said. '*Sons and Lovers!* Although his prose style was slovenly, he was a man of unquestionable genius. But then he became afflicted with Messiahdom, don't you know. Now, what equipment had poor D. H. Lawrence for Messiahdom? He was, in so many ways, a foolish man. He was not fastidious in his friendships. Anyone who took him for a great man he would welcome. He did not stop to question, don't you know, what other qualifications a person had. Anyone who would commune with him on Destiny'—Max capitalized the word with his voice—'he would welcome. As a result, he was always involved with quite inferior people. He was one of those unfortunate men who think that merely because they have done something, it is at once first-rate. Simply because *they* have done it. He had a glowing gift for nature, a real feeling for nature, and in this he was at his best. But through his landscapes cantered hallucinations.'

About the other Lawrence, T. E., the Arabian one, Max said he couldn't talk much, because in that Lawrence the mixture of genius and insanity was too heady for him to do more than sample it. Lawrence had translated the *Odyssey* and then denounced it, as 'pastiche and face powder'. 'He confused the *Odyssey*, you know, with his translation of it,' Max said to me. About Lawrence's translation of the *Odyssey*, Max once wrote to Rothenstein:

> What a strange thing, to be a super-eminent genius and hero, as Lawrence was, plus such streaks of sheer silliness. . . . I have read various extracts from that translation—read them with gasps. And I would rather not have been that translator than have driven the Turks out of Arabia.

Tracing the silver thread led Max to Ezra Pound. Pound had lived for a time in Rapallo, and Max used to see him. He laughed in recollection of one of those meetings. 'Ezra idolized his parents, you know, and they idolized him,' Max said. 'They thought the sun rose and set in him. They came from Idaho. He brought them here, and very nice, simple, unaffected people they were, too. Anyway, one afternoon we were all sitting down there on the terrace of one of the cafés'—Max waved a hand towards downtown Rapallo and the sea front—"and Ezra was talking away. Very entertaining! He was fond of making extravagant statements to amuse his friends, which, of course, he didn't expect them to take seriously. He was in one of those moods. His parents were staring at him, rapt, while he made these utterances. Ezra said, "The greatest master of French literature was Louis the Eighteenth." Ezra's father, who was sitting next to me, nudged me and beamed at me. "That kid," he said, "knows *everything*!" '

I told Max that I had been shown an anti-Semitic poem written by Pound against him. In it the spelling of Max's name was distorted. Max was interested, and not at all surprised. 'I am not Jewish,' he said. 'I cannot claim that. But then, you know, he is crazy. He greatly admired Mussolini. All that Fascist business! He did have one trait, though, that I didn't much care for.' Evidently, Max expected crazy people, outside of their craziness, to live up to some code of gentlemanliness. 'He would start out to rave about some friend, and you thought you were in for a paean of praise. And then the qualifications would creep in. And then you realized that he had begun with the paean in order to conclude with the denigration. The treacle of admiration, don't you know, was always strongly tinctured with the vinegar of envy.'

Max distinguished between people he considered all-out cranks and lunatics and those who were simply idiosyncratic. In his introduction to *Rossetti and His Circle*, he wrote:

> Byron, Disraeli, and Rossetti—these seem to me the three most interesting men that England had in the nineteenth century. England had plenty of greater men. Shelley, for example, was a far finer poet than Byron. But he was not in himself interesting: he was just a crystal-clear crank. To be interesting, a man must be complex and elusive.

On this ground, Max found neither Pound nor D. H. Lawrence interesting. Two complex men Max greatly admired as writers and liked as friends were G. K. Chesterton and Hilaire Belloc. 'They had blind spots,' he said, 'but they were delightful men. Such enormous gusto, you know, such gaiety, and feeling for life.' Max was merely amused by people who had blind spots. Sometimes, when he mentioned a blind spot in conversation, he would tap his forehead to indicate it. Max conveyed the idea that Chesterton and Belloc were men whose minds were vast and hospitable houses, with little dark closets in the attic into which—there were so many other rooms, gay and sunny— you didn't have to go. Robert Speaight, in a biography of Belloc, quotes Max as saying to his hero, 'When you really get talking, Hilary, you're like a great Bellocking ram, or like a Roman river full of baskets and dead cats.' Speaight also repeats a dry observation of Max's when he was told that Belloc had been to a cricket match: 'I suppose he would have said that the only good wicketkeeper in the history of the game was a Frenchman and a Roman Catholic.' Max told me he felt that Belloc was, on occasion, a victim of monomania. 'He had the conviction that there was only a single lane to Heaven,' Max said. 'It suited him, for example, to believe that Dreyfus was guilty. Ergo'—Max tapped his forehead—'Dreyfus *was* guilty.'

Somerset Maugham, in a series of articles on ten great novelists he wrote some years ago, made the flat statement that Balzac was the only one of them to whom he would without hesitation ascribe genius. Commenting on this, Max told me that he thought it was absurd to single out Balzac. 'Tolstoy and Dostoevsky had great genius,' he said, 'and Dickens had it, too, in spite of his dreadful faults.' Nevertheless, except for Turgenev and, at times, Tolstoy, Max had serious doubts about the Russian novelists. He felt that too much of what they wrote was also touched by lunacy. He knew that Dostoevsky was terrifying, and even majestic, but then so was Mont Blanc, and Max wouldn't have liked to live on Mont Blanc. In 1913, Max wrote an essay, 'Kolniyatsch', in which he lampooned the vogue for the Russian novelists among the British intelligentsia. Kolniyatsch (the word is a Russification of Colney Hatch, which was once London's most famous lunatic asylum) is a Russian writer—a composite of Dostoevsky and

Gorky. Kolniyatsch, says Max, developed slowly: 'It was not before his eighteenth birthday that he murdered his grandmother and was sent to that asylum in which he wrote the poems and plays belonging to what we now call his earlier manner.' Was Kolniyatsch an optimist or a pessimist? Max analyses:

> By more than one critic he has been called a pessimist, and it is true that a part of his achievement may be gauged by the lengths to which he carried pessimism—railing and raging, not, in the manner of his tame forerunners, merely at things in general, or at women, or at himself, but lavishing an equally fierce scorn and hatred on children, on trees and flowers and the moon, and indeed on everything that the sentimentalists have endeavoured to force into favour. On the other hand, his burning faith in a personal Devil, his frank delight in earthquakes and pestilences, and his belief that every one but himself will be brought back to life in time to be frozen to death in the next glacial epoch, seem rather to stamp him as an optimist.

Max's great enthusiasms in literature were for Jane Austen, Trollope, Turgenev, George Meredith, Charles Lamb, Henry James, E. M. Forster. He adored Meredith's early manner— *The Adventures of Harry Richmond* particularly—and Henry James's later. *The Golden Bowl* and *The Wings of the Dove* were, Max thought, James's greatest achievements. These writers had no chalets on Mont Blanc, but they took him into realms where he did want to live. Max was on especially good terms with Trollope. 'He reminds us,' said Max, 'that sanity need not be Philistine.' Max told me he thought *The Warden* a perfect novel, and the cello-playing Mr. Harding was one of his favourite musicians, especially when he was playing a cello he didn't have with him. The literature of epilepsy, of cosmic soul-searching, of uncontrollable violence simply had no appeal for him. About the Elizabethans he felt something of what he felt about the Russians. In a Rede Lecture he gave at Cambridge, in which he paid tribute to Lytton Strachey, the only reservation he made was about Strachey's *Elizabeth and Essex*. He said it was a 'brave' thing for Strachey to have tried but that, at best, it was only 'guesswork'. To Max, that far-off world, where murders, sudden decapitations, rushings off to the Tower were part of the climate, as natural as April showers, was incomprehensible and unseizable, and he felt that it must have been so to Strachey also, who was a master of style, and hence of form. He said, 'A very robustious, slapdash writer might convince me that he was in close touch with the souls of those beings whose actions and motives are to me as mysterious as those of wild animals in an impenetrable jungle. You rightly infer that I am *not* a Sixteenth Century man. And I make so bold as to say "Neither was Lytton Strachey". '

Max shied away from lunacy not only in its violent forms but also in its milder forms, one of these being utopianism. 'Good sense about trivialities is better than nonsense about things that matter,' he once said. He had a horror of utopians, a suspicion of 'big' ideas. Some of Shaw's writings bored him, because they were impressments into what he called 'the strait-jacket of panacea'. The effort to force men into this strait-jacket had caused untold misery and suffering to the human race, he thought. Rothenstein once said of Max that he was always amiable except when his sense of sanity was outraged. For Max, even to take oneself entirely seriously was a form of insanity. Listening to Max on the subject, I came to see that what for him constituted sanity was a recognition of one's own limitations. He had—without ever formulating it—a Theory of Limits. Max countered Browning's 'Ah, but a man's reach should exceed his grasp, Or what's a heaven for?' with the statement that many of his friends had gone to hell in just that way. Max liked the attainable, the tangible, the comprehensible, the small in scale.

At the outbreak of the First World War, Max said that it had made life 'epical', but he indicated a distaste for the epical. He wanted life to be liveable rather than epical. Although when he was a boy, he hero-worshipped statesmen—he later recalled those days of veneration in a broadcast, 'A Small Boy Seeing Giants'—he gradually came to be suspicious of 'giganticity'. Napoleon, as an example of overwhelming giganticity, repelled him. Caricatures that Max drew, as a young man, of the great aristocratic politicians of his day were so vivid that he was discharged from two magazines he worked for, the

Bystander and the *Sketch,* because of objections from the adver-
tisers. He cared just as little for 'giganticity' when it doffed its
silk hat and assumed the cloth cap of Labour. Labour resented
his delineations more than the aristocrats did. The latter went
hunting, but Labour, without this resource, stewed in grievance.
Max was on neither side; he punctured the vanities of the
aristocrats, and he didn't see why he should spare those of the
Labourites.

In 1921, he dedicated to Britannia his book of caricatures
called *A Survey,* addressing her formally:

> Madame, I venture to dedicate this volume to you because
> you have always been very kind to me, and because I cannot
> think *why* you have always been so kind to me.

In the dedication, Max is aware that his career as a satirist
must have occasionally irritated his lady. He does not defend
himself but tries to explain:

> In my youth, and indeed until quite recent years, the Court
> was a very dominant factor in your life. A satirist, instinctively,
> goes for what is very strong: the weaker things he derides with
> less gusto, or not at all. But you, Madam, have a great respect
> for strength, and it is the weaker things that are aptest to tickle
> your sense of humour. I myself have a respect for strength, but
> also I am inclined, in my fallen nature, to look for the weak
> points that all strength has, and to point them rudely out.
> I used to laugh at the Court and at the persons around it; and
> this distressed you rather. I never laughed with you at Labour.
> Labour didn't seem to me quite important enough yet. But
> Labour is very important now, very strong indeed; as you have
> found. And I gathered, this year, from a certain mild downward
> curve of your lips when I laid out for you on the yellow sands
> those of my new drawings which referred to Labour, that you
> thought me guilty of not the very best taste in failing to bow
> my knee to your new Baal.
>   Perhaps I ought to exclude these few drawings from a book
> dedicated to you. Do I compromise you by their inclusion?
> I hope not. I *think* not. You have but to say to Labour, 'O
> honoured and darling and terrifying Sir, *I* know you're perfect.
> Don't blame *me* for some drawings done by an utterly absurd
> man who lives ever so far away in a country shaped like a
> jack-boot.' But if such words avail not, and you deem it

expedient to reject the dedication, then reject it, dear Britannia :
I shall not be thereby the less affectionately your old servant,
MAX BEERBOHM.

Max's aversion to giganticity ran through his views on
everything—not only on the aristocrats and Labour but on
dictators, intellectual as well as military (he shrank especially
from totalitarians of the intellect), on skyscrapers, on cities.
The London that Max loved was not the big city but, rather,
what he called the 'congeries of villages'. He wrote about
Bloomsbury, Chelsea, and Bayswater as if they were different
countries, each with its own flavour and idiosyncrasy, producing
different races of people. Bloomsbury he deplored; the pedestrians there didn't seem to have confidence in themselves.
Chelsea he loved, because it had a river, always a freshener; and
Bayswater, because it had Kensington Gardens. He felt that
cities, like egos, became unmanageable when they got too big.
They were no longer on the human scale; you couldn't live in
or with them. His aversion extended even to motor-cars that,
in a temporal form of bigness, went too fast. At the end of a
B.B.C. broadcast he called 'Speed', which he and Miss Jungmann and I listened to that afternoon in 1955, he offered
consolation to those whom he had just berated for exceeding
the speed limit :

> But here is a heartening fact for you. We are all of us travel-
> ling at a tremendous rate, and we shall always continue to do
> so. We shall not, it is true, be able to get rid of our speed-limit.
> But it is a very liberal one. 1,110 miles a minute is not a limit
> to be grumbled at. Our planet is not truly progressing, of
> course: it is back at its starting-point every year. But it never
> for an instant pauses in its passage through space. Nor will it
> do so even when, some billions of years hence, it shall have
> become too cold for us human beings to exist upon its surface.
> It will still be proceeding at its present pace: *1,110 miles a minute.*
> This, Ladies and Gentlemen, is indeed a beautiful and a
> consoling thought—a thought for you to sleep on, to dream of.
> Sleep well. Dream beautifully. In fact—Good Night.

Max's attitude towards bigness was essential to his own view
of himself as an artist. He had a severely topiary intelligence;
he knew where he could go and where he couldn't go, what he

could do and what he couldn't do. 'I am not creative in a big way,' he said to me that day. 'I haven't any powerful invention; I used up all I had. What I really am is an essayist.' In an admiring essay on Whistler's prose style, he wrote, 'An exquisite talent like Whistler's, whether in painting or in writing, is always at its best on a small scale. On a large scale it strays and is distressed. . . . For no man who can finely grasp a big theme can play exquisitely round a little one.' Max ungrudgingly acknowledged the greatness of the wild geniuses who brought up the big guns; at the same time, he felt no obligation to like all that they wrote, and no regret that he was not one of them. Discussing the fact that Lytton Strachey was not one of them, either, he wrote, 'Very exquisite literary artists seldom are men of genius. Genius tends to be careless in its strength. Genius is, by the nature of it, always in rather a hurry. Genius can't be bothered about perfection.' Max could be bothered.

That June, on the next-to-last day I spent with Max, as we sat in our traditional spot in the niche, he talked about his old college, Merton. Once more it was teatime, and once more Miss Jungmann brought us tea. Max told me he thought that of all the novels written about Oxford the best was Compton Mackenzie's *Sinister Street*. 'There is no book on Oxford like it,' he said. 'It gives you actual Oxford *experience*. What Mackenzie has miraculously done is to make you feel what each *term* was like; it was different in each term. Mackenzie notes the separate colour of each term. It evokes for me, more powerfully than anything else that has been written about Oxford, my own years at Merton. It is the epitome of a lifetime, you know—one's history as an undergraduate. It is a life span, from youth in your first year to old age in your last. When you begin, you look up to the third-year men, they are your heroes. By the time you're a third-year man yourself, those heroes are gone, you see yourself inroaded by a horde of younger men, you feel your own youth gone, your time past; you have become a survivor into a time you do not know. Merton was one of the smaller colleges and, with two exceptions, the oldest. It was the most intimate.' Max looked at me almost with an air of apology. 'I still, you know, spend much time in Merton.'

He spent a good deal of time, too, I learned, with his mother and his sisters in Upper Berkeley Street. From Merton, the talk went to those early days in London, and his eyes brightened in recollection. 'Let me tell you about a phrase that was current in our family,' he said. 'My mother, you know, was very amusing and very amusable. When she and my father were separated, they used to write each other long letters, which they tried to make as delightful as they could. Such letters are not written nowadays. It was traditional for my friends to come to Sunday lunch when we lived in Upper Berkeley Street. My friends adored my mother and sisters. My sister Dora was dreamy and abstracted. She became a nun when she was nineteen years old. But my sisters Constance and Agnes were very gay. I still see my mother presiding at those lunches. She was small, you know, and had alert eyes; she always wore a black silk dress and a lace cap—very dignified—but what my friends knew was that she had a volatile humour, and they used to be very gay, those lunches, animated by my mother. Well, we had a catch phrase in the family that had a protean use, for praise or for the reverse—"It's a first-class thing." It came from Johnston Forbes-Robertson. He was somewhere, in some drawing-room, and he noticed a mezzotint of some eighteenth-century admiral that hung on the wall. He reflected how dreary it was. Mrs. Patrick Campbell sailed in. Her eye went at once to the admiral. She began rhapsodizing about him; she became aerated about that admiral—to the delight of the host, of course, who was a bigwig and hadn't realized he had such a master-piece on his wall. Mrs. Campbell couldn't say enough about the mezzotint—it made the room, it transported you. When she had done, she swept down on Johnston. "Don't you agree?" she demanded. Johnston was determined to puncture the tyre of Mrs. Campbell's ecstasy. "Yes," he said calmly, "it's a first-class thing." We never stopped using it. When I was drama critic on the *Saturday* and came back to Upper Berkeley Street after a play and my mother asked me about it, that phrase would save me more ample criticism. It was a wonderful short cut for settling so many questions. My sister Constance came home one day and summoned my mother and me; she was quivering to tell us what had happened. She knew in advance it was the kind of thing my mother would adore. Well, Constance had been walking along the street and met Willie Wilde —Oscar's brother. In one hand he was carrying a huge leg of mutton by the narrow part; with his free hand he swept off his hat and bent over double in a grand, ceremonial bow. There was something so grotesquely funny in the way she did it, conveying both the mutton and the bow. We decided it was a first-class thing.

'Willie Wilde, in one of those rare intervals when he was in funds, took my sister Dora to lunch. Willie was in one of his euphoric moods.' Max, who loved to imitate the grandiose, slid into an affectation of grandiosity. ' "Dora," Willie said, "I feel most imperial this morning, rampantly imperial. I like the feeling of getting up in the morning and thinking, Well, I've got Egypt, I've got Ceylon, I've got Singapore, I've got large areas in Africa. . . ." ' Max brought his hands to the little tea table in front of him in a climactic gesture that was almost devotional; his voice dropped to an awesome whisper. ' "And now, dear Dora, you are the first to know—I've got India!" In something of a flurry, Dora reported the whole thing to Constance. Constance comforted her. "Well, my dear, don't worry. Willie hasn't *really* got India, you know." '

I had lent Max a book about Mrs. Frank Leslie, the widow of an American nineteenth-century newspaper tycoon. Mrs. Leslie had married Willie Wilde, and for this reason I thought the biography might interest Max. He had the book on the tea table next to his chair. He picked up the book and a pencil and, on the inside of the back cover, rapidly sketched Oscar and Willie for me. These are probably the last drawings Max ever did, though he did not regard them as drawings. 'Scratches,' he called them, and yet they are quite remarkable, too. You see that the two men are brothers, all right: Willie, flabby and amiable, hoping for the best, and doomed; Oscar, grinning in Hades, ghastly, and doomed. After giving me the now illustrated book, as a kind of thanks for lending it to him, Max went on talking about Willie Wilde, who, I found, interested him more than Oscar did. Even when it came to failures, he preferred the small ones to those on the heroic scale. There in the niche, he brought back to life a scene in a restaurant between him and Willie.

'I made an engagement with Willie to have a drink in a little restaurant we used to like to go to,' Max said. 'The waiter, who was an old friend of ours, was called Bismarck. He did not resemble the other Bismarck in any way; his name just happened to be Bismarck. Well, we were sitting there talking about literature and life when, abruptly, Willie revealed that his mind was not really on aesthetics. "Beerbohm," he said, "I'd like you to lend me ten shillings." I said that I would. Exhilarated by a sudden feeling of affluence, Willie decided to order something, and whistled for Bismarck. He didn't mean anything by it. It was just that he had been put off balance—he was childish, you know—by the prospect of unearned increment; it was pure high spirits. But Bismarck was affronted. He turned angrily on Willie. "Don't you whistle for me," he said. "I am not a dog. My name is Bismarck." You know, I will never forget it. Everything went out of Willie. He began to stammer out apologies to the waiter. "But, my dear fellow," he kept mumbling, "my dear fellow . . . I didn't mean . . . I meant nothing. . . ." It was awful, you know—that sudden capitulation. In that moment, I believe, he really saw, and perhaps for the first time, the dingy failure of his life; even behind the bulwark of that ten shillings, he saw himself facing tragedy and defeat, he saw that there was nothing ahead for him, that he would never recover, that he would never find a clearing in the shambles he had made for himself. He saw the end, and I saw it, too. It was very painful.'

Max told me some more about Willie. 'He was, as I said, childish. I mean childish in the sense that a child is happily free of any thought of the future and seizes upon what is immediately before him and desirable. It is curious how often one encounters the phenomenon among grown men. Willie had been working for the *Telegraph*, but after he had gone to America to marry Mrs. Leslie, and then been divorced and returned to England, the *Telegraph* no longer wanted him. He began doing drama criticism for unimportant papers and writing general articles in which he would mention tradespeople and get perquisites; I daresay that's how he got the leg of mutton he was carrying when he met my sister in the street. He came to know a delightful lady, a widow with two children, who was greatly interested in him. She was very well off, and we thought we should no longer have to worry about Willie. Willie had really a wonderful way with children. He used to go up to the nursery and play with these two children, and they couldn't wait for his visits, because his affection for them was genuine and they felt it. He used to impersonate a bear. He was enormous, you know, but he would get down on his hands and knees, and he made a really wonderful bear. He was a tame bear, and the children rode him. One day he came—it was just before Christmas—and said, "Now I am a burglar come to rob you, and you must catch me and tame me just as you did when I was a bear." There was a bank affixed to the wall in which the children, all year, had collected pennies, and from time to time their elders had dropped into it coins of larger denomination—even sovereigns. It was not to be opened till Christmas. The burglar advanced on the bank. The children, in a state of great excitement, were about to catch him and denounce him. And then, suddenly, obeying some imperious impulse of childhood, Willie ripped the bank off the wall and ran out of the room and out of the house, and was never seen there again.'

Miss Jungmann had told me that between my last visit to Rapallo and this one two old friends had come to call on Max at the Villino—Somerset Maugham and Max's one-time fiancée Constance Collier. I asked Max what he and Maugham had talked about.

'Oh, old times,' Max said. 'Maugham and I recalled a couple we knew—the Davises. Mr. Davis was a questionable character from the City, who took pride in his vulgarity. Still, the Davises were art collectors and patrons, and very hospitable, and Maugham and I used to enjoy their hospitality. They were very kind, for instance, to Charles Conder. He was an exquisite artist, Conder. He used to go in, you know, for glades, with princesses and fairies appearing at intervals. People would flock to the Davises'. They were always giving fancy-dress balls. For one of them I engaged a costume at the costumier's; I went as a cardinal—a rather second-rate cardinal. When I arrived, I found Mr. Davis on the steps of a throne, dressed as Queen Elizabeth. He used to take these costume parties very seriously. He would put on his costumes the night before so as to get used to them: he had probably been Queen Elizabeth all night. Also on the steps, just below Mr. Davis, there was a really magnificent cardinal. I was fascinated by what I saw. The cardinal on the steps was, I knew, a business rival of Mr. Davis's. Mr. Davis had been hounding him, and now, as Queen, he had him by the throat. The cardinal had come to plead; the Queen forced him to the wall and told him that the only resolution of his dilemma was to commit suicide. Mr. Davis had worked the whole thing out. He had suggested to his rival to come as a cardinal; he wanted to have his revenge in style. When the magnificent cardinal passed me on his way out, his face was ashen. He was a lost man. And, do you know, he did commit suicide. I told Maugham it was a story after his own style; I wondered he had never used it.'

A Mr. and Mrs. Steevens emerged from the shades. 'When Maugham and I were young, we were both hard up, you know,' Max said, 'and we used to go every Tuesday night to dinner at the house of a delightful couple named Steevens. Mr. Steevens was quite a different cup of tea from Mr. Davis. He was a first-rate classical scholar and became a prominent journalist; he was really a remarkable man. At the end, he was working for Lord Northcliffe, who sent him to South Africa at the time of the Boer War. Mrs. Steevens was an American, and owned a fortune. She devoted herself to general and private philanthropies—especially on Tuesday nights. It was a great comfort in those days to know that on Tuesday night you could count on a really good dinner. Mrs. Steevens would invite Maugham, G. S. Street, Reggie Turner, and myself. Maugham and I recalled those Tuesday nights. Among Mrs. Steevens' public philanthropies was an orphanage she supported; when her charges grew up and went out into the world from the orphanage, she used to employ various of them on her household staff. She had a very well-run house, don't you know, but I remember that it used to be somewhat disconcerting to hear her say to the butler, for example, "Dearest, will you bring in the cocktails?" or "Darling, will you give Mr. Beerbohm one of those nice little cakes?" Of course, she had known all her staff from their infancies. Still, it used rather to startle us. When Maugham was here, he and I laughed over it.'

'And what about Constance Collier, Max?' I asked. 'Elisabeth tells me that just a few months before she died she sat in this very chair and had tea with you.'

'We talked mostly of our days in Dieppe, when the future was becomingly veiled, don't you know, and when youth seemed a natural state, the only imaginable state,' Max said. 'Dieppe was a simple fishing village then, and very cheap. Constance used to come there with her mother. It was there that Constance and I became engaged. It was also in Dieppe that I finally decided to be a writer. Maupassant and Meredith were my heroes. Meredith I could not hope to emulate, but Maupassant, since he was so cunningly simple, deceived me into thinking that I *could* emulate him. I have described it all in an essay.'

The essay is called 'A Relic'. Max describes how, rummaging about in an old trunk, he came upon the fragments of a fan. The moment he came upon these fragments, he heard himself murmuring a sentence: 'Down below, the sea rustled to and fro over the shingle.' He goes on to recall an incident of his youth. Max was nineteen. He was sitting at a table of the café on the terrace of the casino in Dieppe, drinking a bock, when he beheld a startling scene. A woman of about thirty rushed by him, pursued by a short, fat man of about fifty-five. '*Écoute, Angélique*,' gasped the perspiring bourgeois. '*Écoute, je te supplie.*' But Angélique wouldn't. She rushed through the swinging doors, the suppliant following. The waiter picked up the remnants of a fan Angélique had broken in her anger, and gave them to Max. After paying for his bock, he followed them; they were nowhere to be seen. Next day, he waited for them, but they did not appear. He never saw them again. Nevertheless, the vision of their faces, Angélique's 'positively dull with rage', made an inescapable impression on him. He tried to reconstruct their story in his imagination, and this reconstruction, he fancied, would make a *conte*, like a *conte* of Maupassant's. He decided to call it 'The Fan'—very Maupassantish. Maupassant would have needed no more; why should he need more? He felt very cynical and worldly, and, after all, Maupassant was so simple; Maupassant was just an observer, like him. Of course, Maupassant was much older than Max and had observed more, but Max had the advantage of having soaked up all of Maupassant's observations in Maupassant. Day after day, Max sat at the table of the terrace café, with a bock and the fan fragments before him, and at last he wrote the first sentence of the first story by the English Maupassant: 'Down below, the sea rustled to and fro over the shingle.' Max liked these words; he liked them so much that he decided they would end his story, too. He began to feel sorry for Maupassant. Could Maupassant brook a rival? He had the '*chose vue*', just as Maupassant so often had; the problem was to get the '*chose à figurer*'. He went to the café every night, he kept fingering the fragments of the fan, but, he is forced to confess, 'the plum did not ripen'. He had the provocative beginning ('Down below, the sea rustled to and fro over the shingle'), he had the mournful ending ('Down below, the sea rustled to and fro over the shingle'); what he couldn't get was the intervening material. Max could never finish that story, but he did finish the essay he wrote about not finishing it: 'The chord this relic strikes in me is not one of curiosity as to that old quarrel, but (if you will forgive me) one of tenderness for my first effort to write, and for my first hopes of excellence.'

I told Max that I knew the essay, and that it was lucky he hadn't finished 'The Fan', because it would have deprived us of 'A Relic'.

Max smiled. Then he said, 'Please find Elisabeth and ask her to give you the little snapshots of Dieppe.'

When I brought in the snapshots, Max took them and we looked at them together. He concentrated on one in particular.

'There it is,' he said. 'The very terrace, the very café—not the very bock—and Constance and myself sitting there. Walter Sickert, I believe, took this snapshot.' Constance is wearing a beribboned, flowered, floppy straw hat and a light summer dress. A parasol is slung over her shoulder. Max is wearing a white flannel suit, with a flower in the buttonhole; his straw hat is in front of him on the table, and his hand is resting on the head of his walking stick. Somehow he endows the *plein-air* costume with an aura of urban elegance.

I remarked on how lovely Constance looked.

'Doesn't she? Doesn't she?' Max said. 'She was beautiful, you know, and with everything before her. My brother Herbert had great plans for her; Coquelin adored her and gave her acting lessons. And I—well, I was on the verge of supplanting Maupassant.'

During her recent visit, Max said, Constance had reminded him of a 'wicked joke' he had played on her in Dieppe. 'Wicked,' Max repeated, full of unashamed guilt.

I inquired, of course, about this lapse.

'Well, you know, there used to be visiting theatrical companies who came there from Paris and played,' he said. 'It was a holiday for the actors, too. I took Constance to a matinée of one of these performances—a comedy. Now, Constance didn't know a word of French. The audience started to laugh, and as Constance hadn't the faintest idea of what was going on and as I imagined she felt stupid at not seeing anything to laugh at, I began to improvise the play for her. I converted it into a drama, so there would be nothing to laugh at. My drama was so heartbreaking, you know, that Constance began to cry. But the audience kept laughing, and this laughter seemed callous and incomprehensible to Constance. She asked me what the others were laughing at. I explained to her that this was a provincial audience, very crude and insensitive to pathos. By the time the curtain fell, Constance was so *émotionnée* that I confessed what I had done. It took some time before she forgave me, but the other day we laughed over it.'

I asked Max whether Constance had mentioned the man she finally did marry, the actor Julian L'Estrange.

'No, we didn't talk about anything, really, that happened after Dieppe,' Max said. 'We remembered all the people who used to come to Dieppe: Aubrey Beardsley and his sister; the painter Pissarro—he was an old man then; Reggie Turner, who went there before we did, Tommy Chaine; Will Rothenstein; my brother Julius. We remembered the English church where Constance and I decided to be married and where we weren't. We remembered them all—and it was delightful to remember them. We talked about Titine.'

'Who was Titine?' I asked.

'She was Mme Lefèvre and ran the hotel Chez Lefèvre, where we all lived in those days,' Max said. 'Sickert was very taken with her. Titine was the soul of Chez Lefèvre. She was enchanting, Titine. We did everything through Titine. We all shamelessly curried favour with her. The food was wonderful. When I was in favour, Titine would see to it that I got something special. I would crow over Sickert. Since Sickert would share the dish, I was not slow to point out the advantage to him of having me for a friend.'

I asked Max whether he had shown Constance the snapshots.

'Oh, yes,' he said. 'She was very shortsighted, you know. She held them close to her eyes. "Is that *us*, Max?" she said. "Are they really *us*?" '

Miss Jungmann came into the room to pick up the tea things, and Max and I, half in Dieppe, half in Rapallo, said good night.

The following day, a friend of mine, Mr. Stanley Marcus, of Dallas, Texas, who is a lover and collector of books, arrived in Portofino and called me to ask if he might meet Max. Mr. Marcus had with him a sheaf of assorted, non-consecutive pages of a printing of *The Happy Hypocrite* by the eminent typographer Bruce Rogers. Rogers had done these as sample pages for a fine edition, had been unable to find a publisher, and had done no more. Mr. Marcus hoped that Max would write his name in this curiosity. Max said that he would be delighted to receive Mr. Marcus, and that he knew and admired the work of Bruce Rogers. As it happened, I was at that time called away from Rapallo for several days, but the visit took place and, Miss

9

Jungmann later reported, went off handsomely. Max asked Mr. Marcus to leave the Bruce Rogers with him, because he wished to make certain emendations in it.

Max's careful labour on these random pages was the last literary task that he ever undertook. The task he set himself was to make the sense carry over from one page to the next as if he had originally written them that way, and it required great ingenuity. For example, one page ended, 'And in the middle of this vain galaxy hung the pre-' The next page, since it was far away, gave you no idea of what it was that hung in the middle of the vain galaxy. At the bottom of the first of these pages, Max added, in his strong and beautiful handwriting, 'sent writer's eviscerated book'. One page ended, 'Presently he heard a footstep in the hall beyond, and a pair of'. The next page began, 'soon forgot him'. Max caused these disparities to coalesce: 'Presently he heard a footstep in the hall beyond, and a pair of *boots appeared with nobody in them, and at sight of them he uttered a piercing scream. But he soon forgot them—and they, it appears,* soon forgot him.'

Max was to work for weeks on this. When it was finished, he was to send it to Mr. Marcus, in Texas, with the following inscription:

> DEAR MR. STANLEY MARCUS:
> Here is the book that you left with me. I have dared to amend, here and there, what seemed to me a lack of continuity in the narration.
>
> Yours very sincerely,
> Rapallo, 1955.   MAX BEERBOHM.

When, long before Max's self-imposed task was completed, I came back to Rapallo, it turned out to be for only one day. I found that I had to leave immediately for New York. That afternoon, I went to the Villino to bid Max good-bye. Miss Jungmann, without saying much, took me to the terrace. We stood in the middle of it.

'Look,' said Miss Jungmann, pointing to the open door of Max's blue-walled study.

I looked. Max, completely unaware of us, was bent over his work-table, writing. He was wearing glasses; he looked very tiny. He was using pen and ink, and the pen kept dipping into the inkpot. He was supplying Bruce Rogers' sample pages of *The Happy Hypocrite* with a continuity. He was working with the avidity and the concentration of a writer slaving to meet a deadline at the end of which glitters a pot of gold. Again, and for the last time, he was working to amuse one reader.

'I hate to disturb him,' I said.

'Oh, no,' said Miss Jungmann. 'He knows you are going. He's waiting for you. Go in. I'll wait for you downstairs.'

I walked into the study. Max finished the sentence he was working on, and looked up. He showed me what he had done to the Rogers pages. I told him that I thought it was ingenious as well as funny, and he was pleased at having solved a technical problem of a kind that had not theretofore been presented to him. We walked out on to the terrace and took up our familiar post at the parapet, and looked for a moment or two at the Swinburne tree. For once, a silence fell between us. I became conscious—and, I feel sure, so did he—that this might be a long farewell. To quench this feeling, to stave it off, I began asking him about *The Happy Hypocrite*.

The Happy Hypocrite is a fantasy, set in the time of the Regency, about a dissolute nobleman, Lord George Hell, who falls in love with a stage performer of great beauty and innocence named Jenny Mere. Jenny won't have anything to do with Lord George; his reputation, not unearned, is truly dreadful, and his personal appearance, which reflects his dissoluteness, is also dreadful. Lord George suddenly sees himself in the light of Jenny's aversion and shares it. He goes to a famous mask-maker and commissions from him a saintly and beautiful mask, which is fitted to him so cunningly that none of his friends know him. Miss Mere herself doesn't recognize him. Wearing his mask, he proposes to her, and she accepts him. Lord George gives away his money, his houses, and all his other possessions, and lives with Jenny in the country, idyllically happy. At the end, a former mistress exposes him to Jenny. The mask is removed, and—lo and behold!—Lord George's face has been transformed into what the mask was; he *is* saintly, and he *is* beautiful.

I said to Max that Jenny Mere seemed to me like one of the two girls in white in his cherished photograph, and like the little girl laughing up at the Abbé, only without freckles.

Max looked pleased. He stared out across the Gulf of Genoa, still and blue. 'I have always been interested in masks, you know,' he said. 'So was Yeats. I once began to collaborate with Aubrey Beardsley on a book about masks. We never finished it.'

'It would be easy,' I said, 'if just by buying a mask of goodness, a mask of beauty, you could achieve them both.'

'But, oh, you have to live *up* to the mask, you know,' said Max. 'Lord George lived *up* to the mask. His love for Jenny made it possible for him to do it.'

I remembered, not with total irrelevance, a caricature of Max's on good and evil. It is called 'Things in General'. It shows 'The Principle of Evil', a satanic figure in a kirtle, doing a Devil's dance around the personification of 'The Principle of Good', a matronly woman, with plaited braids, who is obese from being habitually sedentary. In fact, she is plain slobby. The legend reads:

> THE PRINCIPLE OF GOOD: How is it that you always seem to get the best of it?
> THE PRINCIPLE OF EVIL: Because I'm *active*, my dear.

I mentioned this caricature to Max. He stroked his moustache. He was staring across the gulf as if it were eternity. 'Well,' he said, 'Lord George Hell found a way of making The Principle of Good active, I suppose. Of course, we're all caught up in a chaos of evil impulses. There are many Lord Georges. In fact, there are more Lord Georges than there are masks.'

Another silence fell between us. I knew I had to leave. I hated to leave. Max went on, 'Do you know my favourite line of Henry James?'

I could see that he was not really expecting an answer from me—that he was communing with himself.

'It is "Be generous and delicate and pursue the prize".' Max's eyes were still fixed on the sun-dotted sea. 'He didn't always live up to it, of course. Who can? But in his work he did live up to it. It was *his* mask.' There was a pause. Max looked at me and smiled. 'If you live up to a good manner long enough, don't you know, perhaps it will become first nature to you, instead of second, or third.'

Miss Jungmann called from the foot of the stone steps. Charlie had arrived and was waiting with my taxi.

I shook hands with Max. I told him that I was planning to be in France for the winter, and that it would be a happy day for me when next I crossed the threshold of the Villino.

'I wish you everything you could wish for yourself,' said Max. We stood in silence for a moment. Max looked across the gulf. He turned to me again, with a little smile and a little gesture towards the horizon. 'The same old sea,' he said.

It was not until April of 1956 that I was able to sail for France, and from there I planned to go immediately to Rapallo. The letters I had been receiving from Miss Jungmann were alternately depressed and cheerful, depending on Max's spirits and how he seemed in strength on a particular day. In the last letter I received from her before I sailed, she asked me to bring a special kind of vitamin pill, which was unobtainable in Rapallo. I stocked up on these pills. Just after I checked into my hotel in Paris, on the seventeenth of April, I put in a call to Miss Jungmann. There was no answer at the Villino. Several hours later, she returned my call. Max had been taken to a hospital in Rapallo. He had not been sleeping, and his heart was weak; he had consented to go. She asked me if I had the vitamin pills. I told her to tell Max that I had enough to make it possible for him to enter the Olympic Games. She asked me please to come, and I said that of course I would. She did not seem unduly depressed; she felt that Max had a good chance to pull out of it.

I left the next morning, by car. From the road, I called Miss Jungmann at the hospital. She said Max was delighted that I was coming, and had laughed at the idea of entering the Olympic Games. In the evening of the next day, as I was having dinner at the Grand-Hôtel du Cap, in Antibes, I was called to the telephone. Miss Jungmann said that Max had not had a good night, that he was scarcely eating anything, that he was suffering. I told her I was leaving in the morning by car and would arrive at the hospital in the early evening.

Next evening, I was there, in Rapallo and at the hospital. Miss Jungmann had a small room next to Max's, on an upper floor. Max was asleep. She felt that I probably shouldn't see him that evening, even if he woke up; she was afraid that the excitement might be harmful. The next evening might be better, she said. As things turned out, I was never to see Max again.

That first evening, she told me everything that had happened. The week before, Dr. Rau, Max's doctor from London, in whom she and Max both had great faith, had come for a few days. He had wanted to take Max to London, but Max had refused to go. 'I do not wish to go back to London as an invalid,' he had said. Dr. Rau had then suggested taking him to a hospital in Rome, but Max had not consented to go there, either. The Rapallo hospital, Miss Jungmann told me, was under-staffed and under-equipped. Max suffered acutely. He suffered from bed-sores, and she knew—Dr. Rau had told her—that modern hospitals have a kind of electrified bedding that, by making a ripple of tiny undulations, somehow prevents bed-sores. Miss Jungmann had been on practically twenty-four-hour duty since they had arrived at the Rapallo hospital. Max did not have a private nurse; it was impossible to get one. She was the private nurse.

Everything came out of her in geysers of speech. There was the terrible problem of getting Max to eat anything. When she had prepared his tray that day and put it before him, he had made a little sound of distaste. She had reproached him for his attitude towards the food. 'It's not exactly the sound that lions make when they are confronted with food, is it?' he had admitted. He had made an effort to eat, but it hadn't come to much. The bedclothes bothered him. His covering, Miss Jungmann assured me, was very thin, like gossamer, but he was conscious of great protuberances; he couldn't find a comfortable way to lie. The sound of the spoon on the glass when she brought his medicines grated on him. Miss Jungmann put gauze on the spoon to muffle this sound. There was a green label on the hospital glassware, and this irritated him. 'An ugly green, isn't it?' he said. After that, Miss Jungmann turned the utensils so that he couldn't see the green label. 'And yet, you know,' she said, 'with all his suffering, only the other day I came in at about sunset and he called my attention to a beautiful lavender shadow cast by the cupboard, and he wouldn't let me put the light on, to give that shadow a slightly longer life.'

Every once in a while, Miss Jungmann would go out into the hall and peer into Max's room. She would return and tell me he was sleeping, and then continue her story of these awful weeks. She reproached herself for having gone to Milan nearly two months before, to see a performance of Max's own dramatic version of *The Happy Hypocrite*. It was her first evening out in two years. The local doctor had been there that day and had said that it was all right for her to go, since there was a maid in the house who could call him, if necessary. Miss Jungmann went. She did not find out until the next day that Max had had some sort of attack and that the maid had had to summon the doctor again. When she returned from Milan, Max said nothing about this second visit of the doctor. He reached out his hand to her and said, very casually, 'Oh, you're back, are you?' There had been some puppets before *The Happy Hypocrite* went on, and when Miss Jungmann told Max this, he sat up in bed. His eyes lit up at the mention of the puppets, and he began to talk about the singular enchantment of puppets, and recalled a puppet show he had seen in Venice when he was young, and described the effect of it at great length. 'He remembered the puppets in *Don Quixote* and asked me to bring him the book,' Miss Jungmann said. 'He read me the passage—how Don Quixote is so carried away by the puppet show, it is so real to him, that he jumps on the stage and slashes the poor puppets to pieces. When he came to Sancho's protests—"What do you mean, Sir? These are no real Moors that you cut and hack so, but poor harmless puppets made of pasteboard"—he let the book fall on his lap.'

Miss Jungmann complained about the difficulty of reaching the overworked local doctor. Sometimes he came when he was sent for; sometimes he couldn't. 'He blows in and out of harbour,' Max said of him. Miss Jungmann asked me to call

Dr. Rau, in London, and ask him if he wouldn't come again. I said I would. Then Miss Jungmann thought better of it and suggested that I wait until morning, because the good sleep Max was having might make him feel stronger the next day. Miss Jungmann had been standing; I asked her to sit down and to try to rest for a few minutes. 'Once, the doctor came,' she said—and I was happy to see her smile, almost. 'Max had taken to reading Swinburne, the *Poems and Ballads*. The doctor, you know, has almost no English and Max less Italian. Max was reading aloud to me from *The Garden of Proserpine*: "That even the weariest river/Winds somewhere safe to sea." ' Miss Jungmann stopped for a moment, as if to catch her breath, and got up, went into the hall, and returned. 'The doctor came, and Max read those lines to him, and the doctor, who didn't know what Max was talking about, said, through me, as interpreter, "What I want to know is how you are feeling, Sir Max," and Max, with his eyes far away, recited another verse.'

A nurse came in and said that Max was stirring. I embraced Miss Jungmann and left, telling her that I would call her in the morning.

The next morning, Miss Jungmann asked me over the telephone if I could get Charlie to pick her up at the hospital and drive her to the Villino, because she had to fetch some things. She was somewhat calmer; Max had had a good night. The reason she had been in a state the night before, she said, was that Max had said to her, before he fell asleep, 'I do not see how I can possibly live through this night.' But he had; the doctor had given him a sedative, and he had slept peacefully. She had told Max that I was there, and he had been pleased. She said nothing more about calling Dr. Rau. It was to Dr. Rau that Max said, the last time the doctor saw him, 'I have watched my mother die, I have watched my sister die, but this is different.'

I had said that I would come along with Charlie, and on the way to the Villino Miss Jungmann told me some of the troubles she had had since Max entered the hospital; it was as if by dwelling on these little things she found relief from the contemplation of the appalling, unfaceable fact that was facing her.

Later, we sat in the living-room of the Villino. I sat in my usual place, beside the Merton chair. The niche was as it had always been. The bronze girl with the averted head, the two girls in white, the little girl and the Abbé were on the mantelshelf. Miss Jungmann had packed in a small valise what she had come to get. I asked her whether she would mind if I sent Charlie back to the hospital with her, because I wanted to sit in Max's study for a few minutes. Then I would come on to the hospital, and, if she could manage it, I would take her to lunch. She readily consented to my staying behind, but she did not feel that she could go out to lunch.

'Do you know what was worrying Max before he left for the hospital?' Miss Jungmann said. 'You wouldn't believe what was worrying him!'

I asked what it was.

'Well,' she said, 'you know, he had a letter from your friend Mr. Marcus, to thank him for what he had done with the Bruce Rogers. You remember?'

I said I remembered perfectly.

Miss Jungmann went on, 'Well, it was such a nice letter. It couldn't have been nicer. Mr. Marcus was so appreciative of what Max had done. And still it worried Max.'

I asked why.

'Because,' she replied, 'he said he couldn't tell from your friend's letter whether he had realized that what Max had done was *funny*. He didn't say that it had made him laugh.'

I assured Miss Jungmann that Mr. Marcus probably had laughed but, since Max was, perhaps as much as any writer in the world, the personification of the comic spirit, had thought it *infra dig* to say so.

Miss Jungmann felt better. 'I'll tell Max,' she said. 'He'll be so relieved.'

She was on the point of leaving the room when she hesitated, returned, and sat down beside me. She took my hand in hers and pledged me to secrecy about what she was going to say. She then told me her news. She had been married to Max some days before, in the hospital room. She was Lady Beerbohm.

I said it was wonderful.

'It *is* wonderful,' she said, her eyes brimming with tears.

I asked her how it had come about.

'Oh, you mean the proposal?' she said. 'Well, darling Max, out of a clear sky—— He was lying there, and looked so serene, and I heard him say, "What would you think of the idea of our getting married?" I was startled, but when I recovered I said that I adored him more than anyone else in the world and that I thought it *would* be a good idea. And Max said, "I am so delighted you think it *is* a good idea." '

There was a moment's silence. 'I must return to Max,' she said, and went out. The new Lady Beerbohm was to survive Max by less than three years.

I went out and walked up the steps to the terrace. It was flooded with sunlight. There I remembered a line of Max's: 'The past is a work of art, free of irrelevancies and loose ends.' I crossed the terrace and went into Max's blue study, where I sat for a few minutes. It was cool there. I walked around the bookshelves. I was again tempted to take out *The Poetical Works of Thomas Henry Huxley* and *The Complete Works of Arnold Bennett* but, instead, I picked a book at random—a real book—from the shelf. It was a presentation copy of Henry James's *The Aspern Papers*. Max had drawn James on the title page; the drawing showed him doubled up in a state of acute physical discomfort, and Max's neatly written legend below explained why: 'Mr. Henry James in the act of parturiating a sentence.'

I walked out of the study and crossed the terrace to the parapet. Charlie had returned; his taxi was standing against the wall of the Villino. I looked across the road; the Swinburne tree was leaning far backwards, and beyond it stretched the same old sea.

Three weeks later, on the twentieth of May, Max died. That day, the Old Self could safely have taken off the mask of the character that the Young Self had created—the character of Max Beerbohm. The discrepancy between the man and the mask was always slighter in Max than in most people, and by that time the two had become indistinguishable. Under the Maxian mask was, ultimately, Max.

INDEX